Race and Education

The Roles of History and Society in Educating African American Students

William H. Watkins
University of Illinois at Chicago

James H. Lewis
Roosevelt University

Victoria Chou
University of Illinois at Chicago

Allyn and Bacon

Boston ∎ London ∎ Toronto ∎ Sydney ∎ Tokyo ∎ Singapore

Executive Editor: *Traci Mueller*
Series Editorial Assistant: *Bridget Keane*
Marketing Manager: *Kathleen Morgan*
Editorial Production Administrator: *Deborah Brown*
Editorial Production Service: *Nesbitt Graphics, Inc.*
Composition Buyer: *Linda Cox*
Manufacturing Buyer: *Megan Cochran*
Cover Administrator: *Jenny Hart*
Electronic Composition: *Galley Graphics, Ltd.*

Library of Congress Cataloging-in-Publication Data

Race and education: the roles of history and society in educating African American
students / [edited by] William H. Watkins, James H. Lewis, Victoria Chou.
   p. cm.
Includes bibliographical references and index.
ISBN 0-205-32439-8
   1. Afro-Americans—Education—Congresses. I. Watkins, William H. (William Henry),
1946– II. Lewis, James H. (James Hoffman) III. Chou, Victoria.
LC2717.R23 2001
371.829′96073—dc21   00-056927

Printed in the United States of America

10 9 8 7 6 5 4 3 2 1   05 04 03 02 01 00

CONTRIBUTORS

A. Wade Boykin	Howard University
Enora Brown	DePaul University
Signithia Fordham	University of Connecticut
Michele Foster	Claremont Graduate University
Vivian Gadsden	University of Pennsylvania
Janice E. Hale	Wayne State University
Annette Henry	University of Illinois at Chicago
Asa G. Hilliard III	Georgia State University
Cynthia Hudley	University of California, Santa Barbara
Gloria Ladson-Billings	University of Wisconsin
Carol D. Lee	Northwestern University
James H. Lewis	Roosevelt University
Laurence Parker	University of Illinois, Urbana-Champaign
Margaret Beale Spencer	University of Pennsylvania
William H. Watkins	University of Illinois at Chicago

LIST OF ILLUSTRATIONS

CONTENTS

PREFACE

As America entered the twentieth century, the first generations of newly freed slaves found a sociopolitical environment in which racial subservience, segregation, economic subjugation, and social privilege prevailed. It was within this context that the education of Blacks was contested as the hopes of a downtrodden people for freedom and uplift clashed with the power structure's agenda for accommodation and containment.

Despite the official ending of American apartheid in 1954, racial division, economic inequality, and a host of social problems continue to undermine progress and change. In light of this, education continues to be a pivotal issue in our society. This is compounded by the fact that broad masses of people view the schools as culturally hostile and "savagely" unequal to people of color.

Current battles against "mis-education" of the poor and people of color are being waged on different fronts. In local schools and communities, heroic teachers, involved parents, caring administrators, and students themselves reject the alienating formulas and rigidities of yesteryear. Correspondingly, a new group of black educational scholars and researchers participate in this war. This book samples views and voices of today's African American educational criticism.

Oppositionist black educational thinking can be found in the practices and utterances of teachers dating back to the early nineteenth century when many participated in independent, illegal, and self-help schooling. Into the twentieth century, a new group of highly educated black scholars such as Dr. W.E.B. DuBois, Dr. Carter G. Woodson, Dr. Anna Julia Cooper, Dr. Kelly Miller, Nannie Helen Burroughs, and others entered the scene. Their scholarship influenced, and was influenced by, the early twentieth-century protest. After World War I, the number of educators increased as more African Americans gained access to higher education, especially in the South. We must never forget the magnificent scholars trained in the historically black colleges and universities whose contributions have not been fully acknowledged by the mainstream research community.

In the "Civil Rights" era and the period immediately following, black enrollment in institutions of higher learning skyrocketed. During the late 1970s to early 1980s, a substantial group of newly minted black Ph.D.s, notably women, received appointments to major universities, contributed to established journals, and engaged in scholarly research. Acceptability in established scholarly circles is not the measure of their worth, it is simply coincidental to their accomplishments. This book is largely written by such people.

A historical example may help us understand today's work. In the 1930s and 1940s, although blacks had long contributed to literature, fiction, poetry, and theater, the Harlem Renaissance represented the coming together of a new and large group of black writers and artists. They told the story of black literature, music, plays, and so forth through the eyes of black people. Similarly, we now have a renaissance of theorizing and writing in black education. History and time have rendered this new group of scholars, practitioners, and researchers distinct. Some are in a position to inform policy making and the policy makers. Many have been in the classroom, many have been in the "movement," and many have been in both. All, without exception, have been tempered and shaped by the modern "Civil Rights Movement" and accompanying struggles. This group has the advantage of all the great work that preceded them. They are able to stand on the shoulders of giants.

They (we) were weaned on militancy and the discourses and struggles for human dignity, social justice, and racial equality. Theirs is a "post-Malcolm" scholarship and these are "post-Malcolm" scholars. Rejecting the canon of the academy, this scholarship is not "objective." Rather, it is a discourse for the people. This scholarship is unapologetically partisan. It opposes racism, colonialism, oppression, and inequity. It opposes any social system that desires to subjugate one people to another. It stands for the uplift of oppressed people.

Today's scholars live in a dynamic setting, unimagined by former generations. It is a crossroads in history. If equitably shared, advanced technology and the creation of great wealth can reconfigure the world, improving the lives of all. If not, the continuation of racism, ignorance, privilege, and greed will condemn us all. If societies are judged by their lowest strata, then this book is important. Will we break through ethnocentrism, racism, and the colonial practices of the past? Can schools change? Can teaching practices, the curriculum, and the school organization be made to serve blacks and other underserved populations? These are the crucial questions addressed in this work.

William H. Watkins

Acknowledgments

This volume began with a two-day conference cosponsored by the Chicago Urban League and the University of Illinois at Chicago in March, 1999. The authors would like to thank the Spencer Foundation, and in particular John Williams, for their assistance and support for this work. Maria Makkawi and Teresa Vargas-Vega at the University of Illinois at Chicago and Cynthia Jordan-Hubbard, Ryan Tyler, and Todd Rosenkranz of the Chicago Urban League provided valuable assistance facilitating the conference. Traci Mueller and her colleagues at Allyn & Bacon displayed extraordinary patience and were helpful at each step in the publication process. Finally, the authors thank Chicago Urban League President and CEO James W. Compton for his persistent advocacy for the education of all our children.

Support for Chapter 7, Identity, Achievement Orientation, and Race: "Lessons Learned" about the Normative Developmental Experiences of African American Males, was made possible through funding from the Ford, W.K. Kellogg, and W.T. Grant Foundations; the Office of Education, Research and Improvement (OERI); the National Institutes of Mental Health (NIMH); and the Commonwealth Fund.

The Search for New Answers

James H. Lewis

In March, 1999, seventy Chicago-area scholars and educators convened for two days to discuss the impact of race on our educational system and on the outcomes that our educational system produces. The conference, entitled Race and Education: Creating a Research Agenda, was convened by the Chicago Urban League and scholars at the University of Illinois at Chicago, and was supported by the Spencer Foundation. Conference presenters and selected commentators were asked to produce scholarly papers on their subject areas, which have become the content of this volume.

That insufficient progress has been made in recent years to improve schools argues for innovation. As districts across the nation proceed with reforms based on higher levels of accountability, site-based management, learning standards, basic skills curricula, and various types of school choice, one question that must be asked is whether these reforms will provide the framework for educational programming that will best address the needs of all students. As a whole, the chapters in this volume synthesize a broad literature on the role of race and culture in the education of children. That synthesis argues that the multitude of school reforms under way—be they school choice, charter schools, enhanced local control, or more rigorous standards—are likely to succeed to the extent that they provide the framework within which culturally appropriate, development-sensitive, and individually supportive education can take place. New learning standards, site-based management, and rigorous accountability will not succeed by themselves.

The Search for New Answers

This volume is intended to bring under one cover the cutting-edge thinking of many leading scholars in the educational field. These scholars believe that the educational achievement of African American children will not be improved by narrowing the curriculum or achieving desegregation of schools, or through better funding alone. Rather, the best chance for significant improvement in the performance of low-achieving African American students lies in innovations based on replacing constructs rooted in past white hegemony and its current vestiges and building educational programs and communities consistent with children's ethnic, cultural, social, and developmental needs.

In considering issues of race, a major contribution of critical race theory, the multiculturalists, and others has been to mitigate the power of deficit interpretations of race. As Asa Hilliard argues in Chapter 1, however, race has come inexorably to be associated with deficit, first in the construction of racial categories by dominating societies in past centuries and then perpetually as members of racial groups have come to identify with the type cast. The work of John Ogbu and Claude Steele describes how minority individuals, and perhaps especially those who might have achieved more or come from a higher economic class, disqualify themselves from the highest levels of achievement by accepting caste positions or placing excessive amounts of pressure on themselves to overachieve their stereotype (Ogbu, 1978; Steele & Aronson, 1995).

The problem of how to address the needs of all students is becoming increasingly complex because of the wide variety of settings in which students find themselves and because of their diverse backgrounds. A growing body of literature tells us that the instructional approaches suitable to one setting or to one group of students is not necessarily best for another (Delpit, 1995, p. 28). As complicated as this makes the educational mission in a society where most students attend class with others of the same race or of similar socioeconomic background, a significant number of students do attend school in racially desegregated settings. A layer of complexity is added when we consider that a variety of cultures of learning exist within the members of any racial group that are based on the group's history, expectations, and levels of parental expectations.

Students across America attend school in a wide variety of racial settings yielding a complex matrix of different mixes of students and teachers with different racial, cultural, and experiential backgrounds. The most common type of student body is racially homogenous. A recent study of enrollment patterns in Illinois public schools reported that 70 percent of African American children attended schools that were at least 75 percent minority students. Sixty percent of Latino students attended schools that were at least 75 percent minority. Only 8 percent of African American children and 18 percent of Latino children attended school in districts that were less than 25 percent minority (Lewis, 1995, p. 14).

The national pattern is similar to that of Illinois. Gary Orfield and John Yun of the Harvard University Civil Rights Project have found "large and increasing numbers of African American and Latino students enrolled in suburban schools, but serious segregation within these communities, particularly in the nation's large metropolitan areas" (Orfield & Yun, 1999, p. 1). Orfield and Yun found that black student enrollment in majority white schools peaked during the 1980s but retreated to 1960s' levels during the 1990s (Orfield & Yun, 1999, p. 12). Latino segregation in schools has increased during the past three decades, owing in large measure to significant increases in Latino population in particular localities. Nationally, about one third of African American and Latino students attend schools that are 90 to 100 percent minority (Orfield & Yun, 1999, p. 13).

As Janice Hale points out in this volume, African American communities must develop strategies and institutions that will afford their children the same educational opportunities as the children of the white middle and upper classes. The high correlation of race and poverty in the United States means that African American and Latino students who attend school districts characterized predominantly by members of their own race or ethnicities are also likely to attend school with other poor children. The average black student attends a school that is 42.7 percent poor, the average Latino student attends a school that is 46.7 percent poor, but the average white student attends a school that is only 18.7 percent poor (Orfield & Yun, 1999, p. 16). The vast majority of schools that are over 70 percent minority also have low-income populations ranging from 50 percent to 100 percent (Orfield & Yun, 1999, p. 17).

The racial/ethnic heterogeneity of our school systems presents profound challenges for educators. It is no longer sufficient for teachers to utilize curriculum and instructional methods that might once have been suited for classrooms filled with white, middle-class students. A majority of America's schools have some kind of racial/ethnic mix. Orfield and Yun find that the average white student attends a school that is 81.2 percent white, the average black student attends a school that is 54.5 percent black and 32.6 percent white, and the average Latino student attends a school that is 52.5 percent Latino and 29.9 percent white (Orfield & Yun, 1999, p. 15).

Integration of African Americans and whites has stagnated in most of the nation's largest cities during the past two decades, however, and there is little if anything to suggest that this pattern will change in the next decade or more. Beginning in Oklahoma City, school districts across the country have been declared legally to have attained unitary status, a judicial affirmation that they are no longer culpable for any racial segregation that remains within their districts and are therefore no longer required to provide remedies such as student assignment plans that create racially mixed schools (Orfield & Eaton, 1996).

The persistence of school racial segregation means that the field of education must develop strategies that address the needs of children whether they are found in classrooms that have a racial and economic mix or in classrooms that are racially and economically homogenous. And this has significant implications for the preparation of teachers. It is becoming increasingly clear that in our society, where racial/ethnic identification carries so much meaning for how we view ourselves and how others view us, teachers must be well prepared to communicate effectively with and gain the acceptance and respect of students who may not be of the same racial or ethnic identification.

It is the overarching message of this volume that innovative approaches are needed in classrooms and school communities that attend to the cultures and histories of African American students—not a return to methods that produced the race gap in quality of education that we must now contend with. Clearly one response to the perception of inadequacy of educational performance has been the return to "basics" and attempts to "teacher proof" curriculum by providing teachers with detailed prescriptions of what to teach and detailed lesson plans. To the extent that these strategies are limited to accomplishing narrow educational objectives, they may achieve limited success. However, the lesson of much of the emerging research and of the essays contained in this volume is that curriculum and teaching must be shaped to accommodate the unique needs of students from a variety of backgrounds.

Numerous studies have been conducted that span the terrain of the needs of African American students, but in some respects the scholarship has ranged widely but not sufficiently deeply. The *Reaching the Top* report noted the impact of racial and ethnic discrimination on children, the impact of cultural differences, expectations of success, fears of "whiteness," and cultural attributes related to experience as possible sources of the gap (*Reaching the Top*, 1999, pp. 14–18).

The conclusions of numerous authors of *The Black–White Test Score Gap*, edited by Christopher Jencks and Meredith Phillips, point to sociocultural explanations for much of the black–white gap in test scores—explanations explored by the authors in this volume. Jencks and Phillips argue that "successful" explanations of the gap between African American and white student achievement will likely have three major attributes that will vary from much of the work that has gone before. First, they will likely incorporate interactions of family members and friends, and their interaction with the outside world; second, they will focus on differential responses of African American and white children to classroom experiences; and third, they will look much more closely at psychological and cultural issues (Jencks & Phillips, 1998, p. 43). Phillips and coworkers (1998a, p. 138) argued that racial differences in attitudes and experiences of parents and grandparents, household size, and parenting practices likely have an impact on the size of the test score gap. Phillips, James Crouse, and John Ralph concluded that neither "traditional socioeconomic differences" between African American and white children's families nor differences in schools provided strong explanations for the gap, and they counseled future researchers to search elsewhere (Phillips et al., 1998b, p. 256).

Particular landmark studies direct us toward key issues. In some instances, findings generated ethnographically need to be further validated by quantitative work. Theories such as Asa Hilliard's, that a transition from a race orientation to an ethnic orientation is essential to improve academic achievement, need to be rigorously explored and tested. Questions regarding the salience of learning styles in explaining outcome differences or for developing teaching strategies need to be resolved (see the chapters by Janice Hale and Gloria Ladson-Billings. The work of Margaret Spencer, Signithia Fordham, Enora Brown, Annette Henry, and Vivian Gadsden points to the necessity of addressing children's needs for support systems that respond to the different stages of child development, different types of acculturation, different outsider expectations—especially surrounding gender—and different personal experiences and family histories. Additional studies in these areas must be conducted to synthesize these and related theories and to refine the research so that it has the same political currency as theories regarding the efficacy of school choice, decentralized decision-making, need for learning standards, or accountability generated through high-stakes testing.

Collectively, the authors argue that what happens in the school must align with the child's experiences in other contexts. This may involve creating the nurturing environment called for by Margaret Spencer, Gloria Ladson-Billings, Janice Hale, and Carol Lee, or developing curriculum that accurately represents the African American student's experience, as described by William Watkins. The school as a part of a system of educational administration is important to accomplishing this. Teachers may or may not be recruited and developed with these concerns in mind. Schools may not be structured to permit address of the individual learning needs of each child. Schools and districts may or may not be open to creating learning environments that will nurture a student's ethnic and historical background. The efficacy of these approaches, as well as how needed changes can be implemented, must be further researched.

Michele Foster's and Cynthia Hudley's chapters argue for more work on the impact of schooling on the future socialization of children once they become adults. Historically, the mission of our educational system has been considered to include not only academic achievement, but also the molding of citizenship. Recent scholarship has been devoted almost entirely to studies of how the former occurs. As minority groups move toward collectively becoming a majority of our nation's population, however, schools will become increasingly important for helping children to learn to live and work effectively with people of races and cultures different from their own. Because of the persistence of separation of racial groups residentially, most children will continue to be educated for that multicultural era in schools populated by children of their own race/ethnicity. As Foster and Hudley point out, future research must locate the school's contribution within the larger social community in which the child operates, including family, neighborhood, peers, and media.

REFERENCES

Delpit, L. (1995). *Other people's children: Cultural conflict in the classroom.* New York: The New Press.

Lewis, J. H. (1995). *Preserving privilege: Inequity of the Illinois educational finance system.* Chicago: Chicago Urban League.

The NAEP 1998 reading report card: National & state highlights. (1999). Washington, DC: Office of Educational Research and Improvement, U.S. Department of Education.

Ogbu, J. U. (1978). *Minority education and caste: The American system in cross-cultural perspective.* New York: Academic Press.

Orfield, G., & Eaton, S. E. (1996). *Dismantling desegregation: The quiet reversal of Brown v. Board of Education.* New York: The New Press.

Orfield, G., & Yun, J. T. (1999). *Resegregation in American schools.* Cambridge, Massachusetts: The Civil Rights Project, Harvard University.

Phillips, M., et al. (1998a). Family background, parenting practices, and the Black-White test score gap. In C. Jencks & M. Phillips (Eds.), *The Black-White test score gap.* Washington, DC: Brookings Institution Press.

Phillips, M., et al. (1998b). Does the Black-White test score gap widen after children enter school? In C. Jencks & M. Phillips (Eds.), *The Black-White test score gap.* Washington, DC: Brookings Institution Press.

Reaching the top: A report of the national task force on minority high achievement. (1999). New York: College Entrance Examination Board.

Steele, C. M., & Aronson, J. (1995). Stereotype threat and the intellectual test performance of African Americans. *Journal of Personality and Social Psychology, 69,* 797–811.

1 "Race," Identity, Hegemony, and Education

What Do We Need To Know Now?

Asa G. Hilliard III

Everyday People: An Introduction

Dr. Hefny, to whom the following letter is addressed, has begun to really learn about the global system of thought and classification of human beings, and even about some of its linkages to education.

October 2, 1987

Mostafa Hefny
5130 Neckel
Dearborn, MI 48126

Dear Mr. Hefny:

Be advised that the Michigan Department of Education collects racial and ethnic data as prescribed in Directive No. 15, 'Race and Ethnic Standards for Federal Statistics and Administrative Reporting.' This directive provides standard classification for record keeping, collection, and presentation of data on race and ethnicity in federal program administrative reporting and statistical activities.

According to this directive a white person is a person having origins in any of the original peoples of Europe, North Africa, or the Middle East. Since you come from Egypt (a North African and Middle Eastern country) you are white, not black.

You are directed to change your classification on the Race/Ethnic Identification Card. Be advised that failure to do so will have serious repercussions for your career, and will constitute insubordination, which may result in suspension and discharge.

Sincerely,

Mrs. Teresa D. Myers

Director, Human Resources
cc: Dr. William Simmons
        (Wayne County Intermediate School District, Michigan)

This contemporary example of "race" and education shows how deeply "race" matters are embedded in the structures we use. It also shows how power is at the center of belief and behavior. Even in the response of the victim, Dr. Hefny, aspects of the "race" construct have begun to be used as the main basis for identity. How many other examples could we find if we really looked?

The absurdities reflected in this letter should be obvious. I fear, however, that they may not be. What is "race?" Who decides what it is, and how is it determined? Is this letter about "race," ethnicity, or both? What is the role of the United States government in making the determination, and how will this be done? Will those who are classified have any say in the matter?

Dr. Hefny, a very dark-skinned Nubian Egyptian native, from Aswan, descendant of a people who have lived at Aswan for thousands of years, even before Egypt was a nation, wrote a four-page, single-spaced letter in response on January 14, 1988. Among other things, he said the following.

> I am a black man at five levels, the biological, social, psychological, political, and ideological levels. I want to reconcile my strong black identity with my classification. . . . As a black man and as an African, I am proud of this (my African) heritage. My classification as a white man takes away my black pride and my black heritage.

This issue had not been resolved legally for Dr. Hefny the last time that I spoke with him a year ago. It has affected his life negatively in a direct way. This nightmarish conversation is a virtual tower of "babble." Yet, as irrational as it is, it is no more so than hundreds of thousands of other conversations that professionals hold every day.

Many people in Hitler's Germany, especially the Nazis, were deep into the "race" conversation. Some say that the contemporary concept of "race" started there (Bernal, 1987). Adolf Hitler was definitely aware of the "race" matter and was the person who most clearly saw its full political potential.

Hitler said to Rauchning, "Just as well as all these tremendously clever intellectuals, that in the scientific sense there is no such thing as race, but you, as a farmer and cattle breeder cannot get your breeding successfully achieved without the conception of race. *And I as a politician need a conception which enables the order which has hitherto existed on historic basis to be abolished and an entirely new and anti-historical order enforced and given such an intellectual basis. . . .* With conception of race, national socialism will carry its revolution abroad and recast the world." (Weinreich, 1946, p. 50) [*Italics mine*]

Hitler was very clear about "race" as a *fabrication,* as *anti-historical,* and as a *political* power tool. His scholars were too, as Weinreich documents so thoroughly in his book *Hitler's Professors: The Role of Scholarship in Germany's Crimes Against the Jewish People.* How did Hitler's dialogue about "race" become mainstream? How did victims and targets of his propaganda come to embrace parts of it? How did the "race" dialogue become legitimate?

Working in the topic areas related to "race," we could spin our wheels by using the same popular language, definitions, constructs, paradigms, and problem definitions that are so typical of past work on the problem. However, there are some fundamental issues that we tend to sidestep when dealing with "race" and with identity. Then we can and must tie "race," identity, hegemony, and education together in our analyses just as they are in the real world.

Although my presentation here is primarily from an African perspective, the "race" matter extends to all others as well, since the "race" makers were classifying the whole world, and for the same reasons.

Naming Africans: The Race Card

I have witnessed several transitions in the ethnic group name used by people of African ancestry. I was born during the time when it was popular to use "colored" when referring to African people. "Negro" was also used. During the 1960s, many people felt that a major new shift had been made when "black" became popular, with the predictable addition that the "b" in black be capitalized, just as the Spanish version of the word for black (*negro*), had gradually evolved to the status of capitalization. We even became "Black and proud," that is, we made black a positive rather than a negative name. We challenged the attribution of negative meaning to one facet of our "racial" marker, our pigmentation. This was "much ado" about something, but what?

Obviously these changes represented fresh struggles within the African community to take control of our naming and self-definition process away from our oppressors, or anyone else, and to imbue our collective ethnic name with positive meaning. We wrestled with the ascribed terms, "colored," "negro," and "black" as if we had no other choices. We fought for capitalization as a sign of respect. We embraced the terms "negro" and "black" and gave them new positive meanings.

Yet we had forgotten by that time what we had called ourselves before slavery, other more ancient, even divine, ethnic names. *These names were based upon our natal and cultural bonds and thousands of years of heritage. The names were based upon our collective history and creativity.* Worse, we had forgotten why we named ourselves and how we came to be given alien names in the first place.

Given the sacred nature of names to African people, and given the association of a name with our identity as a family, this was a tragedy of enormous proportions. Our focus on names became a barren one, a focus without the benefit of awareness of our rich cultural traditions. Therefore, we were unprepared for the conversation about "race" naming and identity.

We had come to a point where we, *as a people,* were named by others. Most of us had lost control of this, the most fundamental of human processes, the self-determining process of naming ourselves, of *telling,* not *asking,* the world who we were (Powell, 1937; Moore, 1992).

In the 1980s at a national leadership conference in New Orleans, led by Rev. Jesse Jackson and Dr. Ramona Edlin Hodge, the name "African American" was advocated, followed by a growing, widespread acceptance of that designation within the African community. We did not know that the Jackson-Edlin–led dialogue was actually the third time in our recent history in the United States that we had chosen to call ourselves Africans.

During the 1800s, the records will show that we called ourselves *Africans* in our churches, in our schools, in our lodges, in our self-help societies, and so forth (Anderson, 1988; Hilliard, 1995). We attended *African* Methodist Churches and *African* Baptist Churches. We attended *African* Free Schools and joined the *African* Lodge (Masonic).

Later, in the late 1950s, a movement out of Harlem reintroduced the name *African* to our community (Moore, 1992). So the 1980s' initiative was the third massive self-renaming of us as *Africans.*

Few of us in the 1980s were prepared to deal with this weighty matter in any substantive way. Few of us were well informed about the history of our people before our enslavement by Europeans. We did not understand our history as a whole and healthy ethnic people, not merely as a pigmented people. We certainly were a pigmented people, but without a preoccupation about that, anymore than about any other part of our phenotype. In fact, the record will show that we liked our image, and so did others. We did and still do use our typical physical features as the sign that we probably have spotted an ethnic family member. However, there simply was so very much more to *who* we were than our pigment. So how had we come to become preoccupied with *what* rather than *who* we were, with our political and economic struggle rather than with our essence and our destiny? How had we become individuals rather than family? How did we become a temporal rather than an eternal people, a local rather than a cosmic people? We had seen ourselves as a collective, as divinities, as subjects (Erny, 1973).

In these recent debates about our names, we did not understand how and why we were coerced by Europeans to change our ethnic names to names that caused us to become preoccupied with aspects of our phenotype, mainly our skin color, hair texture, and facial features. *The Europeans were looking for names that dehumanized and subordinated us,* names that *contained* us in our physical being, names that *separated us from our minds, souls, and spirits.*

We did not understand how they, the authors of this specious system, were using their "race" construction in irrational and pseudoscientific but calculated political ways. Above all, we have been unfamiliar with the thoughtful and scholarly homework that was done by some of our own greatest scholars, to reveal to us what was happening in this mind game and why, work that should have punctured the "race" balloon.

Perhaps the most extensive and notable contribution to and under-standing of how we came to be in this predicament of an ethnic "no man's land," one of the only groups in the world, was made by a great group of conscious African scholars in Harlem (Moore, 1992). Richard B. Moore led the research and policy effort, writing the report of the group, which included the late Dr. John Henrik Clarke. Moore's book, *The Name Negro: Its Origins and Evil Use,* first published in 1960, answered most of the questions mentioned earlier. They agreed that the name *African* would be applied to all of the traditional ethnic groups on the African continent and to the descendants of those Africans in the global diaspora.

The names "colored," "negro," "black," "African," and "African Ameri-can" are terms that have more or less been accepted within the African family. They do not exhaust all of the possibilities that we have examined.

My own strong preference is for *African.* For reasons that will become more clear, it fits our actual historical, cultural, and even political circum-stances more precisely than does any other name. As Sterling Stuckey (1987) has shown, *the western experience has fused Africans from all over the diaspora into a new family that still shares the African root culture at the core,* in the same way that diverse ethnic groups of European descent in America are tending toward a common European ethnic identity after having spent so many years believing that they had no ethnicity or that they were "just Americans" (Alba, 1990). Therefore, the African continental name reflects the reality of a common cultural heritage, at the deep structural level, and a common political need. We recognize that cultural change in response to new environ-ments will continue to happen to Africans as to others.

Non-Africans have used and proposed euphemistic specific designators to refer primarily to people of African ancestry. Nonethnic terms such as "minority," "the disadvantaged," "culturally deprived," "culturally disadvan-taged," "inner-city," and "at-risk" are *ascribed* and amorphous "identities, identity designations that detach Africans from time, space, and the flow of human history." Occasionally, African people actually pick up these all but pejorative terms and make them a part of their own definition of themselves. At least no one has yet suggested that they be capitalized—as yet.

Note that these terms emphasize numerical status, social class, and *political* status, that is, how many we are, how wealthy we are, how powerful we are, but not ethnic identity, not *who* we are. In fact, these names apply easily, potentially, to any ethnic group. Almost without exception, the group names ascribed by Europeans to Africans are adjectives, never proper nouns. Significantly, they are *adjectives* that suggest no respect for *who we are* or for our uniqueness as an ethnic family.

The record will show that, in the case of African people, the use of demeaning language was unconscious for some and intentional for others. At the conscious level, naming was a strategy to commit "cultural genocide," a strategy to destroy ethnic family *solidarity,* a strategy to place emphasis on individual rather than family behavior, or a strategy to confuse Africans about their ethnic identity (Ben Jochannan, 1972; Patterson, 1970). Why? As Dr. John Henrik Clarke has so often said, "It is impossible to continue to oppress a consciously historical people." These names have the effect of destroying consciousness and constructing vulnerability. Even when the use of the terms by Europeans was not conscious, the terms had the effects intended by the strategists. The intended effects were to break family bonds, to create *individuals* and *isolates.*

Addressing the Real Problem: Hegemony

Most Africans share a phenotype. This sharing may even have some meaning for us. It is certainly a part of who we are. However, it leaves major things out.

As far as I can tell, there have been few meetings like "Race and Education: Creating a New Agenda," held in Chicago in March, 1999, where group identity designations were analyzed and discussed, for any groups other than Africans. That by itself needs some reflection. For example, I am not aware of meetings to discuss "German identity, race, and education," or "English identity, race, and education," or "Japanese identity, race, and education." *German, English,* and *Japanese* are clearly regarded as *ethnic* or national designations, as proper names reflecting cultural integrity and continuity. It is also clear that the topic "race and education" does not conjure up notions of looking at "white people and education." So when we hear "race and education," most people assume that the speaker is referring to Africans, in the same way that many people assume that "bilingual education" refers to Latinos or Hispanics.

Most of our dialogue about this delicate matter is transacted using euphemistic terminology. That is why it is good for us to gain clarity, first about the *meaning* of the topic "race and education" and then about the *nature of the problem* in education that is related to it.

The matter of ethnic designation or group identity cannot be resolved until the question of *identity* is situated in its historical, cultural, and sociopolitical context. We must understand how the idea of "race" emerged and how it came to be associated with and embedded in education. Then we must also admit that the poison of "race" and hegemony or white supremacy is now a part of global *ideology* and *structure* and is increasingly internalized among the victims of the system. Most of us are in denial about "race" and hegemony and do little serious thinking about these matters. *Our response to the problem ultimately must target ideology and structure, not merely everyday individual behavior.* Then we can deal with both.

The family business of resolving African identity issues can be resolved only within the African family. No one outside a given ethnic family has the right or responsibility to do that for or with that family, any more than Africans can insert themselves into the family discussion of identity matters in other ethnic groups.

If we were in an African family meeting, in addition to the present content, which I will discuss further, I would expect to go into detail about African history and culture in order to ground the discussion in truly meaningful information. I would look especially at the aims, methods, and content of our ancient, traditional, and contemporary independent systems and structures for socialization, both continental and diasporan. I would look at changes to these systems that have occurred in the diaspora. It is here that we can come to grips with matters of belonging, purpose, and destiny. Finally, I would deal in great depth with the nature of European and Asian cultural hegemony in historical perspective.

It is significant that current African preoccupation with pigment (race) has preempted and obscured our awareness of our normal intergenerational transmission of our cultural socialization processes and structures, so that we have little conscious knowledge of them and virtually no use for them. We Africans are looking in the wrong places for our redemption!

These matters of "race," identity, and hegemony are very difficult to discuss because they are so difficult to acknowledge and because of the guilt and fear that are still associated with them. Yet the ideology of "race" drives much of what happens in the world and in education. It is like a computer software program that "runs in the background," invisible and inaudible. However, our silent and invisible "racial" software is not benign. It is linked to issues of power or hegemony, the domination of a given group by another. *That is what this has all been about!* "Race" thinking has no reason for being except for the establishment of hegemony.

As long as there are hegemonic rules running in the background, there is no possibility whatsoever that there can be clarity in the foreground. It is useful to ask, first, "What is the *origin of the idea* of 'racial' identity?" Second,

"Was it common for groups in ancient times to have a 'racial' identity?" What is the *function* of "racial identity"? Why should we pursue it now?

The History of "Race" and Hegemony

Many years ago I did a study of some aspects of this problem in a research project for the Office of Naval Research (Hilliard, Jenkins, & Scott, 1979). I have continued to pursue my interest in this question, the question of "race," hegemony, and education.

There is a large body of literature on the history and analyses of the idea of "race." An examination of that history puts us in an excellent position to understand and to approach the questions of ideology and structures of hegemony and education.

Color prejudice associated with white supremacy appears to be quite old, according to Vulindela Wobogo (1988), one example of which occurred several thousand years ago in India and resulted in the dehumanizing caste system, with human beings referred to as untouchables a form of hegemony and genocide. This hegemonic and genocidal attempt to remove the lower caste from agency or independence was a key aspect of their oppression (Rajshekar, 1987; Ghuyre, 1963). However, "race" as a "scientific" construct or concept as we understand it is quite recent (Kly, 1990; Barzun, 1965; Biddiss, 1970; Blauner, 1972; Friedman, 1970; Shipman, 1994; Stanton, 1960; Hodge, Struckmann & Trost, 1975; Bernal, 1987; Hofstader, 1971; Montague, 1968, 1974; Willhelm, 1971; Zindgrist, 1992; Spiegel, 1988). While Europeans were committing cultural genocide on Africans, they were shoring up their own cultural solidarity (Spindler & Spindler, 1998; Huntington, 1996; Kotkin, 1993).

Perhaps no one has written more clearly about these matters and their structural nature than Sidney M. Willhelm. Staughton Lynd (1970) summarized some of Willhelm's thinking in the preface of *Who Needs the Negro*:

> It does not follow that, because racism is economic in origin, racism can be overcome by economic change. The racism of white Americans has become, in Professor Willhelm's words, a "dominant and autonomous social value." In his repeatedly expressed formulation, racism expresses itself within economic limits created by the white American's need for the black American's labor. If the white American no longer needed the black American labor, this does not mean that the white American would no longer be racist. On the contrary. As Professor Willhelm views the situation, if the white American no longer needed the black American's labor, he might then feel free to express his racism fully: not merely to exploit the black American, as in the last 300 years, but to kill him.
> . . . The ultimate destiny of the Afro-American is likely to be extermination, not assimilation. His situation is less like that of the European immigrant than like that of the American Indian. Black militants have not fully understood

the economic basis of what they perceive, but in prophesying genocide they have accurately grasped the end to which the logic of automation leads.

Indians were economically useful so long as Europeans wanted furs rather than land for farming, and militarily useful so long as the North American continent was divided between several European powers. When they were no longer useful in either way, they were destroyed. What reason have American blacks to expect a different outcome?" (pp. xi and xiii)

Willhelm was not alone by far in raising these issues. Samuel Yette (1971) also raised the issue of genocide. He believed that he was fired from his job at the *Washington Post* because of what he wrote in his book *The Choice*. One of his chapters is entitled, "A plan to destroy obsolete people." It is interesting that the policy chapter in the popular *The Bell Curve*, by Charles Murray and Richard Herrnstein, speaks about the intellectual ability of the lower quartile in IQ test scores, the bottom 25 percent as being *"worthless and expendable people."* The surviving author of this book has been an influential advisor to a president and a prominent presence in conservative think tanks (Edwards, 1997). In the two authors' own words,

What happens to the child of low intelligence who survives childhood and reaches adulthood trying to do his best to be a productive citizen? Out of the many problems we have just sketched this is the one we have chosen to italicize. *All of the problems that these children experience will become worse rather than better as they grow older, for the labor market they will confront a few decades down the road is going to be much harder for them to cope with than the labor market is now. . . .* People in the bottom quartile of intelligence are becoming not just increasingly expendable in economic terms: they will sometime in the not-too-distant future become a net drag. In economic terms and barring a profound change in direction for our society, many people will be unable to perform that function so basic to human dignity: putting more into the world than they take out. . . . For many people, there is nothing they can learn that will repay the cost of the teaching. (Herrnstein & Murray, 1994, pp. 519–520)

The concept of "worthless" people is reintroduced in this book, which was on the *New York Times* best seller list for ten weeks. *The Bell Curve* cannot be dismissed as the crank thoughts of some outcast. The thinking is mainstream, even elite professional (Snyderman & Rothman, 1990). Middle-class families around the country gave Murray standing ovations for *Bell Curve* presentations.

There is a consensus among historians of the "race" concept that the idea, the construct, is a product of Europe's colonization of Africa and other parts of the world, of its enslavement of Africans, and of the development of apartheid, segregation, and the supporting ideology of white supremacy. Other ethnic groups such as Indians and Asians, indeed groups of color around the whole world, came under the umbrella of the construct of "race, and experienced the dehumanizing colonial treatment." Hegemony was also at the root of the creation and adoption of the construct as it was applied to these other groups. Even European ethnic groups were divided into "races" and ranked, to establish domination of the "superior European race." In Germany the ultimate realization was the fabrication of the "Master Race" (Chase, 1977; Weinreich, 1946; Leary, 1992; Lifton, 1986; Muller-Hill, 1988; Proctor, 1988).

It is profoundly meaningful that prior to the 1700s, the concept of race, as we know it, did not exist! This leads immediately to the question of, *What was the historical nature of group identity, when "race" was not in the picture? What is the normal basis for group identity in world history?* Why do we seek to get a "racial" identity in the face of the illegitimate origin of the concept and in the absence of current validity for the construct? Our physical similarities are a given. Healthy Africans are quite comfortable with this aspect of themselves, even proud. But what next?

Examining the nature of group identity prior to the introduction of the concept of race gives us the opportunity to determine the parameters that should be used for naming *ethnic* families. It will also allow us to raise the question, "Why and how did we acquire the ideology and structure of white supremacy, a structure that is based on this 'racial' classification system?" How did it become a part of global thinking?

Looked at in these ways, it can be seen that the hegemonic problem for Africans must never be reduced to the simple matters of "stereotyping," "prejudice," and "human relations," important though these may be. There are much more serious issues here, issues having to do with dependence and independence, issues having to do with life and death.

"Race" Is New and Western

A sample of some of the homework on the history of "race" and its place in the social and political context is instructive. The origin of "race and racism" as a western idea is discussed by Kovel (1984). But more important than this idea and its origin in the west are its violent nature and its abuse of power.

> . . . Racism is a category of western civilization, and western civilization is saturated, not merely with racism—that is obvious enough—but with the elementary gesture out of which racism is constructed: splitting the world in the course of domination. It follows that:
>
> - Racism antecedes the notion of race, indeed, it generates the races;
> - Racism supersedes the psychology of prejudice, indeed, it creates that psychology for its purposes;
> - Racism evolves historically, and may be expected to appear in different phases in different epochs and locales;

- Racism cannot be legislated out of existence, since what is put into law always serves to legitimate the system which generates racism and is defined by it;

Let me put it another way. A society's racism is not comprised by its degree of racial segregation, or how racially prejudiced the population may be. These are manifestations of racism, but the *racism itself is the tendency of a society to degrade and do violence to people on the basis of race,* and by whatever mediations may exist for this purpose. (pp. ix–x)

Science Used to Legitimate "Race" and Oppression

Ruth Benedict (1959) was one of the earliest scholars to show that the idea of *"race" and the violence of its actualization were supported by all of the respectable sciences and many of the most prestigious scientists as well.* This amounts to a "full court press," since the end product is *legitimation* of the belief, behaviors, and structures of domination, where religion and superstition had been before. To explain the horrors of white supremacy in the past we have referred to the overt signs of it, such as separate drinking fountains, rest rooms, and seats on busses. *But to these visible signs must be added more powerful, silent, and invisible permeating structures of domination and dehumanization.* Scientists were there to help them to create, to maintain, and to legitimatize the structures. Many are still there, doing the same thing (Ani, 1994; Carruthers, 1995; Guthrie, 1998; Thompson, 1998; Barzun, 1965; DuBois, 1973; Diop,1991; Van Dijk, 1993; Shipman, 1994; Stanton, 1960; Tucker, 1994; Weinreich, 1946; Selden, 1991; Muller-Hill, 1988; Nunn, 1997; Leary, 1992; Lewis, 1973; Lutz & Collins, 1993; Lieberman, Hampton, Littlefield & Hallead, 1992; Kamin, 1974; Hegel, 1991; Gould, 1981; Chase, 1977).

> It was left for high European civilization to advance such a reason for war and persecution and to invoke it into practice. In other words, racism is a creation of our own time. It is a new way of separating the sheep from the goats." (Benedict, 1959, p. 4)

Profound Critique of "Race" Thinking Goes Ignored

Ashley Montague has written extensively on the problem of validity with the concept of "race." For the most part, scholars such as Montague are ignored by scholars who continue to use the race construct, a legacy of pseudoscience (Yee, 1983; Fairchild, 1991; Helms, 1992). This shows that race is a *political construct,* and that the problem of hegemony is far more intractable than "dialogues on race" suggest.

> The modern conception of "race" owes its widespread diffusion to the white man. Wherever he has gone, he has carried it with him. The rise of racism is

associated with slavery and the growing opposition to it so that it is not until the second half of the 18th century that one begins to encounter its development. This is not to say that discrimination against (personal) groups on the basis of skin color or difference did not exist in the ancient world; there is plenty of evidence that it did. But it is to say that such views never became the officially established doctrine, upon any large scale, of any ancient society.

. . . Here the word "race" is used for the first time in a scientific context, and it is quite clear after reading Buffon, that he uses the word in no narrowly defined, but rather in a general, sense. Since Buffon's works were widely read and were translated into many European languages, he must be held at least partially responsible for the diffusion of the idea of a natural separation of the "races" of man, though he himself does not appear to have had such an idea in mind. (Montague, 1974, pp. 33–34)

Montague is devastating in his critique of the concept of race and in the characterization of the use of the construct as pseudoscience.

The Concept of Race

The history of science is littered with the relics of oversimplified theories and outmoded methodological devices. For example, phlogiston was a substance supposed to be present in all materials given off by burning. Advanced in the late seventeenth century by the chemist J. J. Beecher, everyone believed in phlogiston as a demonstrable reality until the true nature of combustion was experimentally demonstrated by Lavoisier a hundred years later. It is an illuminating commentary on the obfuscating effect of erroneous ideas that Joseph Priestley, who, all his life, stoutly defended the phlogiston theory, was unable to perceive that he had discovered a new gas in 1774, which according to the (Fall) theory he thought to be "dephlogisticated air," but which Lavoisier correctly recognized and named oxygen. "Race is the phlogiston of our time" (Montague, 1970, p. xii).

Race and Global Hegemony

It remains for someone like Mills (1997) to situate the "race" matter in its *global* political context. Few people at the bottom of the pyramid of world power have an understanding of how the whole system or structure operates.

One could say that the Racial Contract creates a transnational white polity, a virtual community of people linked by their citizenship in Europe, at home and abroad (Europe Proper, the Colonial Greater Europe, and the "fragments" of Euro-America, Euro-Australia, etc.), and constituted an opposition to their indigenous subjects. (p. 29)

Economic structures have been set in place, causal processes established, whose outcome is to pump wealth from one side of the globe to another, and which will continue to work largely independently of the ill will/good will, racist/anti-racist feelings of particular individuals. This globally color coded distribution of wealth and poverty has been produced by the racial contract and in turn reinforces adherence to it in its signatories and beneficiaries. (p. 36)

Others besides Mills have noted the tribal nature of world power (Kotkin, 1993; Huntington, 1996). Some of the tribal power is based on racial thinking.

The Problem of "Race" and the Fact of Ethnic Plurality: The Political Problem

Kly (1990) puts some of the current issues on the table. *Assimilation, pluralism,* and the problem of *nationalism* with a *multiethnic* population are faced squarely. Kly tries to argue for a possible future, given the unavoidable fact of diversity. Kly says that international law now grants the right of *self-determination* and *cultural integrity,* the very targets of attack in structures of domination. All nations, especially in the age of diversity, recognizing the power of ethnicity and the needs of nationality, find themselves in a quandary about tolerance for and protection of ethnic diversity.

> This book points to a fourth option, one apart from nationalism, assimilation or self-determination, that does not deny the possibility of these options, while still encouraging national unity.
> . . . The central text of international human rights laws states: "In those states in which ethnic, religious or linguistic minorities exist, persons belonging to such minorities shall not be denied the right, in community with the members of their group, to enjoy their own culture, to possess and practice their own religion, or to use their own language." (Article 27 of the United Nations Covenant on Civil and Political Rights: 1, 2, 3)

Ideology as the Legacy of Hegemony

An interesting and provocative analysis of the domination problem, including "racial" domination, is given by Hodge, Struckmann, and Trost (1975). Some scholars argue, I among them, that *greed* and/or *fear* are the elemental sources of the drive to dominate others. Hodge, Struckmann, and Trost argue persuasively that there is more to it than that. They argue that the greedy and fearful actions lead to the creation of *definitions, assumptions, and paradigms, which are embedded in the belief system, which then dictates domination or hegemonic behavior!* This is a critical matter, especially if we are to seek remedies. Where do we start if the problem is to be defined as Hodge, Struckmann, and Trost define it, as ideology?

> A common Western notion occasionally expressed, usually implied, is that Western culture is superior to other cultures. In the West, Western culture is generally considered to be identical with "civilization," and the non Western world is considered to be in varying states of development, moving toward civilization. "Primitive" and "uncivilized" are terms frequently used by Westerners to refer to people in cultures which are unlike the West.
>
> That the people of a culture should view themselves as culturally superior is certainly common. But not so common is the feature contained in Western cultural thinking, that the superior *should control* the inferior. It is this kind of thinking which emphasizes the value placed on control, that produces the missionary imperialism. The notion of "white man's burden" is also derived from this type of thinking. Western control over non Western people is thereby often considered morally defensible.
>
> . . . Westerners identify themselves with reason; they identify non Western people with nature. They therefore conclude that they are justified in dominating and controlling non Western people. (Hodge, Struckmann, & Trost, 1975, p. 3)

How do schools fit into this picture? Which ideas do they manifest and reinforce? To what extent are our school's messages culturally and/or ethnically democratic and nonhegemonic?

Changing Ethnicity to Phenotype: Hegemonic Masterstroke

And so, as shown above, this business of "race" that seems so natural to many today is very new. Prior to the 1700s identity was fundamentally an *ethnic* identity, an identity based on *cultural traditions, linguistic traditions, historical traditions,* and so forth. This does not mean that physical features or phenotypical diversity went unnoticed. It simply means that phenotype was not the core of ethnic identity!

Obviously, phenotype was *correlated with culture.* The farther back we go, the more correlated, the less "mixture." However, there were no "races." There was only one race, the human race.

"Race," or phenotypical diversity, did not become the core of ethnic identity, or, more accurately, a substitute for ethnic identity, until there was a political necessity to make it so. How then do we explain our continued use of "race" in research, in education, and in politics? What should be done about it?

The writers on the history of the idea of race are virtually unanimous in ascribing its origin to Western Europe, with particular emphasis on Germany, France, and England, but not limited to these countries. It is here that politicians, with the aid of the most prestigious scientists and the most prestigious higher education institutions, created the ideology. Blumenbach, at Göttingen University in Germany, was among the earliest Europeans to put a "scientific" foundation under the study of "racial" differences (Bernal, 1987). "Racial" difference studies proliferated and became standard fare as Europeans carried the message to all parts of the world with their slavery and colonial activities.

It must be emphasized that it was not only "race" that was a problem, but also the *ideology associated with race* that derived from the study of race, which itself derived from the politics of domination. Hodges, Struckmann, and Trost, above, say that the study of racism is really not the study of race but the study of domination.

This is not to suggest that domination was exclusive to Europeans, only that using race as a scientific concept, as the rationale for the development of domination, is the special product of Europe. It is the combination of the concept of race with the ideology of white supremacy that produced the designations that we see today.

Perhaps the most significant force for the expansion of racism and white supremacy was the successful attempt by Europeans to shift the basis of group designation from its traditional cultural and ethnic base to an exclusively physiological one. They treated phenotype as if it were "race," and they treated "race" as if it were the primary explanatory factor in human social behavior. *Even "nonracists" continue to use the construct. It is a fixation!*

What is the *purpose* of the use of this invalid construct? What are the *consequences* of the use of the construct? How is society *structured* to project and to legitimatize the construct? I believe that these are the fundamental questions that we should be following with research. I believe that these questions must be addressed in order that our discussion of the subject of race, identity, and education will not be hopelessly confounded.

Unfortunately, we have been following the detour of "race," as if it is real, rather than the ideology that propels it. Some of my most respected friends, all brilliant scholars and major contributors to African progress, have made the study of "racial identity" a core piece of their academic work (Cross, Parham, & Helms, 1998). Implicit in the study of "black racial identity" is the idea that "race" is real, that it is valid and meaningful to us, and that we should strive to have a "healthy 'racial' identity." Of course, when this type of work is conducted as an antihegemonic exercise to create strategies to counter European defamation, I would be the first to find it of great value. I suspect that these scholars tend to use "racial" categories as if they were ethnic categories. This is a confounded meaning of "race," to say the least.

As Africans, we cannot ignore the negative teachings about us in a racist and white supremacist society. However, I do not believe that the appropriate response to the error of the use of invalid "racial categories" is to *reify the categories,* by having the victims create a better use of the categories.

The older basis for family identity is more meaningful. To pursue it forces changes in the nature of the dialogue in profound ways.

Should the goal of the prisoner who is falsely accused be to make the jail better or to get out of jail? In other words, I believe that the search for a "racial identity" leads us in the wrong direction. It is not a matter of research methodology, of assessment instrumentation, of educational theory. *It is simply the wrong question!* The right question is, "How do we restore a healthy ethnic identity to the African family?"

This does not mean that problems with respect to our *perception* of our phenotypical characteristics do not exist. Centuries of propaganda and defamation have definitely taken their toll. The continuing brisk sales of Nadinola and Porcelana skin-lightening or -bleaching creams in the United States and even in Africa itself (but now legally banned in Nigeria) is evidence of the acute nature of the problem. Users experience frequent loss of pigmentation with a growing incidence of skin cancer. Something is dreadfully wrong!

The idea among some of our youth that academic achievement is "acting white" is a testimonial to the absence of systematic socialization by a strong ethnic family. Spike Lee's movie *School Daze* tells us that the issue is potent now, not merely "back then" (Fordham, 1996).

We know that these problems with respect to phenotype do continue, since the phenotype of the African has undergone decades of onslaught through negative projections, such as ridicule of African hair, skin color, lips, and so on. This, of course, results in serious consequences, of which we are all aware, especially when victims of systematic, ongoing, pervasive degradation internalize these meanings. Naturally we must pay attention to these consequences. But the end toward which we strive should be the decolonization of minds, to purge them of images created by white supremacy ideology, and the restoration of the African family, not the search for "racial identity." Rather we must clarify our African family identity. This restoration must include a move to restore our ethnic base, in keeping with the requirement of any healthy group, from antiquity to the present. We must have a healthy ethnic identity. Then the question of our obvious phenotype will take care of itself.

We do not need and should not have an *oppositional* ethnic identity. We are not a "civil rights" people, even though we have fought to the death in heroic struggles for our rights. *We do not exist merely because we are oppressed. We existed long before our oppression. We experience oppression; however, our identity is not "the oppressed."* The essence of our identity does not depend on our oppressors. Who would we be if they did not exist? Our *condition* may find disproportionate numbers of us in poverty; however, our *identity* is not "the poor or the lower class."

Genuine identity is based on collective culture and traditions, not on opposition to white supremacy, no matter how necessary that struggle is. This realization by Africans makes those who seek to control us uneasy, even fearful. Mentally and physically, the captives are freeing themselves! That is an awesome reality.

The question therefore becomes, "Are the victims of extended periods and deep pressure of white supremacy now ethnic neuters?" "Can we restore a sense of our ethnic selves?" These are important questions, of course.

My research reveals that the core family of African people never lost its ethnic core. Even though modified and developed, the core is still there. Only our awareness of it has dimmed. Only our embracing of it has waned. Many family members have left the fold altogether. Many more may. Yet the core remains, as all advertisers for corporate products know, even if educators do not. They "segment the market," targeting specific groups. Otherwise they would fail.

The Current Agenda in Education

Where does this bring us? I believe that it is important that we arm ourselves with the tools of analysis. We must know the history, purposes, consequences, and structure of the racial paradigm. And I believe that we should all be engaged in dismantling that evil paradigm brick by brick. Then I believe it is our obligation to go about the process of healing ourselves. We have been pushed off our center.

We cannot make ourselves whole merely by studying problems of "human relations," "stereotypes," "prejudice," "bigotry," and so forth. That vocabulary tends to trivialize the *hegemony* problem, to misdirect attention from the root problem, and to falsify its nature. The real problem will never be remedied by capitalizing the word "black," making Africans the only group in the world's list of ethnic groups named by an adjective instead of a proper noun (Moore, 1992; Wynter, 1992).

Healing the distortions will require an understanding of the history of *hegemony*, an analysis of the strengths and weaknesses of those who have practiced it, and an analysis of the consequences of hegemony on the behavior of victims. We need to do whatever is necessary so that our children and our people accept themselves, with all our magnificent phenotypes, as people of beauty, as natural, as normal. But to stop there is a gross mistake. To use phenotypical features, including the ones not normally associated with race, as the essence of identity is literally to remove the bearer, or the bearer's ethnic family, from time and space. Indeed, it is to remove us from the human historical and cultural process. That is *the ultimate in dehumanization and cultural genocide*.

Ethnicity implies history, culture, location, and creativity (Obenga, 1998). Color does not. The trick of oppressors' causing victims to become pathologically preoccupied with phenotype, to the exclusion of an understanding of their place in the cosmos and thus leading to a lack of understanding of the evolution of the ethnic family and a lack of creating stronger bonds among ethnic family members, will lead our people down the wrong pathway. This is a curriculum issue.

The fundamental question, as I have stated elsewhere, for people of African ancestry is, "To be or not to be African?" For some of us, ethnicity does not matter at all. In fact, some run from it as fast as is humanly possible. I have no message for them, nor will I argue for or against their position. Their struggle, if any, is of a different order.

Nothing in what I have said will or should prevent any African or other person from making a choice with respect to his or her family membership. What if Africans choose not to be Africans? That is a choice that they can certainly make. To be an individual, with no recognition of membership in any ethnic family, or to attempt to be a member of someone else's ethnic family is an option that everyone is free to explore and attempt. Such choices are as old as the human family. They will continue to be made. Similarly, to commit to family, to find one's destiny with that family, is also a choice.

Ethnicity in Global Perspective and the Structure of Domination

There are certain global realities that few of us are called on to consider. *An ethnic imperative is at the heart of how the world is organized!* I have frequently referred to Kotkin (1993) and Huntington (1996), whose works, though somewhat controversial, provide analyses that are quite compelling about the way the global world actually functions. While large parts of the world's population are becoming more diffused, Kotkin and Huntington argue that a few ethnic groups rule the world's "global tribes or civilizations." *According to Kotkin and Huntington, they do so because they preserve a strong sense of ethnic identity. This is the basis of the trust within that permits collaboration in economic and political arenas.*

I have gone into some detail in this discussion about "race" and "racial identity." The topic "race and education" cannot be addressed in the absence of such an analysis. In fact, to continue with traditional analyses of the problem of "race" and education focus on biology rather than on hegemony is, in my opinion, to actually contribute to the negative consequences of the existing structures of domination.

Elsewhere I have dealt with the question of the *structure of hegemony* (Hilliard, 1988; Pine & Hilliard, 1990; Hilliard, 1997), in the case of people of African ancestry being under white supremacy, especially during the past 400 years. In my speaking and writings, I have identified, from my own experience, from research, and from the general literature on race, education, and domination, common elements in structures of domination anywhere. Specifically, dominating populations *crush or suppress the history* of their victims, *destroy the practice of the culture* of their victims, *prevent the victims from coming to understand themselves as a part of a cultural family,* teach systematically *the ideology of white supremacy, control the socialization process, control the accumulation of wealth,* and *perform segregation and apartheid.*

It is very important to keep in our consciousness the fact that these things are *matters of structure, matters of systematic practices founded on ideology.* No attempt to remedy problems in education can occur apart from an understanding of these things; in fact, as I have indicated in other places, one of the reasons that we have been so unsuccessful in producing educational equity is that our understanding of the structure of hegemony was focused on a single element, that of segregation of "the races." This left the other elements largely untouched since they were not prominent in our understanding of segregation. Otherwise, remedies would have jumped out at us immediately. For example, if the suppression of history is an element of hegemony, then the restoration of history is the antidote. Similarly, the same thing holds true with the other elements.

Race, Identity, and Hegemony in Education

Now we turn to "race" and education. In common professional dialogue, when "race" is mentioned, it is most frequently associated with questions of intellectual capacity, questions of inequity in the provision of services, and questions regarding the type of services provided, for example, ethnic specificity. These are mostly matters that pertain mainly to students. There are also issues that have to do with equity in employment, with the linkage between school and community.

Education, like the matter of "race," is situated in a context. There should be no need to go into great detail about the history of the education of Africans under slavery, colonization, apartheid, and white supremacy ideology (Woodson, 1969; Anderson, 1988; Shujaa, 1994; King, 1971; Spivey, 1978). The record is clear. The treatment of Africans was not a matter of negligence or accident. It was not benign. Massive and strategic attempts were made to use educational *structures* to destroy "critical consciousness" (Freire, 1970), to alienate Africans from tradition and from each other, to teach African inferiority and European superiority.

The record will also show that there have been many different *forms of all of the above.* For example, tracking is a form of in-school segregation that followed separate schools. This and other forms of hegemonic devices have been rationalized by respected scholars (Snyderman & Rothman, 1990; Herrnstein & Murray, 1994; Weinberg, 1977; Hilliard, 1997).

So we have two major concerns. First, there is the need to access and to *dismantle* a tremendous array of aggressive negative beliefs, behaviors, and strategies. Second, there is the need to construct normal nurturing. There is no mystery about how to provide a high quality of teaching to people of African ancestry or to anyone else. There is only the matter of will (Hilliard, 1995).

Again, the problem is not technical, but political. There are no technical solutions to political problems.

In healthy societies, the school is an extension of family and community. Students are precious resources (Erny, 1973, 1981; Fu-Kiau & Lukondo-Wambo, 1988; Suzuki, 1984; Mathews, 1988). When students become commodities or isolates, detached from family, lost from a strong sense of belonging to a family, trouble lies ahead.

We have an enormous task before us. We must cleanse our thinking of gross error. We must apply ourselves to correct our systems and structures. We must inform our scientific and general communities of what we are about. We must support a healing process for offended and damaged ethnic families. We must focus the spotlight on hegemony and its practitioners so that we can see it coming and take actions against it.

Scholarship is a double-edged sword. It can cut two ways, for good or for evil. We must guarantee that it does the former.

REFERENCES

Anderson, J. D. (1988). *The education of blacks in the south, 1860–1935.* Chapel Hill: The University of North Carolina Press.

Alba, R. D. (1990). *Ethnic identity: The transformation of white America.* New Haven: Yale University Press.

Ani, M. (1994). *Yurugu: An African centered critique of European thought and behavior.* New York: Africa World Press.

Arnold, M. (Ed.) (1978). *Black consciousness in South Africa.* New York: Random House.

Asante, M. K. (1987). *The Afrocentric idea.* Philadelphia: Temple University Press.

Azibo, D. A. (1996). *African psychology in historical world perspective and related commentary.* Trenton, NJ: Africa World Press.

Backler, A., & Eakin, S. (1993). *Every child can succeed.* Bloomington, IN: Agency for Instructional Technology.

Barzun, J. (1965). *Race: A study in superstition.* New York: Harper Torchbooks.

Benedict, R. (1959). *Race, science and politics.* New York: Viking Press.

Ben Jochannan, Y. (1972). *Cultural genocide in the black and African studies curriculum.* New York: Alkebu-Lan.

Bernal, M. (1987). *Black Athena: The Afroasiatic roots of classical civilization: Volume I, The fabrication of ancient Greece 1785–1985.* See especially chapter 4 "Hostilities to Egypt in the 18th Century." pp. 189–223.

Berry, M. F. (1971). *Black resistance/white law.* Englewood Cliffs, NJ: Prentice-Hall.

Biddiss, M. D. (1970). *Father of racist ideology: The social and political thought of Count DeGobineau.* New York: Weybright & Talley.

Blauner, R. (1972). *Racial oppression in America.* New York: Harper & Row.

Bulhan, H. A. (1985). *Frantz Fanon and the psychology of oppression.* New York: Plenum Press.

Cabral, A. (1973). *Return to the source: Selected speeches by Amilcar Cabral.* New York: Monthly Review Press.

Carlson, L. H., & Colburn, G. A. (1972). *In their place: White America defines her minorities, 1850–1950.* New York: John Wiley & Sons.

Carruthers, J. (1995). Science and Oppression. In D. Azibo (Ed.), *African psychology in historical perspective and related commentary.* Trenton, NJ: Africa World Press.

Chase, A. (1977). *The legacy of Malthus: The social costs of the new scientific racism.* New York: Alfred A. Knopf.

Chinweizu (1987). *Decolonizing the African mind.* London: Sundoor Press.

Conrad, E. (1966). *The invention of the Negro.* New York: Paul S. Exilison, Inc.

Crick, B. (1996). *Race: The history of an idea in the West.* Baltimore: Johns Hopkins University.

Cross, W., Parham, T., & Helms, J. (1998). Nigrescence revisited. In R. Jones (Ed.), *Advances in black psychology,* Oakland, CA: Cobb & Henry Publishers.

Cruse, H. (1967). *The crisis of the negro intellectual: From its origins to the present.* New York: Morrow.

Delpit, L. (1995). *Other people's children: Cultural conflict in the classroom.* New York: The New Press.

Diamond, S. (1995). *Roads to dominion: Right wing movements and political power in the United States.* New York: The Guilford Press.

Diop, C. A. (1974). *The African origin of civilization: Myth or reality.* Westport, CT: Lawrence-Hill & Co. (First published 1955, in Paris.)

Diop, C. A. (1991). *Civilization or barbarism: An authentic anthropology.* Brooklyn, NY: Lawrence Hill.

Drake, S. C. (1987). *Black folk here and there: Volumes 1 & 2.* Los Angeles: University of California, Center for Afro-American Studies.

DuBois, W. E. B. (1973). *Black reconstruction in America: An essay toward a history of the part which black folk played in the attempt to reconstruct democracy in America 1860–1880.* New York: Harcourt Brace & Co.

Dubow, S. (1995). *Scientific racism in modern South Africa.* New York: Cambridge University Press.

Edwards, L. (1997). *The power of ideas: The heritage foundation at 25 years.* Ottowa, IL: Jameson Books, Inc.

Erny, P. (1973). *Childhood and cosmos.* New York: Black Orpheus Press.

Erny, P. (1981). *The child and his environment in black Africa.* New York: Oxford University Press.

Fairchild, H. H. (1991). Scientific racism: The cloak of objectivity. *Journal of Social Issues, 47*(3), 101–115.

Fanon, F. (1967). *Black skin, white masks.* New York: Grove.

Fanon, F. (1969). *A dying colonialism.* New York: Grove. (First published 1959.)

Feagin, J. R., & Herman, V. (1995). *White racism: The basics.* New York: Rutledge Press.

Felder, C. H. (1991). Race, racism and the Biblical narratives. In C. H. Felder (Ed.), *Stony the road we trod: African American biblical interpretation* (pp. 127–145). Minneapolis: Fortress Press.

Fontaine, P. M. (Ed.). (1991). *Race, class and power in Brazil.* Los Angeles: University of California, Center for Afro-American Studies.

Fordham, S. (1996). *Blacked out: Dilemmas of race, identity and success at capital high.* Chicago: The University of Chicago Press.

Freire, P. (1970). *Pedagogy of the oppressed.* New York: Herder & Herder.

Friedman, L. J. (1970). *The white savage racial fantasies in the Post Bellum South.* Englewood Cliffs, NJ: Prentice-Hall.

Fu-Kiau, B. I., & Lukondo-Wambo, A. M. (1988). *Kindezi: The kongo art of babysitting.* New York: Vantage Press.

Fu-Kiau, B. I. (1991). *Self-healing power and therapy: Old teachings from Africa.* New York: Vantage Press.

Garcia, J., & Goebel, J. (1985). A comparative study of the portrayal of Black Americans in selected U.S. history textbooks. Unpublished manuscript.

Ghurye, G. S. (1963). *The scheduled tribe of India.* New Brunswick, NJ: Transaction Books.

Gould, Stephen J. (1981). *The mismeasure of man.* New York: Norton.

Greene, E. (1998). *Planet of the Apes as American myth: Race, politics, and popular culture.* Hanover: Wesleyan University Press.

Griffith, E. E. H. (1998). *Race and excellence: My dialogue with Chester Pierce.* Iowa City: University of Iowa Press.

Guthrie, R. (1998). *Even the rat was white.* New York: Harper & Row.

Hacker, A. (1995). *Two nations: Black and white, separate, hostile and unequal.* New York: Ballentine Books.

Harding, S. (Ed.). (1993). *The racial economy of science: Toward a democratic future.* Bloomington: Indiana University Press.

Hare, N. (1970). *The black Anglo-Saxons.* Boston: Collier.

Hegel, G. W. F. (1991). *The philosophy of history.* New York: Prometheus Books.

Hehir, T., & Latus, T. (Eds.). (1993). *Special education at the century's end: Evolution of theory and practice since 1970.* Cambridge: Harvard Educational Review Reprint Series, No. 23.

Heller, K., Holtzman, W., & Messick, S. (Eds.). (1982). *Placing children in special education: A strategy for equity.* Washington, DC: Academy Press.

Helms, J. E. (1992). Why is there no study of cultural equivalence in standardized cognitive ability testing? *American Psychologist, 47,* 1083–1101.

Herrnstein, R., & Murray, C. (1994). *The bell curve: Intelligence and class structure in American life.* New York: The Free Press.

Hilliard, A. G. (1988). Conceptual confusion and the persistence of group oppression through education. *Equity and Excellence, 24,* 1.

Hilliard, A. G. III (1990). *Fabrication: The politics and sociology of knowledge in the study of Ancient Kemet (Egypt) and Greek and Roman world.* Presented at Temple University, Symposium on Martin Bernal's Black Athena, Department of African American Studies and Department of Classics. Philadelphia: Temple University.

Hilliard, A. G. (1995). Either a paradigm shift or no mental measurement: The nonscience and nonsense of *The bell curve. Psych Discourse, 76*(10), 6–20.

Hilliard, A. G. III (1994). What good is this thing called intelligence and why bother to measure it? *The Journal of Black Psychology, 20*(4), 430–444.

Hilliard, A. G. III (1995). *The Maroon within us: Essays on African American community socialization.* Baltimore: Black Classic Press.

Hilliard, A. G. III (1997). Psychology as political science and as a double edged sword: Racism and counter racism in psychology. In *Psych Discourse, 29*(5)(6), 6–20.

Hilliard, A. G. III (1998). *SBA: The reawakening of the African mind.* Gainesville, FL: Makare Publishers.

Hilliard, A. G. III, Jenkins, Y., & Scott, M. (1979). *Behavioral criteria in research and the study of racism: Performing the jackal function. Technical Reports I and II.* (Contract No. N00014-177-C0183). Washington, DC: Office of Naval Research.

Hodge, J. L., Struckmann, D. K., & Trost, L. D. (1975). *Cultural basis of racism and group oppression: An examination of traditional "western" concepts, values and institutional structures which support racism, sexism and elitism.* Berkeley: Two Riders Press.

Hofstader, R. (1971). *Social Darwinism in American thought.* Boston: Beacon Press.

Huggins, W. N., & Jackson, J. G. (1999). *Introduction to African civilizations.* Baltimore: Black Classic Press. (See especially chapter XX, "That word "NEGRO' (negro)," pp. 155–161. (First published 1937.)

Huntington, S. P. (1996). *The clash of civilizations and the remaking of world order.* New York: Simon & Schuster.

Jones, R. (1998). *African American Identity Development.* Hampton, VA: Cobb & Henry.

Jordan, W. (1968). *White over Black: American attitudes toward the Negro. 1550–1812.* New York: W. W. Norton & Co.

Kambon, K. K. K. (1992). *The African personality: An African-centered framework.* Tallahassee, FL: Nubial Nation Publishers.

Kamin, L. (1974). *The science and politics of I.Q.* New York: John Wiley.

King, K. (1971). *Pan-Africanism in education: A study of race, philanthropy, and education in the southern states of America and east Africa.* Oxford: Clarendon Press.

King, M. L., Jr. (1968). The role of the behavioral scientist in the civil rights movement in "King's challenge to the nation's social scientists." *Monitor* (American Psychological Association). January, 1999, 26–29.

Kly, Y. N. (1990). *International law and the black minority in the U.S.* Windsor, Canada: Clarity International.

Kotkin, J. (1993). *Tribes: How race, religion, and identity determine success in the new global economy.* New York: Random House.

Kovel, J. (1984). *White racism: A psycho history.* New York: Columbia University Press.

Leary, W. E. (1992, November 10). Exhibition examines scientists' complicity in Nazi-era atrocities. *The New York Times.* B-8.

Lewis, D. (1973). Anthropology and colonialism. *Current Anthropology,* 14, 581–602.

Lieberman, L., Hampton, R. E., Littlefield, A., & Hallead, G. (1992). Race in biology and anthropology: A study of college texts and professors. *Journal of Research in Science Teaching, 29*(3), 301–321.

Lifton, R. J. (1986). *The Nazi doctor's medicine: Killing and the psychology of genocide.* New York: Basic Books.

Lutz, C. A., & Collins, J. L. (1993). *Reading National Geographic.* Chicago: University of Chicago Press.

Margo, R. (1990). *Race and schooling in the south: 1880–1950: An economic history.* Chicago: University of Chicago Press.

Mathews, J. (1988). *Escalante, the best teacher in America.* New York: Henry Holt & Company.

Maxwell, F. J. (1975). *Slavery and the Catholic Church: The history of Catholic teaching concerning the moral legitimacy of the institution of slavery.* Chichester: Barry Rose Publishers.

McCulloch, J. (1995). *Colonial psychiatry and the African mind.* Cambridge: Cambridge University Press.

Memmi, A. (1967). *The colonizer and the colonized.* Boston: Beacon Press.

Mills, C. W. (1997). *The racial contract.* Ithaca, NY: Cornell University Press.

Muller-Hill, B. (1988). *Murderous science: Elimination by scientific selection of Jews, Gypsies and others: Germany 1933–1945.* New York: Oxford University Press.

Montague, A. (1968). *The concept of the primitive.* New York: The Free Press.

Montague, A. (1970). *The concept of race.* London: Cathier Books.

Montague, A. (1974). *Man's most dangerous myth: The fallacy of race.* New York: Oxford University Press.

Moore, R. B. (1992). *The name "negro": Its origin and evil use.* Baltimore: Black Classic Press. (First Published, 1960.)

Nunn, K. B. (1997). Law as a Eurocentric enterprise. *Law and Inequality Journal of Theory and Practice, IV,* 323–371.

Obenga, T. (1998). Who am I? In J. H. Carruthers & L. Harris (Eds.), *African world history project: The preliminary challenge* (pp. 31–46). Los Angeles: Association for the Study of Classical African Civilizations.

Osborne, N. G., & Feit, M. D. (1992). The use of race in medical research. *Journal of the American Medical Association, 267*(2), 275–279.

Patterson, W. L. (1970). *We charge genocide: The historic petition to the United Nations for relief from a crime of the United States government against the negro people.* New York: International Publishers.

Pine, J., & Hilliard, A. G. III. (1990). RX for racism: Imperatives for American schools. *Phi Delta Kappa, 71,* 593–600.

Poliakov, L. (1974). *The Aryan myth: A history of racial and nationalistic ideas in Europe.* New York: Meridian.

Powell, R. (1937). *Human side of a people and the right name.* New York: Philemon.

Proctor, R. N. (1988). *Racial hygiene: Medicine under the Nazis.* Cambridge: Harvard University Press.

Quigley, C. (1981). *The Anglo-American establishment: From Rhodes to Cliven.* New York: Books in Focus.

Rajshekar, V. T. (1987). *Dalit: The black untouchables of India.* Atlanta: Clarity Press.

Saunders, W. L., & Rivers, J. C. (1996). *Cumulative and residual effects of teachers on future student academic achievement. Value Added Research & Assessment.* Knoxville: University of Tennessee.

Schwartz, B. N., & Disch, R. (1970). *White racism: Its history, pathology and practice.* New York: Dell.

Selden, S. (1991). Selective traditions and the science curriculum: Eugenics and biology textbook, 1914–1949. *Science Education, 75,* 493–512.

Shipman, P. (1994). *Evolution of racism: Human differences and the use and abuse of science.* New York: Simon & Schuster.

Shujaa, M. J. (Ed). (1994). *Too much schooling, too little education: Paradox of black education in white societies.* Trenton, NJ: African World Press.

Snowden, F. M. (1983). *Before color prejudice: The ancient view of blacks.* Cambridge: Harvard University Press.

Snyderman, M., & Rothman, S. (1990). *The iq controversy: The media and public policy.* New Brunswick, NJ: Transaction.

Spiegel, M. (1988). *The dreaded comparison: Human and animal slavery.* Philadelphia: New Society Publishers.

Spindler, G., & Spindler, L. (1998). Cultural politics of the White Ethniclass in the mid-nineties. In Y. Zou & E. T. Trueba (Eds.), *Ethnic identity and power: Cultural contexts of political action in school and society.* Albany: State University of New York Press.

Spivey, D. (1978). *Schooling for the new slavery: Black industrial education, 1868–1915.* Westport, CT: Greenwood.

Stanton, W. (1960). *The Leopard's spots: Scientific attitudes toward race in America 1815–59.* Chicago: The University of Chicago Press.

Stuckey, S. (1987). *Slave culture: Nationalist theory and the foundations of black America.* New York: Oxford University Press.

Suzuki, S. (1984). *Nurtured by love: The classic approach to talent education.* Smithtown, NY: Exposition Press.

Tatum, B. D. (1997). *"Why are all the black kids sitting together in the cafeteria?": And other conversations about race.* New York: Basic Books.

Thompson, A. (1998). Developing an African historiography. In J. H. Carruthers & L. Harris (Eds.), *African world history project: The preliminary challenge.* Los Angeles: Association for the Study of Classical African Civilizations.

Tucker, W. H. (1994). *The science and politics of racial research.* Chicago: University of Illinois Press.

Van Dijk, T. A. (1993). *Elite discourse and racism: Volume 6 in Sage Series on Race and Ethnic Relations.* London: Sage Publications.

Ven Norden, L., & Pollock, J. (1985). *The black feet of the peacock: The color-concept "black" from the Greeks through the Renaissance.* New York: University Press of America.

Wa Thiong'o, N. (1987). *Decolonizing the mind: The politics of language in African literature.* London: Heinemann.

Walker, S., Spohn, C., & DeLonc, M. (1996). *The color of justice: Race, ethnicity and crime in America.* New York: Wadsworth Publishing Company.

Weinberg, M. (1977). *A chance to learn: The history of race and education in the United States.* New York: Cambridge University Press.

Weindling, P. (1989). *Health, race and German politics between national unification and Nazism 1870–1945.* New York: Cambridge University Press.

Weinreich, M. (1946). *Hitler's professors: The part of scholarship in Germany's crimes against the Jewish people.* New York: Yiddish Scientific Institute.

Welsing, F. C. (1991). *The Isis papers: The keys to the colors.* Chicago: Third World Press.

Willhelm, S. (1970). *Who needs the Negro?* New York: Anchor.

Willhelm, S. (1983). *Black in a white America.* Cambridge: Schenkman.

Wilson, A. N. (1990). *Black-on-black violence: The psychodynamics of black self-annihilation in service of white domination.* New York: Afrikan World InfoSystems.

Wilson, A. N. (1993). *The falsification of Afrikan consciousness: Eurocentric history, psychiatry and the politics of white supremacy.* New York: Afrikan World InfoSystems.

Wilson, A. N. (1998). *Blueprint for black power: A moral, political and economic imperative for the twenty-first century.* New York: Afrikan World InfoSystems.

Wobogo, V. (1988). *The prehistoric origins of white racism.* San Francisco: Unpublished manuscript.

Woodson, C. G. (1969). *Miseducation of the Negro.* Washington, DC: The Associated Publishers. (First published 1933.)

Wynter, S. (1992). *Do not call us Negroes: How "multicultural" textbooks perpetuate racism.* San Francisco: Aspire.

Yee, A. H. (1983). Ethnicity and race: Psychological perspectives. *Educational Psychologist, 18*(1), 14–24.

Yette, S. (1971). *The choice: The issue of black survival in America.* New York: Berkley Medallion Books.

Zindgrist, S. (1992). *Exterminate all the brutes.* New York: The New Press.

Zou, Y., & Trueba, E. T. (1998). *Ethnic identity and power: Cultural contexts of political action in school and society.* Albany: State University of New York Press.

2

Comment

The Social "Destruction" of Race to Build African American Education

Laurence Parker

The film "Black is . . . Black ain't," by Marlon Riggs (1995), provides a useful summary context for my response to the excellent paper by Asa Hilliard III. Hilliard questions the fundamental definition of race and how it has developed from the white European American experience related to discrimination, hegemony, and control of persons of color. Hilliard also shows how racial ideology and hegemony framed the debate around the wrong issues in education (e.g., at-risk, cultural-deficit model) related to race. Instead, Hilliard argues for defining an African ethnicity linked to current and historical aspects of identity regarding people of African descent in the United States. A direct implication of the African ethnicity position in education is how it positions itself against racially discriminatory school policies and practices. This viewpoint also looks to existing models of successful African-centered education with African American students.

Given the perspective articulated by Hilliard, I would partially echo some of his concerns about the problematic use of race and how ethnicity would be a term that more accurately describes African Americans.[1] To that end, my brief chapter response seeks to build on Dr. Hilliard's work regarding his criticism of the use of the term *race* and replacing it with *ethnicity*. *Ethnicity* may be a more accurate term to use because *race* has had such a strong hegemonic effect on the racial subordination of persons of color. Yet, the historical use of the term has also been problematic regarding its use against African Americans (Omi & Winant, 1994; Sleeter, 1992). My response will

---

[1]Hilliard uses the term *people of African descent who live in the United States.* Throughout this paper, I will also make reference to this term but will also use African American or black as well, even though I acknowledge the problematic nature of the debate surrounding the definitions of these terms. See for example, Martin's (1991) discussion on this topic.

briefly address some of the key aspects of racial categorization and ethnicity and their link to modernity. My response chapter concludes with a call for critical theories of race in connection with educational policy issues that have had harmful effects on African American students.

Tracing the Origins of "Race" and Its Connection with Modernity

Hilliard correctly points out that the white Eurocentric perspective of superiority related to race and racism has historically dominated the knowledge base in the social and behavioral sciences. Under this intellectual framework, African Americans have been continually viewed as psychologically inferior to white European Americans, based on a socially constructed racial status that elevated the use of race as a term linked with notions of inferior and superior judgments of racial hierarchy. The psychological and anthropological theories based on racial identity development have been grounded on dangerously faulty ideological and epistemological assumptions about the inferiority of African Americans (Baker, 1998; Malik, 1996; Smedley, 1999). Furthermore, one must fully acknowledge the centrality of race in modernity and how race has shaped intellectual history and culture (Goldberg, 1993).

I agree with Hilliard in that the term "race" has a problematic etymological past rooted in the period of the scientific racism–eugenics movement at the turn of the twentieth century. Hilliard argues instead for replacing "race" with the term "ethnicity" since peoples of African descent are ethnically and culturally linked to Africa as an ethnic group. This is an important shift in thinking as some see "ethnicity" as a more accurate term to define the myriad experiences of African Americans as a cultural group. For example, Alex M. Johnson (1996) argues, in the *California Law Review,* that racial identifications, particularly through the legal classifications of the U.S. Census, simply serve to ossify the psychological and ideological connection white European Americans have assumed regarding negative physical and cultural traits associated with African Americans. Johnson sees an analogy with trademark law in commerce since products are viewed as representing a brand name particular to their product for consumers. Johnson argues that if "ethnicity" is adopted as the more correct term of classification, it will result in destabilizing the daily ideological and psychologically biased categories most people have about the meaning of race and its association with the status of African Americans (Johnson, 1996, p. 929). The use of ethnicity would also allow African Americans to claim a central ethnicity of African descent, as well as multiple ethnicities (e.g., Irish, English, French), therefore disrupting the ethnic definitions white European Americans hold for themselves and causing them to question the validity of racial discrimination.

I would ideally like to believe that, at some point in time, this definition could be used as a categorical lens to replace race. However, I think more elaboration and explanation are needed to distinguish the more general definition of ethnicity, with that of the previous assumptions related to ethnicity based on ethnocentric notions of White European American superiority over persons of color.[2] If the term "ethnicity" is used to replace "race," careful research needs to follow this shift in order to document how African American ethnic experiences were qualitatively different from those of white European Americans. This becomes particularly important with respect to using education for academic achievement and upward mobility in the face of white American philanthropic attempts at control and virulent southern racial discrimination (Anderson, 1988; Siddle-Walker, 1996).

As Christine Sleeter (1992) commented in her review of two books on the White European ethnic experience (Perlmann, 1988; Alba, 1990), many of the current problems in urban education can be attributed to an unquestioned assumption of a generalized white European American view (or "whiteness," see Delgado & Stefancic, 1997) related to assimilation into mainstream society.[3]

According to this perspective, all racial and ethnic groups, regardless of the particulars of their histories, should emulate "the one best model" of the white European American ethnic group success in the United States. This general assimilationist ethnicity pattern was established by social scientists who argued that all groups progress through similar stages in "pulling themselves up by their bootstraps" and that the experiences of African Americans will not be radically different from those of white European immigrants (Myrdal, 1944; Glazer & Moynihan, 1963). Furthermore, the ethnic identity politics of the early twentieth century would merely take on symbolic importance in the form of cultural or ethnic holiday pride. This would be due to the fact that many white European American ethnic groups would intermarry with each other and thus lessen the group need for ethnic solidarity and even consideration as a particular ethnic group (Hout & Goldstein, 1994).

The assumption of the "one best model" of ethnicity has also ruled social science methodology, as Omi and Winant (1994) articulated in their criticism of the ethnicity paradigm related to research and the lack of attention paid to

[2]Racial appearance and national origin are often the major determinants of power relations and discrimination based on race. However, as van Dijk (1993) points out, *ethnicism* can also stem from differentiation based on cultural characteristics or religion, etc., which in turn leads to the process of categorization, prejudice, and eventually discrimination.

[3]Sleeter stated that some of these problems were low student achievement among African Americans, poor relations between white European American administrators and the African American community, and white European American teacher biases against African American students. For more on white teacher biases against African American students, see Kailin (1999).

race. Under the ethnicity paradigm, Omi and Winant believed that group norms and common circumstances have acted as the independent variable in many studies that have compared how different ethnic and racial groups have used education for upward mobility. Omi and Winant asserted that because "the independent variable is the 'norm,' the idea of 'differences in status' being affected by factors outside or even unrelated to the group is ruled out at the level of assumptions" (p. 21). Therefore, if African Americans fail to do well in school, it is due to their poor values, norms, and cultural deficiencies, as opposed to institutional or structural racism. Omi and Winant also discussed how common circumstances (e.g., poor schools, hard neighborhood conditions) faced by all ethnic groups become the "dependent variable" in that these are the universal conditions all ethnic groups have to encounter in order to do well and achieve success (p. 21). This success is dependent on how the minority ethnic group is willing to accept the norms of the majority ethnic group. Omi and Winant made important criticisms of the traditional ethnicity paradigm in social science research regarding how it does not pay attention to the enduring consequences of race and racial discrimination.

A Call for a Critical Race Theory for Education

If we take Hilliard's call seriously for using ethnicity regarding persons of African descent, then follow-up is needed to document the differences in ethnicity experiences. The white European ethnic experience is *not* and should not be the norm for judging African American student success and failure. Furthermore, as Omi and Winant illustrated, race still does matter as a socioeconomic and political construct that in turn plays a deciding role in shaping the life chances of African Americans in the United States.

This is where I would argue for a critical theory of race applied to educational policy that does indeed "deconstruct" the problematic history, discourse, and "unconscious racism," and its current harmful effects on racial minorities (Lawrence, 1995). Critical race legal scholars such as Kimberlie Crenshaw and associates (1995), Richard Delgado (1995), Derrick Bell (1992), and Adrian Wing (1997) have been in the forefront of exposing how the law and policy have been intertwined with the historical definitions of race that has subjugated people of color. This has resulted in the historical use of the problematic definitions of race and racism to justify equating white European Americans as a race with property rights over American Indians and African Americans, or the current federal courts' support of "color-blind" U.S. constitutional and statutory civil rights laws. Similarly, Ladson-Billings and Tate (1995), Tate (1997), Solorzano (1997), and Parker, Deyhle, and Villenas (1999) utilized critical race theory in education. These works call for bringing critical race theory into analyzing how educational policies and practices in the areas such as graduate education, school funding, curriculum and instruction, and bilingual education have had a negative racial impact on African Americans, Chicanos/Chicanas, and the Navajo Nation. So while I agree with Hilliard to a great extent, I would argue that the many problems associated with the terms "race" and "racism" are used against our children in schools. Therefore, we need critical theories and praxis related to race in order to critique racially discriminatory policies and take positive actions for African American and other students of color.

REFERENCES

Alba, R. D. (1990). *Ethnic identity.* New Haven: Yale University Press.

Anderson, J. A. (1988). *The education of blacks in the south: 1860–1935.* Chapel Hill: University of North Carolina Press.

Baker, L. D. (1998). *From savage to Negro: Anthropology and the construction of race: 1896–1954.* Berkeley: University of California.

Bell, D. (1992). *Faces at the bottom of the well: The permanence of racism.* New York: Basic Books.

Crenshaw, K., Gotanda, N., Peller, G., & Thomas, K. (Eds.). (1995). *Critical race theory: Key writings that formed the movement.* New York: The New Press.

Delgado, R. (Ed.). (1995). *Critical race theory: The cutting edge.* Philadelphia: Temple University Press.

Delgado, R., & Stefancic, J. (1997). *Critical white studies: Looking beyond the mirror.* Philadelphia: Temple University Press.

Glazer, N., & Moynihan, D. P. (1963). *Beyond the melting pot.* Cambridge: MIT Press.

Goldberg, D. T. (1993). *Racist culture: Philosophy and the politics of meaning.* Oxford: Blackwell.

Hout, M., & Goldstein, J. R. (1994). How 4.5 million Irish immigrants became 40 million Irish Americans: Demographic and subjective aspects of the ethnic composition of white Americans. *American Sociological Review, 59,* 64–82.

Johnson, A. M. (1996). Destablizing racial classifications based on insights gleaned from trademark law. *California Law Review, 84,* 887–952.

Kailin, J. (1999). How white teachers perceive the problem of racism in their schools: A case study in "liberal" Lakeview. *Teachers College Record, 100,* 724–750.

Ladson-Billings, G., & Tate, W. F. IV (1995). Toward a critical theory of race. *Teachers College Record, 97,* 47–68.

Lawrence, C. R. III (1995). The id, the ego and equal protection: Reckoning with unconscious racism. *Stanford Law Review, 47,* 819–848.

Malik, K. (1996). *The meaning of race: Race, history and culture in western society.* New York: New York University Press.

Martin, B. L. (1991). From Negro to black to African American: The power of names and naming. *Political Science Quarterly, 106,* 83–107.

McIntyre, A. (1997). *Making meaning of whiteness: Exploring racial identity with white teachers.* Albany: SUNY Press.

Myrdal, G. (1944). *An American dilemma: The Negro problem and modern democracy.* New York: Harper & Brothers.

Omi, M., & Winant, H. (1994). *Racial formation in the United States, 1960–1990. 2nd ed.* New York: Routledge.

Parker, L., Deyhle, D., & Villenas, S. (Eds.). (1999). *Race is . . . Race isn't. Critical race theory and qualitative studies in education.* Boulder: Westview Press.

Perlmann, J. (1988). *Ethnic differences: Schooling and social structure among the Irish, Italians, Jews, and Blacks in an American city, 1880–1935.* Cambridge: Cambridge University Press.

Riggs, M. (Director-Producer). (1995). *Black is . . . Black Ain't* [Film]. (Available from California News Reel, 149 9th St., San Francisco, CA 94103).

Siddle-Walker, V. (1996). *Their highest potential: An African American school community in the segregated south.* Chapel Hill: University of North Carolina Press.

Sleeter, C. E. (1992). The white ethnic experience in America: To whom does it generalize? *Educational Researcher, 21,* 33–36.

Smedley, A. (1999). *Race in North America: Origin and evolution of a worldview. 2nd ed.* Boulder: Westview Press.

Solorzano, D. G. (1998). Critical race theory, race and gender microaggressions, and the experience of Chicana and Chicano students. *International Journal of Qualitative Studies in Education, 11,* 121–137.

Tate, W. F. IV (1997). Critical race theory and education: History, theory, and implications. In M. Apple (Ed.), *Review of Research in Education* (pp. 195–250). Washington, DC: American Educational Research Association.

van Dijk, T. A. (1993). *Elite discourse and racism.* Thousand Oaks, CA: Sage.

Wing, A. K. (Ed.). (1997). *Critical race feminism: A reader.* New York: New York University Press.

CHAPTER

3 Blacks and the Curriculum

From Accommodation to Contestation and Beyond

William H. Watkins

Early Black Education: A Sociopolitical Analysis

The ideological debates between Booker T. Washington and W. E. B. DuBois have frequently been used to introduce the study of late nineteenth- and early twentieth-century black education. Underlying those polemics, the forging of race and class relations for the new industrial society occurred. Black education was, and continues to be, a politically charged endeavor involving power brokering at the highest levels. This chapter seeks to overview and summarize salient ideological, political, and intellectual forces impacting the 150-year curriculum "struggle" in black education.

Curriculum has been a defining feature of black education. From the outset the white "architects" of black education (Watkins, 2001) understood the power of ideas. They carefully *selected* and *sponsored* knowledge, which contributed to obedience, subservience, and political docility. The battle over what African Americans learn has been long-standing and inextricably connected to national politics, civil rights, labor economics, and social justice. Few disagree that the status of black education serves as a barometer of our people's plight.

While there are many ways to approach this issue, Herb Kliebard's notions of "struggle" and contestation have been chosen as a conceptual and discursive framework. Kliebard's (1987) *The Struggle for the American Curriculum* begins with the end of the nineteenth century. He journeys through several decades where we learn of the different intellectual, ideological, and political forces influencing the traditional school curriculum. He demonstrates that the official curriculum is the result of a battle of ideas and social views. School knowledge is a product of complex power politics, popular ideas, ideological struggle, negation, consensus, and compromise. Along the way powerful individuals and groups affect the process.

From the Civil War onward, the "Negro question" occupied a central place in the social and political unfolding of America. Far beyond the narrow issues of teaching and learning, the education of black Americans became entangled in the complicated questions of nation building, regionalism, colonialism, labor economics, and the socio-moral development of an emergent and influential world power. From De Tocqueville to DuBois, social theorists observed that racial questions would occupy America henceforth.

Reconstruction represented the critical period during which the South was forcibly rejoined to the Union. Victorious northern industrial hegemonists agreed on social, political, and legal policy that granted citizenship to blacks without disturbing the racial and social class traditions of the South. This was no easy task, given the passionate demands for freedom coming from blacks and northern liberals alike.

Surrounded by these complex, delicate, and even antithetical demands, the education of blacks emerged as central in the effort to structure a segregated yet stable South. Northern industrialists turned their considerable financial and institutional resources to the establishment of Negro schools (Arnove, 1980; Berman, 1980) and curriculum. This occurred at a time when there were demands by blacks for citizenship in the racist South (Anderson, 1988; Carruthers, 1994; Watkins, 1993).

Prior to the Civil War, self-help efforts combined with activities of benevolent and altruistic white Christians to provide rudimentary education for blacks. By the mid-1860s Congress established the Freedman's Bureau, which joined the efforts of the missionary, Sabbath, and private black schools already existing throughout the south.

Beyond literacy and basic education, southern black leaders had additional demands. The quest for self-determination (Anderson, 1988) demanded knowledge of society, citizenship, and vocation. The cultivation of teachers, leaders, ministers, managers, and skilled tradesmen were objectives of early black education. Many black educators were attracted to the New England–styled classical liberal curriculum (Anderson, 1988), as it promised participation in the social life of the new America.

From the defeat of Reconstruction (Peery, 1975) to World War I, curriculum occupied a place of importance in black education. Beyond reading, writing, and arithmetic, the curriculum became an object of contestation (Tyack, 1974). The politics of colonialism and subjugation thrust schooling, especially the curriculum, into the center of the sociopolitical and ideological struggle. Northern hegemonists and southern "moderates" took interest in the racial and power arrangements of the new South. What would be the social, political, and economic status of blacks? How would a middle or compradore class, requisite to any group's stability, be cultivated? What models of education and curriculum could be utilized? The particular features of the South's internal colonization (Peery, 1975), the inherited political and cultural forms of its racial structure, and the possibilities for corporate wealth to influence public policy all contributed to a "special kind of education" (Bullock, 1967) for southern blacks. This education attempted to reconcile Negro subservience with the new arrangements of power, defuse potential turmoil, and pacify diverse elements.

Accommodationist-styled education and curriculum models, which were similarly introduced to other colonial and semicolonial peoples (King, 1971; Watkins, 1989), now gained favor among those shaping the new south. With General Samuel Armstrong as field commander, Dr. Thomas Jesse Jones as bursar, and Booker T. Washington in charge of public relations, the shaping of Negro education took form. The battle for a "black curriculum" was now under way.

Accommodationist education, simply stated, meant blacks had to adjust themselves to the existing racial and social class structure of the South. Guiding black education in that direction required considerable resources and political skill. Proponents of accommodationism opposed, but could not ignore, self-help and missionary education programs identified with liberal and classical notions of citizenship education, uplift, and individual betterment. Many Blacks viewed European middle-class liberal education as the ideal.

The tasks of the northern hegemonists and their southern supporters were to reconcile the growing black demand for education with the political realities of peonage and oppression. Colonial education had to be *fitted* to the American South. This undertaking required the efforts of both the ideologists and the financiers. Corporate philanthropists joined forces with racial sociologists to design seventy-five years of education for blacks.

Anderson (1988) described the mid-nineteenth–century transition of missionary philanthropy to industrial philanthropy as it influenced black education. The missionary movement had its roots in abolitionism. Belief in the dignity of humankind, the possibility of redemption, and the need for socialization drew church missionaries to Reconstruction-era black education. Anderson (1988) writes:

> The missionary philanthropists basically egalitarian in their views of civil rights and race relations launched their campaign for black higher education as a means to produce a college-bred black leadership that would lead the black masses in their struggle for equal rights. Certainly, as has been pointed out, individual missionaries varied greatly in their socio-political and racial creeds. The dominant liberal leadership, however, held the mission societies to a belief in human equality, a concern for civil and social justice, and a faith in moral and cultural improvement through classical liberal education. Hence, missionary ideology supported the struggle for black civil and political equality within the existing economic order. (p. 149)

While missionary philanthropy kept black education within safe ideo-logical parameters, it could not satisfy the monumental political demands of the northern industrialists, who required a conquered South with a subdued black population. Containment and subjugation became the objective of imposed Negro education (Bullock, 1967).

As the twentieth century was drawing closer, several questions had to be addressed. How much of the black population should be given formal education? How should education be structured? How could potential social upheaval, sparked by liberally trained blacks, be avoided? Enter Samuel Armstrong with his program of "special education" for the Negro.

Armstrong, who was familiar with his father's work in Hawaii (Harlan, 1983), understood education, colonialism, and the political objectives of the industrialists. His view of the Negro fit the reactionary cultural politics of the time. In a series of speeches delivered to the National Education Association beginning in 1872, Armstrong declared that the Negro could acquire knowl-edge but not digest it. His philosophy of "special education" for the Negro combined the rhetoric of improvement with social control. Throughout his writings and lectures while Principal of Hampton Institute, Armstrong suc-cessfully argued that the Negro could best be morally and socially uplifted through labor and character training. Armstrong's ideas and legacy provided a foundation to further build colonial education for blacks.

The Lake Mohonk Conferences of the 1890s further solidified Negro education. Here is how Jacob Carruthers (1994) described those meetings in a section entitled "Deciding What's Best for the Negro":

The Negro education system was carefully planned and implemented. As a case in point consider the Lake Mohonk Conferences in the Negro Question. Some of the leading White educators of this country met at Lake Mohonk, New York (a resort area) on June 4–6 1890, and June 3–5, 1891, to read papers and discuss what they officially called the "Negro question." By the time the second conference ended they had decided that the primary goals of education for Blacks should be morality and the dignity of labor (i.e. working for White folks) . . . Rutherford B. Hayes, former president of the United States, was credited with proposing the conference and was elected to chair it in 1890. In his opening address, Hayes expressed optimism that the African could be lifted to "the full stature of American manhood." Moreover, he exhorted the conference partici-pants to take "full encouragement" from the "brighter side" of the Negroes' experience, which he described in the following manner: A century or two ago the ancestors of the great majority of the present (Negro) population of the United States were African barbarians and pagans of the lowest type. They had no skill in any kind of labor, nor industrious habits, and knew nothing of any printed or written language. This heathen people, brought from the Dark Continent, after several generations in bondage, understand and speak the English language. All of them have been taught the first, the essential lesson in civilization: they can all earn their own living by their own labor. A "platform" intended to influence education policy related to Negroes was adopted at the close of the 1891 conference. Its first 4 planks were: [1] The accomplishing of the primary education of the Negro by the States themselves, and the further development of means and methods to this end, till all Negroes are creditably trained in primary schools. [2] The largely increased support of schools aided by private benevolence, which shall supply teachers and preachers for the Negro race. [3] The grounding of the vast majority of these teachers and preachers in common English studies and in the English Bible, with the further opportunity for any of them to carry on their studies as far as they may desire. [4] The great extension of industrial education for both men and women. The emphasis on industrial education for African-Americans in the 1890's had very little to do with the DuBois and Washington debates. The well-known philosophical argument between W.E.B. Dubois and Booker T. Washington came after the Lake Mohonk Conferences. General Samuel Armstrong, who founded Hampton Institute, was among the leading figures at the Lake Mohonk Conferences. Armstrong recommended Booker T. Washington, his best pupil at Hampton, to be the principal of a new school at Tuskegee in 1881, and developed the educational model that Washington implemented at Tuskegee. DuBois and Washington never addressed the issue of White control over African-American education and indirect White control of the Black population through an educated Negro elite. These fundamental issues had been decided upon by the powerful Whites who participated in the Mohonk Conferences and in other similar discussions of "the Negro question." (pp. 46–48)

The northern industrialists' political mandate was soon to be carried out by experienced administrators. Further rationale needed to be developed. The emerging and newly defined social science community, which included Columbia University sociologist Franklin Giddings among its leaders, offered theories of education and race well suited to the politics of the day. In general, their notion was that Blacks were genetically inferior, capable of rudimentary vocational education, and urgently in need of "character building."

Blacks and the Curriculum in the Early Twentieth Century: The Hampton Social Studies

Several events bolstered colonial black education in the early twentieth century. In the legal and political arena, *Plessy v. Ferguson* guaranteed the legal consolidation of America's apartheid. The Atlanta Compromise and Booker T. Washington's increased prominence suggested a significant sector of the black population would support accommodationism. Refined industrial training and vocational education curricula were designed to morally uplift the "childlike" black. Finally, America's embarkation on imperialist world conquest, especially in the Caribbean and Western Hemisphere, signaled new initiatives against colored people and the intention to oppress, exploit, and control colored peoples at home *and* abroad.

Relating to black education, policy initiatives were becoming more clearly focused even though finances were eroding in the early twentieth century (Butchart, 1994). Funds for teacher training, buildings, and programs were becoming more difficult to obtain, but the colonial imperative continued. Industrial education gathered new momentum from philanthropists and curriculum theorists alike.

The Hampton Social Studies (HSS) became the *primer* for Negro education. More than a body of classroom curriculum, it was a statement of political philosophy. HSS taught the Negro of his "place" in a society transitioning from agricultural slavery to mechanical industrialization. It addressed the vexing questions of how black Americans should fit into the new social order without disruptions. The HSS was a treatise on politics, economics, and the sociology of race.

The *Southern Workman* became the vehicle and organ through which the HSS would be introduced. In the December 1905 issue a rationale entitled "Social Studies in the Hampton Curriculum: Why They Are Needed" was published. It read:

> Slavery and the tribal form of government gave the Negro and Indian but little opportunity to understand the essentials of a good home, the duties and responsibilities of citizenship, the cost and meaning of education, the place of labor, and the importance of thrift. (p. 686)

Denied knowledge and participation in social and political life, many social theorists felt minorities must be politically socialized or they could become disruptive. Author and Hampton professor Dr. Thomas Jesse Jones noted that morality and a less "emotional" religious orientation must become part of the new training for blacks. He believed the rapidly changing society required that traditional education be scrapped in favor of this new "special education" (Bullock, 1967).

The HSS's "social study" would serve the cause of "race development." It would teach of civil government, economics, democracy, civic responsibility, and race relations. Interestingly, in the HSS, Jones maintained that both the white supremacist position of eternal inferiority and the black's desire for equality were wrong. He blamed evolution for the racial predicament affecting blacks. A catch-up time would be needed for people of color to evolve. He wrote:

> Economics shows the importance of material possessions and of the power to toil as factors of progress. Civil government emphasizes the importance of intelligence and integrity in the members of a democracy, the toil and suffering through which civil liberty has been obtained, and the responsibility resting upon the citizens of a republic. Sociology describes the origins of such human institutions as the home, the school, the church, the government, it states the types of character which strengthen these institutions, and the qualities which

these institutions must possess in order to develop the character of their members. (p. 689)

The first actual component of the HSS appeared in the January 1906 issue of the *Southern Workman* and was entitled "Social Studies in the Hampton Curriculum: Civics and Social Welfare." Jones divided this course into the development of government, government and public welfare, and the machinery of government.

Democratic government, Jones argued, was the product of human evolution. It represented the progress of social organization. He instructed blacks to work that they might soon be fit for democratic civilization. He asserted that "the failure of democracy when tried by the ignorant and irresponsible is proved by reason and example." The explicit and implicit message for blacks was that they must move slowly.

He concluded that government could be useful to the Negro as it could help rationalize agricultural production, conduct studies, and support education. The government offered training in occupations that Jones believed the Negro desperately needed.

After the rationale and government sections, Jones published "Social Studies in the Hampton Curriculum: Economics and Material Welfare." The section subtitled "Consumption or Demand" aspired to make better consumers of the "colored and the Indian." It "scoffed at the Negro's preference for non-nutritious food, expensive garments, and poor consumer choices." Much of this lesson was taken up with the virtue of saving money. If blacks ever wanted to achieve "like the Japanese or the better class of immigrants, they must save and sacrifice for the future." Black families must consider industrial education preferable to take advantage of its immediate possibilities. Higher education was to be considered for a later time.

The second subtopic entitled "Production or Supply" addressed capitalist industrial organization. Jones began by expressing relief that the "socialistic notions so prevalent among the working classes of the North have not proliferated." Jones' discussion focused on agricultural cultivation. He believed blacks (and Indians) were forever wedded to agriculture despite the widespread emergence of commerce and industry. He wrote: "Further the rural life is better adapted to their physical conditions—a fact clearly proved by the very high death rate of colored people dwelling in cities" (p. 115).

Further:

... The general conclusion is usually that as a whole these races have not reached the standard of the white race although in certain communities and in individual cases they are quite equal, and that at the same time the backward races, as a whole, are becoming more efficient, especially in communities where they have a fair opportunity. (p. 116)

Jones concluded the discussion of economics, claiming great flexibility and promise for the industrial organization of society. If the colored races would study the dynamics of credit, transportation, monopolies, profit, interest, rent, wages, labor efficiency, and so forth, they too, could prosper in the new age.

The next lesson, entitled "Social Studies in the Hampton Curriculum: United States Census and Actual Problems," was an outgrowth of Jones' own academic background whereby he believed knowledgeable people should be able to quantify and document demographics, wage status, educational progress, and "local conditions" of the people. His focus in this lesson was on the documenting, charting, and graphing of such statistics.

Among the most important and ideological of the lessons was the fifth, entitled "Social Studies in the Hampton Curriculum: Sociology and Society." Here, Jones framed social and political outlooks on the organization of society and individuals within that organization. He believed that for schooling and other social institutions to be effective, they must understand the "place" of black people. Relying on the teachings of his mentor, sociology professor Franklin Giddings, and the typologies they developed in previous work, he reprised the "social mind" concept, that is, classifying people by "mental and moral" type. The concept held that rational and intellectual types would lead, and all should be cautioned that the impulsive and emotional types possessed the possibility of wrecking society. He believed the impulsive types had been responsible for "some of the most serious mob actions in the world's history" (p. 690).

Retreating to the "scientific racism" of the mid-nineteenth century, Jones chose this lesson to raise the "warm climate" argument:

> The influence of a warm climate in developing the emotional element in a race or community is readily proved by comparing the races in different parts of the world, but more vividly by comparing the people in different sections of this country, or in different parts of the same state. The colored people of Piedmont, Virginia, not only because they have come under the influence of the Scotch-Irish in western Virginia, but because of the more invigorating climate of the mountains of the part, are less irritable, impulsive, and emotional than those of Tidewater, Virginia, with its warm moist, climate. The effect of heat increased ease with which the evangelist can arouse his congregation to the frenzy of a religious revival when his church is well heated or overheated. Other conditions which contribute to emotional, impulsive or mob action are a low average of intelligence or the presence of a large, unwieldy crowd. In the instances of impulsive action given by the students, almost all of these conditions are present. (p. 691)

In part two of this lesson, Jones described what he considered effective social organization. Social organization was defined as family kinship, the state, the church, and the institutions. He argued that social organization was "necessarily coercive" in circumstances of inequality and adversity as only homogeneous society could be truly efficient and fully functioning. In other words, blacks would have to be checked by force.

The sixth and final lesson, entitled "Social Studies in the Hampton Curriculum: The Progress of the Indians," was primarily a statistical census report. Jones looked at population data, disease factors, reservation data, literacy, per capita income, and expenses. He concluded that Native Americans, like America's other minorities, were on an "upward" path to progress.

The HSS became an ideological model for corporate-sponsored black curriculum. It was a politically charged set of classroom lessons. It also became the ideological school course work, aimed at maintaining racial subservience. It would have a fifty-year legacy as corporate-industrial hegemonists successfully forged a segregated society based on African inferiority.

Moving Forward: Race and Identity in the School Curriculum

Since the 1960s there has been an explosion of interest in race theorizing, cultural studies, and "popular culture." The representation of marginalized groups in literature, film, myth, and school knowledge has been of great interest (McCarthy & Critchlow, 1993). Several important questions have been raised in this inquiry. Among them, researchers want to understand race, identity, and their significance in the educational process. These complex issues have been approached in a variety of ways.

While race has often been debated as a biological-genetic concept, it can also be approached as a historically and politically constructed notion. Heagety and Peery (1998) discuss race and racial antagonism as a function of private property. They argue that humans have historically been "bonded by tribal affiliation or religious allegiance," and that racial oppression arose in post-Renaissance Europe. They write:

> As private property developed and spread, "us" and "them" divisions began to appear early on, because they were an efficient way of consolidating conquered territory and enriching one empire at the expense of another. Enslavement and forced labor were integral to the organization of many pre-capitalist empires, both West and East. For most of human history, they were on a continuum with other kinds of labor. In these societies human beings were sold into slavery for many reasons—as the result of conquest and war, as punishment for crimes, because of poverty. Before capitalism, "enslavement could be the fate of any person, no matter his or her color." As Milton Meltzer shows in his book, *Slavery, Throughout History*, "whites enslaved whites by the millions." Divisions in society were not related to color. Who ruled society, who was considered a part of

society, and who was not part of it had nothing to do with racial designations. Such status was instead defined by wealth or by force. (p. 2)

They go on to argue that race division as we know it is defined by markets and conquest:

> And since capitalism is not capitalism unless it can expand, nations also provided a home base from which the rulers of that nation could launch campaigns of territorial aggression and conquest. Using such concepts as "national character," scientists, historians and philosophers sought to identify, describe and ascribe a natural and biological identity, and even biological diverse peoples on the basis of their physical characteristics were used to advance the idea that diversity was a result of fundamental, natural differences in which some peoples were "superior" and others "inferior." It was only part of the natural order of things, so the argument went, that one should rule the other. (p. 2)

The question we are confronted with is the meaning of race in society, politics, culture, and education. We need to know how race is represented in our social knowledge.

Curricularist William Pinar (1993) insists that we go beyond conventional explanations. He writes:

> What is the meaning of race? It is hardly an unchanging, biological concept. Race is a complex, dynamic, and changing construct. Historically, those groups identified as "people of color" have changed according to political circumstance. For instance, before the Civil War, southern Europeans, Jews, even the Irish were considered "non-white" (Omi & Winant, 1983). The racial category of "black" grew out of slavery. "Whites" collapsed the diversity of African-and native-peoples into monolithic, racialized categories. (p. 61)

If race can be described as a constructed phenomenon, what can be said of how it is represented in the culture and more specifically in school knowledge?

The imperial tradition of racial representation is now clear. Western intellectual thought highlights history from the Renaissance onward. The great civilizations of so-called third world people are either obscured or challenged. Historical evidence reveals much about culture and civilization in the Empires of Ghana, dating to the fourth century; the Mali Empire, which flowered in the thirteenth and fourteenth centuries; the Empire of Songhay in the fifteenth century; the Kingdom of Kanem-Bornu of the tenth and eleventh centuries; the Hausa City-States of the ninth and tenth centuries; the Kingdom of Benin in the fifteenth century; the militaristic Oyo Kingdom of the seventeenth century; the Dahomey people of the eighteenth century; and the Ashanti Kingdom of the seventeenth century (Good, 1976).

Beyond the obfuscation of sub-Saharan African peoples, western scholarship continually denies the influences of Kemetic civilization. Some comtemporary scholars argue that Mesopotamia was a transient region and that its contributions should not be attributed to (northern) Africans or African influence. Likewise, the influences of Ancient China, Asia, and the great Incan and Mayan civilizations are similarly tarnished, obfuscated, or denied.

The ultimate objective is to present Europeans as the main contributors to civilizing the world. Europe is credited with bringing modern commerce, art, music, literature, culture, and civility to a world trapped by atavism, ignorance, and uncertainty. In short, Europe is portrayed as establishing order and progress.

The representation of Africans and African Americans looks quite different. School knowledge relegates people of color to savagery and barbarism. Most are now familiar with the negative image representation of African people.

We know historically that oppression breeds protest. Thesis summons antithesis. Position calls into being opposition. Negation leads to negation of the negation (Engels, 1940). So it is with curriculum and race. The critique of black representation in the curriculum, as well as black education in general, has summoned widespread opposition from many quarters.

The American Curriculum: One Hundred Fifty Years of Black Protest

Although it seems black protest thought is a product of Civil Rights–era militancy, such ideology actually dates back to the antebellum period. Many clergymen, missionaries, and teachers among the then emergent black intelligentsia were utterly pessimistic about America's hope for racial redemption. Some were attracted to notions of voluntary separatism, others to black self-sufficiency, and some even wanted return to Mother Africa.

A persistent demand of black protest thought has been education. All understand that the future belongs to the young and that education is a necessity in the struggle for uplift and equality.

While activists and "militants" have identified with different persuasions, commonly felt outrages have served as the building blocks for social and educational theorizing. Among them have been the practices of colonialism, the debasement of Africa, inhumane forms of slavery in the Americas, and a pervasive pessimism that Eurocentrism and racism persist. Many believe American society will not likely change for blacks. Racial uplift, improvement, and separatism continue as common themes in African American protest.

Separatism and Nationalism

Separatist social theory was in evidence from the Civil War until World War I. Two thrusts emerged (Moses, 1978), black nationalism and pan Africanism. Early black nationalists promoted self-help, whereas pan Africanists looked to ally with Africa and the black diaspora. Separatist views persisted following World War I. From World War II onward, separatists played a prominent role in the social and educational thinking of the African American population. A brief summary and overview of their ideological foundations, personalities, and historical evolution offer explanation of the 150-year quest to influence the shape of black curriculum as well as the larger sociopolitical protest.

Rooted in Christian humanism, civilization-building, absolutism, and elitism, black separatism and nationalism evolved to become more relativist, culturalist, and secular in the twentieth century (Moses, 1978). Separatist and nationalist theories run the gamut from movements of identification, racial pride, cultural pluralism, physical separatism, back to Africa, and straight-out race war. In general they have opposed slavery, colonialism, racism, and the Euro-American exploitation and brutalizing of colored peoples. While most separatist and nationalist outlooks cover broad social arenas, it was inevitable that such views made themselves known in the expanding movement for black education.

Alexander Crummell, an early twentieth-century black intellectual and a nationalist of sorts, was among the early advocates of a black-oriented curriculum (Watkins, 1996). Pious and perhaps conservative by today's standards, the educated and well-traveled Crummell matured in the reconstructed South and saw possibility for the education of blacks in the twentieth century. For him, the only hope for the race was education. He declared that the day was past for appeals to the conscience of the white man. It was Crummell (1885), before DuBois, who conceptualized the notion of the "talented tenth." He wrote:

> Who are to be the agents to raise and elevate this people to a higher plane of being? The answer will at once flash upon your intelligence. It is to be affected [*sic*] by the scholars and philanthropists which come forth in these days from the schools. They are to be the scholars; for to transform, stimulate and uplift a people is a work of intelligence. It is a work which demands the clear induction of historic facts and their application to new circumstances—a work which will require the most skillful resources and the wise practicality of superior men. (p. 24)

In 1887 Crummell founded the American Negro Academy. By bringing together the best of libratory science, art, literature, and philosophy, Crummell was assembling a curriculum for emancipation. He challenged Booker

T. Washington, arguing that the southern black did not need to learn to work, but rather to learn the value of his labor. In the true nationalist spirit of his time, Crummell asserted the necessity for blacks to claim a body of intellectual production distinctly their own (Moses, 1978). Education for Crummell meant civilization building. His curriculum was one of racial pride, social progress, and redemption. Schooling, Crummell believed, should uplift and unite his people.

Although aware of the growing criticism of Western capitalism from European and American radical elements, most black nationalists and separatists chose not to incorporate such views in their framework. Their emphasis was on racism as a function of colonial social policy. Greatly influenced by Christian humanism, these turn-of-the-century black theorists accepted America's path to democratic industrialism. Their hope was for black participation in the new economic order.

Early twentieth-century nationalist and separatist outlooks contributed to the foundations of one hundred years of protest thought in education. Their voices have been heard in the urban storefront schools of the 1960s and 1970s, the Black Muslim schools, and other efforts that challenge integrationist and assimilationist thinking. Among separatists and nationalists, a cultural perspective has gained popularity. Culturalism, in this case, focuses on ethnic identity, revitalization, and pride. The purely culturalist outlook sidesteps many important issues in capitalist development. Culturalists fail to link twentieth-century racial subservience to the politics of cheap labor and market economics, choosing instead to focus primarily on the social manifestations of racism.

It was the young DuBois, though initially rejecting the philosophy of Karl Marx, who began to include the dynamics of economic exploitation in his sociological inquiry. By 1908, DuBois' educational commentary differed from that of his mentor, Crummell, and the other cultural nationalists. Dubois might easily be called a black social reconstructionist, as he introduced politics into black educational discourses.

Black Social Meliorism/Reconstructionism in the Curriculum

Kliebard (1987) examined social meliorism in the traditional curriculum. He observed that it was rooted in a view that America's early twentieth-century corporate industrialism was the source of great misery to the less fortunate. American capitalism seemed to be creating great debt, unemployment, poverty, and inhumane social policy as it relied on models of efficiency and productivity.

Educational reconstructionism or social meliorism was a movement led by social democratic professors and educators who believed schools and the curriculum should join, and even lead, the critique of social and economic injustice. For meliorists, schools should serve the cause of change and reform (Cremin, 1961). Never a united movement (Watkins, 1990b), the reconstructionists/meliorists agreed on economic and democratic reform.

Curriculum scholars have never attempted to explore how black meliorist and reconstructionist views appeared in the struggles of black education and curriculum. It should be reiterated that while separatist and nationalist outlooks were aimed at changing social and racial relationships, their focus was primarily cultural. Concerned with slavery, colonialism, and discrimination, the nationalists looked to cultural democracy, often accepting America's corporate industrial order. The meliorists and reconstructionists focused much of their attention on the inequalities caused by unchecked capitalism, the maldistribution of wealth, and a system of socioeconomic stratification that allowed an economic elite to dominate society.

Owing, in part, to his Harvard and Berlin education, DuBois was able to move within the ranks of the radical literary white intelligentsia. Having studied with George Santayana and William James, he was accepted among the radical *avant garde*. Manning Marable (1986) describes his colorful connections:

> The heart of this political and cultural ferment was Greenwich Village in New York City. Between 1911 and 1917, the village was filled with avant-garde and counter cultural institutions . . . new schools, art galleries, free love colonies, clusters of militant socialists, new radical journals. One such gathering point was 23 Fifth Avenue, the celebrated salon of Mabel Dodge, a pioneer in the cult of the orgasm . . . Dodge was not involved in the NAACP but was an important patron and advisor to white liberals and radicals who related both to the early desegregation movement and to other social protest currents. Most of the major American radical intellectuals and activists of the period gave talks in her home; birth control advocate Margaret Sanger, writer Carl Van Vechten, anarchist Emma Goldman, feminist Charlotte Perkins Gilman, and William English Walling were associates of DuBois. Along with socialist editor Max Eastman, these young rebels—called by their contemporaries the "New Intellectuals"—shared many of DuBois' beliefs and ideals. (pp. 83–84)

Within African American education, DuBois was a respected educational theorist. Advancing years brought him closer to Marxian socialism. His view of the role for education in social criticism, egalitarianism, and political justice never waned. DuBois' version of social meliorism called into question the economic and social arrangements of the corporate state. Because of this he would receive little support from the architects and gatekeepers of accommodationism.

Multicultural Education

In recent decades, scattered voices have argued for modernizing the curriculum to reflect America's rapidly changing racial and ethnic mix. The decade of the 1970s, however, provided persuasive empirical research suggesting that public schooling was failing African Americans and other minority youngsters. Unlike previously mentioned reform-minded and radical challenges to the curriculum, this one had significant nurturing from within the community of professional educators.

The multicultural–multiethnic curriculum movement has its roots in the post–World War II protest for civil rights and social justice. Meir and Rudwick's (1970) examination of that period notes the definitive voices for ethnic cultural identification. The call for "black power" and black nationalism and "la raza" differed from the cry for integration.

The civil rights movement of the 1960s is frequently decontextualized and romanticized, ignoring important circumstances underlying events. Piven and Cloward (1977) argue that by the 1960s powerful political and economic forces insisted the South be industrialized and modernized. The absurdity of apartheid and Jim Crow in America made modernization impossible. The civil rights movement occurred during a time when the aims of corporate America, the legal and political bureaucracy, and the aspirations of dispossessed and disenfranchised southern blacks overlapped.

Culturalist arguments resonated loudly during this period. Proponents of cultural pluralism and ethnic identification raised doubts about the possibility of a melting pot or a truly integrated society.

A significant body of research after 1965 focused on public schooling's exclusion of ethnic groups. The work of Ramirez and Casteneda (1974) concluded that Mexican Americans and other minorities had field-sensitive learning styles tied to their cultural backgrounds. Shirley Brice Heath's (1982) Tracton study examined language interactions among rural southern blacks. She found the language dynamics of their culture at odds with the culture of schools. John Ogbu (1978) wrote of the cultural discontinuities between home and school facing minority youngsters. Susan Phillips' (1983) work on "participant structures" suggested that the culture of school was often not conducive to the participation of the Native American.

This movement may be seen as representing an intensified culturalist challenge to the curriculum. Owing to significant advocacy by professional educators, culturalist protest has established definitive rationale and specific lesson proposals to restructure the curriculum. The abundant works of James Banks (e.g., 1995, 1994, and 1993), Donna Gollnick and Phillip Chinn (1990), Christine Bennett (1990), and others have greatly influenced the multicultural curriculum movement. Lacking the abrasiveness and polemics of other protest thought, the movement for multicultural education is inextricably connected to the oppositionist curriculum protest.

The Afrocentric Curriculum

Rooted in 150 years of black nationalism, pan Africanism, separatism, revitalization movements, and African identification movements, Afrocentrism as a foundation for school and curriculum organization has attracted considerable contemporary interest. Both public and private schools in several metropolitan areas have committed to pursue the "Afrocentric idea" (Asante, 1987).

The rationale for Afrocentrism has both a social and educational basis. In the social arena the perpetuation of white racism in America is viewed as cause to turn to African identity outlooks. Also, the research literature in multicultural education has long insisted that minority, and especially black, youngsters are particularly inclined to model and identify with minority teachers and their own ethnic milieu. More interest in school, lower dropout rates, higher achievement scores, and fewer behavioral problems are the objectives. Such accomplishments remain to be verified in the coming years.

How can the Afrocentric curriculum be described and understood? Its philosophic outlook, content, and method must be clarified. It should be stated that proponents of Afrocentrism embrace a broad range of outlooks. Separatists, cultural nationalists, and middle-class educational reformers have staked out territory.

The general philosophy of Afrocentric outlooks rejects views that European and American social and curriculum theories offer the only legitimate models. Such outlooks are seen to be rooted in empiricism, rationalism, "scientific method," and positivism (Asante, 1987). Afrocentrics generally support views that mainstream curriculum is ideologically conditioned by notions of domination, prediction, control, racism, and so on. Afrocentrics deplore the colonization of knowledge. They contend American public schooling and its curriculum have failed African Americans by not providing the African American student the cultural foundation for learning. Afrocentrics further claim American public schooling has relied on negative pathology theories regarding blacks, such as being "permanent underclass," having "at-risk" "cultural deficit," and being "disadvantaged," as theoretical rationale for educational and curriculum policy-making.

Hilliard (1990) points to six areas in which the prevailing school curriculum is deficient in offering a curriculum cultural foundation for students of African ancestry: the very significant history of Africans before the slave trade is ignored; the history of Africa is most often ignored; the history of the African diaspora (e.g., Fiji, the Philippines, and Dravidian India) is not taught; cultural differences as opposed to similarities of Africans in the diaspora are highlighted; little of the struggle against slavery, colonialism, segregation, apartheid, and domination is taught; little explanation of the common origins and elements in the system of oppression during the past 400 years is offered.

Afrocentrics desire a curriculum focused on African themes. Holding Africa forth as the cradle of civilization, they turn to ancient Kemetic (Egyptian) civilization as the model for knowledge, culture, and social development. Afrolian mathematics includes computational formulas predating Euclid and Pythagoras. African models of state craft stemming from the great civilizations are to be preferred over European models of democracy. Traditional African humane and communalistic social structure is viewed as preferred. Indispensable to the African curriculum is the comprehensive study of the continent's art, literature, music, religion, and anthropological development. Additionally, history, geography, and the sciences have a role in the Afrocentric curriculum.

Afrocentric pedagogy and method are more complex. Proponents do not believe methods of teaching must be limited to prevailing practices. They acknowledge a place for orality and spirituality beyond the role of memorization and "drill and kill" so acceptable today. Asante (1987) acquaints us with African ways of knowing. Afrocentric method seeks to legitimize expression, public discourse, feeling, myth-making, and emotion as acceptable avenues of inquiry. Such method seeks out "transcendence which is the quality of exceeding ordinary and literal experience." Asante asserts that the Afrological pursuit of knowledge goes beyond the material world.

Central to the Afrocentric concept is the notion of intellectual emancipation. The teaching and learning experience in this approach is destined to free the learner from the shackles of Western positivistic thought. Asante (1987) argues:

> A second proposition is that the afrologist, by virtue of his perspective, participates in the coming to be of new concepts and directions. His perceptions of political and social reality allow him to initiate novel approaches to problems and issues. Without the Western point of view he is mentally as free as possible. This is not a closed path; it is open to all who would change their perspectives. In fact, the afrologist, typically, is a person who is capable of understanding many points of view because he values such diversity of opinion. He may change his perspective by altering his conditions, or because of some external influences on the object perceived but the perception is always uniquely his. (p. 62)

Culture and School Knowledge: Recent Black Scholarship

Over the past twenty-five years we have witnessed an explosion of curriculum theorizing emanating from African American scholars. A significant strain of that work calls attention to the relationship of knowledge to culture. Several overarching themes have come from the post-Malcolm black intellectual community, althought only a small sampling can be presented here.

These theorists turn our attention to the cultural differences existing in our society. While latter day "melting pot" theorists such as Hirsch (1987) and D'Souza and associates (1991) highlight the macroculture, which they argue binds us together, radical black culturalists point to the difference in cultural orientations. They point to the integrity and tenacity of culture. They highlight the history of imperialism and colonialism and their influence on peoples' development. Furthermore, they argue that not all cultures are equal. There are dominant and subordinate cultures. Cultures are associated with history, power, and racism. Mwalimu Shujaa (1994) writes:

> The failure to take into account differing cultural orientations and unequal power relations among groups that share membership in a society is a major problem in conceptualizations that equate schooling and education. Cultural orientations "involve cognitive, affective, and directive processes in people's strategies to solve problems. . . . They are tenacious, persistent, superorganic principles that resist pressures for change brought about by the institutional transformation of society. However, cultural orientations must be understood to exist in the context of group historical experience. The African-American cultural identity has been and continues to be influenced by the U.S. social context, but it is essential to note that the African-American cultural orientation also represents an experiential context. Thus, while African-Americans exist within the U.S. social context, they also exist within an African historical-cultural continuum that predates that social context and would continue to exist even if the nation-state and its societal arrangements were to transform or demise. (pp. 14–15)

This new scholarship accepts a reproductionist theory, which posits that schools recreate society's existing cultural and power relationships. For example, the Eurocentric world view and value system are transmitted in school knowledge.

Curriculum theorist Beverly Gordon (1995, 1994) has argued that there exists an African American cultural knowledge. This knowledge emanates from the African American "existential" condition and is the product of a people's lived experiences. This cultural knowledge is located in "literary arts, dance, media, theology, athletics, music, cinema and so forth." Gordon acknowledges that while this cultural knowledge has gained some visibility it is for the most part marginalized. Suppressing this body of knowledge in schooling denies students' connectedness. Gordon writes (1994):

> The information, facts, values, stories, legends, ideals mythology, etc. that are passed on intergenerationally, provide students with the world-view/context through which they learn history and cultural and societal identity. The critical issue, however, is the nature of the cultural and historical knowledge included in this process. Such knowledge is the global history of humankind. Moreover,

this knowledge demonstrates definitively that people can engage in action to change societal structures in ways that result in the improvement of their lives. These, I believe, are at least some components of an education that is liberatory. (p. 65)

This group explicitly breaks with the "neutrality" of western scholarship. They declare themselves not only partisan, but advocates for a new kind of education and curriculum that is culturally grounded and, most importantly, culturally relevant.

The Challenge: Toward New Models of Curriculum and Teaching

Opposition to twentieth-century American curriculum, as noted, dates from Crummell, DuBois, and Woodson. The various strains of protest thought have offered prescriptions for revising the curriculum. Post-Malcolm African American cultural theorists have made significant contributions in proposing alternative models.

Joyce King's (1994) Afro-humanity concept is greatly concerned with curriculum change. King proceeds from the notion that the "realities of slavery," the "derogation of Africa," and the inhumanity of American racism have caused great damage to African people. She argues that "racist schooling distorts realities and abducts Diaspora Africans from their Afro/human cultural moorings." The curriculum becomes culpable in this process.

King writes of the "whitening" of Egypt and the denial of African origins in Greek culture among the insults found in the traditional curriculum. Rather than enlightenment, black children are scarred by the curriculum. They are left alienated, disaffected, and isolated. King highlights the affective damage of the school curriculum. She calls for a freeing, or a "BEing free," which requires the "emancipation of human knowledge." She calls for an education that nurtures "cognitive autonomy" and transcends "dysconscious, unfree habits of mind." She calls for a curriculum rooted in the Afro/human legacy. That legacy, for King, offers a pedagogy that "challenges the social justifications of poverty, sexism, human ranking, exploitation, racism and unhealthy environments." It rejects the "colonizing mission" of school as it rejects dominance.

Some of the most interesting recent research has explored the roles of teachers and culture. For example, Foster (1993), Ladson-Billings (1995, 1994, 1990), Lee (1995, 1994), and Henry (1998) focus on teacher success and instruction delivery. This corpus of work has broad curriculum implications, casting the teacher as central to the processes of learning. It explores the effects of cultural background and belief systems on teaching (Ladson-Billings, 1994). Her studies have found that effective teachers embrace African

American cultural norms, establish close personal ties with students, are socially and politically conscious, and attempt to arm students for an alienating world, among other things. Ladson-Billings further theorizes about "culturally relevant teaching" (1994, 1992), suggesting that cultural relevance appears more important and transcendant over partisan models (e.g., direct instruction, experientialism, etc.). She notes that the most effective teachers of black children utilize cultural referents to impart knowledge.

The multiculturalists have been especially active in the recent discourse on curriculum and race. Drawing from the work of Gibson (1976) and Sleeter and Grant (1987), James A. Banks (1995) has identified five "dimensions" of multicultural education. Content integration explores how teaching utilizes information from various cultures in the curriculum. Knowledge construction describes the cultural assumptions underlying the selection of knowledge. Prejudice reduction investigates strategies to help students develop tolerance and democratic values. Equity pedagogy explores techniques to assist low-achieving students to attain greater academic achievement. Finally, empowering school culture examines ways of altering the climate and clutter of the institution itself.

Other African American theorists have been active in the prescriptive curriculum discourse over the past three decades. They have taken up such topics as pluralism and democracy in the curriculum (Gay, 1995), cultural discontinuities (Ogbu, 1978), identity formation (Spencer, 1987), learning styles (Hale-Benson, 1987), school community, and home psychological interventions (Comer, 1988).

Carol Lee's African-centered pedagogy is among the most thoughtful curriculum proposals. Enjoying wide support, it might be viewed as a prototype for African-centered education. It involves both teaching and curriculum. She views it as a "liberation pedagogy." It is geared toward "humanizing"; however, she asserts that there are different conceptions of what that means. Absent universal norms, she calls for a pedagogy that is culturally specific, that is, African centered. The curriculum and teaching practice should have several objectives: to legitimize African stores of knowledge; to embrace positive community and cultural practices; to build on indigenous languages; to reinforce and idealize the family, race, and social relationships; to promote self-determination; and to support critical consciousness.

Lee argues that cultural practices influence cognition. Thinking and learning are shaped by the cultural context. She wants schools to provide a culturally consistent and sensitive curriculum for black children.

Finally, Lee addresses the often-asked question about how black children taught in culturally specific outlooks ultimately relate to the larger diverse population(s). Here is her response (Lee, 1994):

> In the context of a multi-ethnic, democratic society, attention to African-centered pedagogy amidst calls for multicultural education creates serious

tensions. We must address the question of how an African centered pedagogy reinforces intra-ethnic solidarity and pride without promoting inter-ethnic antagonisms. An African-centered pedagogy must include a conceptualization of American society as a culturally diverse entity within which ethnic solidarity is required in order to negotiate, acquire, and maintain power. This pedagogy should promote intra-ethnic solidarity among African-Americans while at the same time providing strategies for coalitions with other groups with similar needs and interests. American society is not a melting pot, but rather a mosaic of diversity. We must honestly address the question of what the implementation of an African-centered pedagogy means in different settings—such as a class-room in which many ethnic groups are represented or a public school whose population is entirely African-American. (pp. 308–309)

This new scholarship is intriguing and represents a step forward in both theory and practice. It can be argued that black protest thought is the original "liberation theology."

Afterthoughts

Issues and problems surrounding the curriculum are at the heart of today's debates on urban education. Significant sections of the African American and Latino populations believe schools are not serving their children. One only has to visit their nearest urban school to find far too many students snoring and ignoring their way through class. Can it be that all of these students are dull and uninspired? Perhaps the answers lie elsewhere.

Despite sometimes strident calls for change, public schools seem to move at glacial speed. The demands for "relevance," "cultural sensitivity," and more experiential learning are being answered with direct instruction, scripted learning, increased testing, teacher proofing, and "back-to-basics."

Perhaps it's time for professional school administrators to break with Taylorian and corporate models of curriculum and education. What effect do the politics of accountability really have? Perhaps it's time to explore the recent research of African American and other scholars, which directs us toward more culturally relevant, sensitive, and humane education.

REFERENCES

Anderson, J. D. (1988). *The education of blacks in the south 1860–1935.* Chapel Hill: University of North Carolina Press.

Apple, M. (1979). *Ideology and curriculum.* London: Routledge & Kegan Paul.

Apple, M. (1982). *Education and power.* Boston: Ark Paperbacks.

Aptheker, H. (Ed.). (1973). *The education of black people: Ten critiques, 1906–1960 by W. E. B. DuBois.* New York: Monthly Review Press.

Arnove, R. F. (Ed.). (1980). *Philanthropy and cultural imperialism: The foundations at home and abroad.* Bloomington, IN: Indiana University Press.

Asante, M. K. (1987). *The Afrocentric idea.* Philadelphia: Temple University Press.

Banks, J. A. (1994). *Multicultural education: Theory and practice.* Boston: Allyn & Bacon.

Banks, J. A., & Banks, C. A. (Eds.). (1995). *Handbook of research on multicultural education.* New York: Macmillan.

Banks, J. A., & Banks, C. A. M. (Eds.). (1993). *Multicultural education: Issues and perspectives* (2nd ed.). Boston: Allyn & Bacon.

Bennett, C. (1990). *Comprehensive multicultural education: Theory and practice.* Boston: Allyn & Bacon.

Berman, E. H. (1969). *Education in Africa and America: A history of the Phelps-Stokes Fund 1911–1945.* Unpublished doctoral dissertation, Columbia University.

Berman, E. H. (1980). *Educational colonialism in Africa: The role of American foundations 1910–1945.* In Arnove, R. F. (1980), 179–201.

Bloom A. J. C. (1989). *The closing of the American mind.* New York: Simon & Shuster.

Bond, H. (1966). *The education of the Negro in the American social order.* New York: Octagon Books.

Bullock, H. (1967). *A history of Negro education in the south: From 1619 to present.* Cambridge, MA: Harvard University Press.

Butchart, R. E. (1994). Outthinking and outflanking the owners of the world: An historiography of the African American struggle for education. In M. J. Shujaa (Ed.), *Too much schooling, too little education: A paradox of Black life in White societies* (pp. 85–122). Trenton, NJ: Africa World Press.

Carruthers, J. H. (1994). Black intellectuals and the crises in black education. In M. J. Shujaa (Ed.), *Too much schooling, too little education: A paradox of Black life in White societies* (pp. 37–55). Trenton, NJ: Africa World Press.

Comer, J. P. (1988). Educating poor minority children. *Scientific American, 259,* 42–48.

Cremin. L. (1961). *Transformation of the school: Progressivism in American education, 1876–1957.* New York: Alfred E. Knopf.

Crummell, A. (1885). *The need of new ideas and new motives for a new era.* p. 24. Quoted in Moses, W. J., (1978) p. 73.

Dove, N. (1994). The emergence of Black supplementary schools as forms of resistance to racism in the United Kingdom. In M. J. Shujaa (Ed.), *Too much schooling, too little education: A paradox of Black life in White societies* (pp. 343–359). Trenton, NJ: Africa World Press.

D'Souza. D. (1991). *Illiberal education: The politics of race and sex on campus.* New York: The Free Press.

DuBois, W. E. B. (1953). *The souls of Blackfolk.* New York: The Blue Heron Press.

Engels, F. (1939). *Anti-Duhring: Herr Eugen Duhring's revolution in science.* New York: International Publishers.

Engels, F. (1940). *Dialectics of nature.* New York: International Publishers.

Foster, M. (1993). Education for competence in community and culture: Exploring the views of exemplary African-American teachers. *Urban Education, 27*(4), 370–394.

Foster, M. (1994). Educating for competence in community and culture. Exploring the views of exemplary African-American teachers. In M. J. Shujaa (Ed.), *Too much schooling, too little education: A paradox of Black life in White societies* (pp. 221–244). Trenton, NJ: Africa World Press.

Foster, M. (1995). African American teachers and culturally relevant pedagogy. In J. A. Banks & C. A. Banks, *Handbook of Multicultural Education* (pp. 570–581). New York: Macmillan.

Foster, M. (1989). It's cookin' now: An ethnographic study of a successful Black teacher in an urban community college. *Language in Society, 18*(1), 1–29.

Gadsden, V. (1994). Literacy, education, and identity among African Americans: The communal nature of learning. In M. J. Shujaa (Ed.), *Too much schooling, too little education: A paradox of Black life in White societies* (pp. 245–261). Trenton, NJ: Africa World Press.

Gay, G. (1995). Curriculum theory and multicultural education. In J. A. Banks & C. A. Banks (Eds.), *Handbook of Multicultural Education.* New York: Macmillan.

Gibson, M. A. (1976). Approaches to multicultural education in the United States: Some concepts and assumptions. *Anthropology and Education Quarterly, 7,* 7–18.

Giddings, F. H. (1896). *The principles of sociology: An analysis of the phenomena of association and social organization.* New York: Macmillan.

Giddings, F. H. (1901). *Democracy and empire: With studies of their psychological, economic and moral foundation.* New York: Macmillan.

Giddings, F. H. (1924). *Perspectives in social inquiry: The scientific study of human society.* Chapel Hill: University of North Carolina Press.

Giddings, F. H. (1932). *Civilization and society: An account of the development and behavior of human society.* New York: Henry Holt.

Giroux, H. (1981). *Toward a new sociology of curriculum.* In H. A. Giroux, N. Penna & W. F. Pinar (Eds.), *Curriculum and Instruction.* Berkeley: McCutcheon.

Gollnick, D. M., & Chinn, P. C. (1990). *Multicultural education in a pluralistic society.* Columbus, OH: Merrill.

Good, K. G. (1976). *From Africa to the United States and then . . . A concise Afro-American history.* Glenview, IL: Scott Foresman & Co.

Gordon, B. M. (1994). African-American cultural knowledge and liberatory education: Dilemmas, problems and potentials in postmodern American society. In M. J. Shujaa (Ed.), *Too much schooling, too little education: A paradox of Black life in White societies* (pp. 57–78). Trenton, NJ: Africa World Press.

Gordon, B. M. (1995). Knowledge construction, competing critical theories, and education. In J. A. Banks & C. A. Banks (Eds.), *Handbook of multicultural education*. New York: Macmillan.

Hale-Benson, J. (1987). *Black children: Their roots, culture, and learning styles.* Baltimore: Johns Hopkins University Press.

Harlan, L. R. (1983). *Booker T. Washington: The wizard of Tuskegee 1901–1915.* New York: Oxford University Press.

Heagerty, B., & Peery, N. (1998). *Moving onward: From racial division to class unity.* Chicago: League of Revolutionaries for a New America.

Heath, S. B. (1982). Questioning at home and at school: A comparative study. In G. D. Spindler (Ed.), *Doing the ethnography of schooling* (pp. 96–101). New York: Holt, Rinehart & Winston.

Henry, A. (1998). *Taking back control: African Canadian woman teachers' lives and practice.* Albany: State University of New York Press.

Hilliard, A. G., Payton-Stewart, L., & Williams, L. O. (Eds.). (October, 1990). *Infusion of African and African American content in the school curriculum: Proceedings of the first national conference.* Morristown, NJ: Aaron Press.

Hirsch, E. D. Jr. (1987). *Cultural literacy: What every American needs to know.* New York: Houghton-Mifflin.

King, J. E. (1994). BEing, the soul-freeing substance: A legacy of hope in Afrohumanity. In M. J. Shujaa (Ed.), *Too much schooling, too little education: A paradox of Black life in White societies* (pp. 269–294). Trenton, NJ: Africa World Press.

King, J. (1990). (Ed.). In search of African liberation pedagogy: Multiple contexts of education and struggle. *Journal of Education, 172*(2).

King, J. (1991). Dysconscious racism: Ideology, identity, and the miseducation of teachers. *The Journal of Negro Education, 60*(2), 133–146.

King, K. (1971). *Pan Africanism and education: A study of race, philanthropy and education in the southern states of America and East Africa.* Oxford: Clarendon Press.

Kliebard, H. (1987). *The struggle for the American curriculum 1893–1958.* New York: Routledge & Kegan Paul.

Ladson-Billings, G. (1992). Liberatory consequences of literacy: A case of culturally relevant instruction for African American students. *Journal of Negro Education 61*(3), 378–391.

Ladson-Billings, G. (1994). *The Dreamkeepers: Successful teachers of African American children.* San Francisco: Jossey-Bass Publishers.

Ladson-Billings, G. (1995). Multicultural teacher education: Research, practice and policy. In J. A. Banks & C. A. Banks (Eds.), *Handbook of multicultural education* (pp. 747–759). New York: MacMillan.

Ladson-Billings, G., & Tate, W. F. (1995). Towards a critical race theory of education. *Teachers College Record, 97*, 47–68.

Ladson-Billings, G., & Henry, A. (1990). Blurring the borders: Voices of African liberatory pedagogy in the United States and Canada. *Journal of Education, 172,* 72–88.

Lee, C. D. (1992). Literacy, cultural diversity, and instruction. *Education and Urban Society, 24*(2), 279–291.

Lee, C. D. (1994). African-centered pedagogy: Complexities and possibilities. In M. J. Shujaa (Ed.), *Too much schooling, too little education: A paradox of Black life in White societies* (pp. 295–318). Trenton, NJ: Africa World Press.

Lee, C. D., Lomotey, K., & Shujaa, M. (1990). How shall we sing our sacred song in a strange land? The dilemma of double consciousness and the complexities of an African-centered pedagogy. *Journal of Education, 172*(2), 45–61.

Lee, C. D., & Slaughter-Defoe, D. T. (1995). Historical and sociocultural influences on African American education. In J. A. Banks & C. A. Banks (Eds.), *Handbook of multicultural education* (pp. 348–371). New York: Macmillan.

Marable, M. (1986). *W. E. B. DuBois: Black radical democrat.* Boston: Twayne.

McCarthy, C. (1990a). *Race and curriculum.* London: The Falmer Press.

McCarthy, C., & Crichlow, W. (Eds.). (1993). *Race identity and representation in education.* New York: Routledge.

Meier, A. G., & Rudwick, E. (Eds.). (1970). *Black protest in the sixties.* New York: Quadrangle Books.

Moses, W. J. (1978). *The golden age of Black nationalism, 1850–1925.* New York: Oxford University Press.

Ogbu, J. (1978). *Minority education and caste: The American system in cross-cultural perspective.* New York: Academic Press.

Ogbu, J. (1995). Understanding cultural diversity and learning. In J. A. Banks & C. A. Banks (Eds.), *Handbook of multicultural education* (pp. 582–593). New York: Macmillan.

Omi, M., & Winant, H. (1986). *Racial formation in the United States.* New York: Routledge.

Peery, N. (1975). *The negro national colonial question.* Chicago: Workers Press.

Phillips, S. U. (1983). *The invisible culture: Communication in classroom and community on the Warm Springs Indian reservation.* New York: Longman.

Pinar, W. F. (1993). Notes on understanding curriculum as a racial text. In C. McCarthy & W. Crichlow (Eds.), *Race identity and representation in education* (pp. 60–70). New York: Routledge.

Piven, F. F., & Cloward, R. A. (1977). *Poor peoples' movements: Why they succeed, How they fail.* New York: Vintage Books.

Ramirez, M., & Casteneda, A. (1974). *Cultural democracy, bicognitive development, and education.* New York: Academic Press.

Shujaa, M. J. (Ed.). (1994). *Too much schooling, too little education: A paradox of Black life in White societies.* Trenton, NJ: Africa World Press.

Sleeter, C. E., & Grant, C. A. (1987). An analysis of multicultural education in the United States. *Harvard Educational Review, 7,* 421–444.

Southern Workman (1906–1908). Hampton, VA: Hampton Institute.

Spencer, M. B. (1987). Black children's ethnic identity formation: Risk and resilience of caste-like minorities. In J. S. Phinney & M. J. Rotheram (Eds.), *Children's ethnic socialization: Pluralism and development* (pp. 103–116). Beverly Hills, CA: Sage.

Tyack, D. B. (1974). *The one best system: A history of American urban education.* Cambridge, MA: Harvard University Press.

Watkins, W. H. (1989). On accommodationist education: Booker T. Washington goes to Africa. In *International Third World Studies Journal & Review, 1,* 137–144.

Watkins, W. H. (1990a). W. E. B. DuBois versus Thomas Jesse Jones: The forgotten skirmishes. *Journal of the Midwest History of Education Society, 18,* 305–328.

Watkins, W. H. (1990b). The social reconstructionists. In T. Husen & T. H. Postelthwaite (Eds.), *The international encyclopedia of education. Supplementary Volume Two* (pp. 589–592). London: Pergamon Press. Reprinted as "Social reconstructionist approach" (1991). In A. Lewy (Ed.), *The international encyclopedia of curriculum* (pp. 32–35). Oxford: Pergamon Press.

Watkins, W. H. (1993). Black curriculum orientations: A preliminary inquiry. *Harvard Educational Review, 63*(3), 321–337.

Watkins, W. H. (1994). Curriculum for immigrant and minority children. In T. Husen & T. N. Postelthwaite (Eds.), *The international encyclopedia of education* (pp. 3840–3848). London: Pergamon Press.

Watkins, W. H. (1996). Reclaiming historical visions of quality schooling: The legacy of early 20th century Black intellectuals. In M. J. Shujaa (Ed.), *Beyond segregation: The politics of quality in African American schooling* (pp. 5–24). Thousand Oaks, CA: Corwin Press.

Woodson, C. G. (1933). *The miseducation of the negro.* Washington, DC: The Associated Publishers.

CHAPTER

4

Comment

Researching Curriculum and Race

Annette Henry

Introduction

In Chapter 3, William Watkins mentions a number of important points regarding the history of curriculum in African American education. (1) History is important in understanding black education; for example, the very right to be educated has been an enormous issue in the historical black struggle. (2) African American education has always been implicated with, and subordinated by, capitalism, the historical processes of European colonization, as well as cultural and political imperialism. (3) Knowledge and knowledge production are sociopolitical. Thus, curriculum constitutes a sociopolitical site of contestation and struggle for transformation.

Watkins evokes a number of epistemological and ontological questions: How do official grand narratives (of national identity, etc.) play out in this struggle? What counts as (valid) knowledge? What and whose knowledge is relevant? For what purposes should African Americans be educated? Using whose and what methods?

In my brief response to Professor Watkins I outline eight principles to consider in constructing research agendas regarding race, curriculum, and education. First, however, I want to highlight an area that was not discussed in Watkins' discussion of race and curriculum.

A Hidden Curriculum of Research on Race?

Maurice Merleau-Ponty called it the knowledge of the body-subject, reminding us that it is through our bodies that we live in the world. He called it knowledge in the hands, and knowledge in the feet. It is also knowledge in the womb. Eve knew it,

but she let on and was exiled from Eden, the world of divine law, for her indiscretion. We, her daughters, have kept silent for so long that now we have forgotten that knowledge from and about the body is also knowledge about the world.
—Madeleine Grumet (1994)
Conception, Contradiction, and Curriculum

Madeleine Grumet names curriculum as a field of utter confusion, perhaps a kind of Tower of Babel. Indeed, as Philip Jackson (1992) explains in the *Handbook of Research on Curriculum,* curriculum is difficult to define and reflects many different theoretical orientations and arguments (traditionalists, reconceptualists, post-structualists, etc.). Curriculum implicates knowledge. But whose knowledge? What knowledge? Referring to the work of Merleau-Ponty in the citation above, Madeleine Grumet (1994) speaks of a body knowledge. . . knowledge about the world. As researchers we gather knowledge about the world and tend to ignore that it is also a body knowledge. As we examine our educational findings, we might need to pay more attention to this sociopolitical category in which all individuals are grouped and through which ideology is all powerful. For example, in the historical analysis by William Watkins, no mention was made of gender ideology in black educational reform.

Black female education in the early twentieth century was shaped by racial ideology and by gender role expectations within the black community (Harley & Terborg-Penn, 1978; Neverdon-Morton, 1989; Werum, 1997). The early twentieth-century black educational reform movement was based on middle-class assumptions about gender roles. W. E. B. Dubois, considered a radical reformer because he endorsed classical education for black men, minimized his ideas on African American women's education. He said little about whether black women should receive academic instruction at all (Meier, 1963). In fact, black educational reformers disagreed over the content and purposes of educating black women.

Werum (1997, p. 231) summarizes three groups of educational reformers. One group supported industrial education for black females because of the potential economic benefits. Some argued that industrial education would improve black women's morality by teaching thrift and discipline and by preparing them for their roles as mothers. Another group of reformers lobbied for combining academic and industrial education in order to prepare black women for a range of domestic and public responsibilities. A third group of black educators, notably educational activist women (e.g., Lucy Laney, Mary McLeod Bethune, and Anna Julia Cooper), supported expanding academic instruction for black women at all educational levels. They argued that schools were the only place where black women could learn languages, math, and philosophy.

Gender as a Category

Similarly, in the latter part of the twentieth century, Patti Lather (1994) remarked on the gender blindness of much of neo-Marxist sociology of education discourse (1994, p. 243). Although the situation has changed somewhat, researchers have pointed out that there is still a reluctance in research on race and class in education to consider the specificities of black women and girls (Henry, 1998b; Mirza, 1993). The category of gender in research on black education has tended to focus on the needs of the black male child, popularly called "endangered." And indeed there are valid reasons for this focus: One has only to look at the high dropout rates and the overrepresentation in special education programs experienced by African American boys, and at some of the brutal experiences in the wider society. In fact, this concern for the education of black boys has provided much of the curricular and pedagogical impetus for culturally relevant and African-centered schooling in the United States (Pollard, 1998). However, as Paul Gilroy (1993) has warned, there is a patriarchal tendency to prioritize the current crisis of black masculinity in the survival of the race. Let me emphasize that there is plenty of room for more systematic research on black males and the educative process in studies on race and education. Indeed, inquiries need to be analyzed by sex, race, ethnicity, sexuality, and social class to provide a more accurate picture of issues, dilemmas, and successes in terms of curriculum, race, and education.

Curriculum, Gender, and Race: Lessons from My Research

My own research with black girls 10 to 14 years of age has shown me how black masculine discourses and dominant Euro-centric discourses help to squeeze out the social and academic needs of middle-class African American and working-class African Caribbean girls (Henry, 1998a, 1998b). These girls that I have studied were at critical developmental and cognitive junctures as preadolescent and young adolescent females. Barrie Thorne (1993) has argued that the transition from being a child to a teen is a time in which girls start negotiating their adult femininity and become more fully inscribed into relationships of power and subordination. Through the explicit and implicit classroom curricula, school ethos, and social interactions, they learn about societal constructions of "female" and "black female."

Questions of race, gender, and education inevitably invoke the question: What are the purposes and intents of education (Gordon, 1997)? What might a competent education for black girls look like? That is, what cognitive and affective training is helpful in moving individuals through life as adult citizens on an independent and interdependent, but not dependent, basis (Jackson, 1976, p. 18)? Although critical studies in education stress the notion of the student voice, the voice of black girls is not examined in any systematic, rigorous way, although there have been a few studies, such as those of Fordham (1996), Fuller (1980), and Brock (2000).

My research findings (Henry, 1998a, 1998b) have shown that black girls do not hold a strong sense of identity in the classroom or express personal points of view or a strong sense of self and purpose that allows them the self-confidence to engage with the classroom topics. These are some of the healthful characteristics of "voice" outlined by Beverly McElroy Johnson (1993), a teacher of African American children. I hope that future research on race and curriculum could help bring about this voice for the many girls who may be in hostile or unfriendly learning environments, beleaguered by sexual harassment (AAUW, 1998) or by teachers' negative evaluations based on nonacademic factors (skin color, hair texture, social skills [see Omolade, 1994]).

Principles for an Agenda on Race and Curriculum Research

I want to conclude by outlining some ways in which a research agenda on race and education could address issues of curriculum in dynamic ways. These eight, interrelated principles are not new, but they envelop notions of collective action and equity so important in researching minority groups. As a qualitative researcher, I find this moment in social science investigation to be exciting: innovative epistemologies from previously silenced groups are emerging; the concept of the aloof researcher is increasingly being abandoned; and possibilities are being opened up for alternative, activist-oriented investigations (Denzin, 1997; Lincoln & Denzin, 1994).

To conclude, then, here are some worthwhile points to consider in future research in race and curriculum:

1. **Collaborative classroom research.** Curriculum research is about process, rather than product; research that helps researchers and classroom teachers systematically study and provide learning opportunities for students is axiomatic.
2. **University-school research partnerships.** This is one kind of collaboration that can help to re-shape the existing knowledge base for research both into classroom teaching and teacher education (Darling-Hammond, 1997; Fullan et al., 1998).
3. **Re-theorizing power and empowerment.** Research needs to be conducted that opens up relationships of participation, collaboration,

and dialogue; and re-theorizes power and empowerment and epistemological questions underlying conventional research methodology (Ristock & Pennell, 1996).

4. **Blurred dichotomies.** Research/practice (researcher/practitioner) binarisms are being blurred by some of the above relationships. Also, as an educational researcher displays her multiple identities (e.g., Muslim, African American, feminist, university professor, etc.), she demonstrates some reflexivity and displays her own biases, interests, and positionings in the research (Reinharz, 1992; Ristock & Pennell, 1996).

5. **Accessible, relevant research.** It follows that the kinds of research on race and education advocated above must directly address the issues that black teachers, students, parents, and other community members define as relevant and urgent and for community empowerment (hooks & West, 1991; King & Mitchell, 1995).

6. **Small-scale, localized studies.** Grand, universalizing narratives of black populations need to be replaced by local, small-scale theories fitted to specific problems and situations.

7. **Race as dynamic and complex.** The range and possibility of issues can be examined in new ways if race, language, and culture are seen as complex and dynamic. Cultures are not self-contained (Bhabha, 1996). Grossberg (1996, p. 88) calls for new ways to think about identity, arguing against the subsumption of identity into a particular set of modernist logics and the assumption that such structures of identity necessarily define the appropriate models and sites of political struggle. Given the role of media (music, movies, etc.) in the lives of youth, studies that capture this relationship may help untangle theoretical and practical pedagogical and curricular issues.

8. **Integrative approaches.** This last point evokes my earlier arguments about the neglected dimensions in studies of race. Fundamental to research on race is what George Dei (1996, p. 55) defines as integrative antiracism. It examines how the dynamics of social difference (race, class, gender, sexual orientation, physical ability, language, and religion) are mediated in people's daily experiences.

REFERENCES

AAUW (1998). *Gender gaps: Where schools still fail our children.* Washington, DC: American Institutes of Research.

Bhabha, H. (1996). Cultures in-between. In S. Hall & P. Du Gay (Eds.), *Questions of cultural identity.* (pp. 53–60). London: Sage Publications.

Brock, R. (2000). *Theorizing away the pain: Hyphenating the space between the personal and the pedagogical.* Unpublished doctoral dissertation, 1999. Penn State University.

Darling-Hammond, L. (1997). *The right to learn.* San Francisco: Jossey Bass.

Dei, G. (1996). *Antiracism education.* New Brunswick, NJ: Fernwood Press.

Denzin, N. (1997). *Interpretive ethnography.* Thousand Oaks, CA: Sage.

Fordham, S. (1996). *Blacked out.* New York: Routledge.

Fullan, M., Galluzzo, G., Morris, P., & Watson, N. (1998). *The rise and stall of teacher education.* Washington, DC: American Association of Colleges for Teacher Education.

Fuller, M. (1980). Black girls in a London comprehensive school. In R. Deem (Ed.), *Schooling for women's work* (pp. 52–61). London: Routledge & Kegan Paul.

Fuller, M. (1983). Qualified criticism, critical qualifications. In. L. Barton & S. Walker (Eds.), *Race class, and education* (pp. 166–190). London: Croom Helm.

Gilroy, P. (1993). *The Black Atlantic: Modernity and double consciousness.* Boston: Harvard University Press.

Gordon, B. (1997). Curriculum, policy and African American cultural knowledge: Challenges and possibilities for the year 2000 and beyond. *Educational Policy* (Vol. II, No. 2), 227–242.

Grossberg, L. (1996). Identity and cultural studies. In S. Hall & P. Du Gay (Eds.), *Questions of cultural identity* (pp. 87–107). London: Sage Publications.

Grumet, M. (1994). Conception, contradiction, and curriculum. In L. Stone (Ed.), *The education feminism reader.* New York: Routledge.

Harley, S., & Terborg-Penn, R. (1978). *The Afro-American woman: Struggles and images.* Port X. Washington, NY: National University Publications.

Henry, A. (1998a). Complacent and womanish: Girls negotiating their lives in an African centered school in the U.S. *Race, Ethnicity and Education, 1*(2), 151–170.

Henry, A. (1998b). Speaking up and speaking out: Examining voice in a reading/writing program with adolescent African Caribbean girls. *Journal of Literacy Research, 30*(2), 233–252.

hooks, B., & West, C. (1991). *Breaking bread.* New York: Between the Lines.

Jackson, J. (1976). *Career options for Black women.* Washington, DC: National Institute of Education. ERIC Document Reproduction No. ED 138 812.

Jackson, P. (1992). *Handbook of research on curriculum: A project of the American Educational Research Association.* New York: Macmillan.

King, J., & Mitchell, C. (1995). *Black mothers to sons: Juxtaposing African American literature with social practice.* New York: Peter Lang.

Lather, P. (1994). The absent presence: Patriarchy, capitalism and the nature of teacher's work. In L. Stone (Ed.), *The education feminism reader* (pp. 242–251). New York: Routledge.

Lincoln, Y., & Denzin, N. (1994). The fifth moment. In N. Denzin & Y. Lincoln (Eds.), *Handbook of qualitative research* (pp. 575–588). Thousand Oaks: Sage.

McElroy-Johnson, B. (1993). Giving voice to the voiceless. *Harvard Educational Review, 63,* 85–104.

Meier, A. (1963). *Negro thought in America: 1880–1915: Racial ideologies in the age of Booker T. Washington.* Ann Arbor: University of Michigan Press.

Mirza, H. (1993). The social construction of Black womanhood in British educational research: Towards a new understanding. In M. Arnot & K. Weiler (Eds.), *Feminism and social justice.* (pp. 32–57). London: Falmer.

Neverdon-Morton, C. (1989). *Afro-American women of the south and the advancement of the race.* Knoxville: University of Tennessee Press.

Omolade, B. (1994). *Rising song of African American women.* New York: Routledge.

Pollard, D. (1998). The contexts of single-sex classes. In *Separated by sex: a critical look at single-sex education for girls* (pp. 73–84). Washington, DC: American Association of University Women Educational Foundation.

Reinharz, S. (1992). *Feminist methods in social research.* New York: Oxford University Press.

Ristock, J., & Pennell, J. (1996). *Community research as empowerment.* Don Mills, Ontario Canada: Oxford University Press.

Thorne, B. (1993). *Gender play: Boys and girls in school.* New Brunswick, NJ: Rutgers University Press.

Werum, R. (1997). Gender ideology in early twentieth-century Black educational reform. In P. Dubeck & K. Borman, *Women and work* (pp. 230–232). New York: Routledge.

5 The Power of Pedagogy

Does Teaching Matter?

Gloria Ladson-Billings

Learning Styles versus Teaching Styles

During the past few decades we have seen educators exhibit a growing interest in the idea that students differ in a personality or cognitive trait called "learning style" (Royer & Feldman, 1984). Klein (1951), one of the early pioneers in this area, proposed a conceptual continuum that extended from what he termed "levelers" to "sharpeners." According to Klein, levelers are learners who hold tight to the categories of perception and judgment and do not change their mental set even when presented with new evidence or changing conditions. Sharpeners are learners who are attuned to change and capable of spotting shades of difference. Witkin (1962, 1977) distinguished between field dependence and field independence. According to Witkin, field-dependent learners rely heavily on environmental support, whereas field-independent learners are less bound by the situations in which they find themselves. Kagan (1964) distinguished between "impulsivity" and "reflectivity" according to the degree to which a learner reflects on the validity of alternative solutions. Ausubel (1968) differentiated between "satellizers" and "non-satellizers"; satellizers have an intrinsic sense of self-worth independent of what they accomplish, whereas non-satellizers lack an intrinsic feeling of self-worth and feel the need to prove themselves through accomplishment.

Domino (1971) moved this inquiry into learning styles further by examining how a personality trait could be used to select an optimal instructional approach. Cronbach and Snow (1977), however, did not find any consistent pattern indicating that students with certain personality traits respond better when taking courses from teachers having corresponding personality traits.

Soon after the learning styles literature began to gain acceptance a somewhat parallel body of literature emerged that began to apply the learning styles notions to racial, ethnic, and cultural groups. Ramirez and Castaneda (1974) translated Witkin's field-dependent/field-independent typology to field-sensitive/field-independent as a way to explain disparities between Latino and Anglo school performance. Cohen (1976) made distinctions between analytical and relational modes of conceptual organization and indicated that while students of color often demonstrated a preference for relational styles, schools generally favor and reward the analytical mode. Hale-Benson (1986) and Shade (1982) have applied the concept of learning style to the particular needs of African American students.

Hilliard (1989) questioned the use of the term "style" to describe (and perhaps justify) the low academic performance of students of color. More importantly, Hilliard questioned the use of the term as an excuse for both low expectations on the part of teachers and substandard delivery of instruction. Hilliard further asserts that although style is cultural (or learned) and meaningful in teaching and learning, we do not know enough about how or whether pedagogy should be modified in response to learning styles.

The learning styles research is open to criticism on several levels. First, only a few styles (e.g., field dependence/field independence, reflectivity/impulsivity) have been researched extensively. Second, this research rarely is linked to issues regarding teachers' learning styles and/or teaching styles. And, perhaps most importantly, there is little evidence to suggest that distinguishing students according to their learning styles makes any significant differences in their academic performances. Each of these areas needs further research before we can accept or reject the saliency of learning styles as a way of addressing the educational needs of students.

Irvine and York (1995) completed a comprehensive review of the learning styles literature as it relates to culturally diverse students and concluded the following:

> Learning-styles research is based on the theory that individuals respond to learning situations with consistent patterns of behavior. When applied to culturally diverse students, learning styles research proposes to explain why children of the same culture or ethnicity often employ similar strategies for learning.
> . . . One core assumption inherent in the learning-styles research is that children outside of mainstream culture learn better when teaching matches their preferred style. However, research on learning styles using culturally diverse students fails to support the premise that members of a given cultural group exhibit a distinctive style. Hence, the issue is not the identification of a style for a particular ethnic . . . group, but rather how instruction should be arranged to meet the instructional needs of culturally diverse students. (p. 494)

Irvine and York (1995, p. 491) point out that there are several questions raised by the notion of learning styles:

1. Is culture the primary variable that influences learning styles of students of color? Are there other significant variables?
2. Do characteristics of the cultural group apply uniformly to individual members of the group?
3. What is the relationship between teachers' instructional methods and students' learning styles?
4. Should students of color always be taught using their preferred learning styles?

Without providing definitive answers to these questions, Irvine and York suggest that the learning styles research is not solid enough to provide direct insights into classroom applications. One concern that arises from the use of learning styles in the classroom is that subordinated students somehow always seem to be identified as those using "less prestigious" or "less rigorous" learning styles. Thus, all learning styles are not created equal.

Much of the learning styles research has as its ideological base the primacy of the individual and individual differences. However, this may be an ideological blind spot that prevents researchers from understanding the role of culture in supporting students' learning and teachers' instructional decisions. Thus, we may need to turn from psychologists to anthropologists for additional insights into school performance.

The Case for Culturally Relevant Teaching

Anthropologists have long had an interest in applying their research methodology to complex social institutions such as schools (Spindler, 1988). In an attempt to examine questions related to the denial of equal educational opportunity, anthropologists have looked at schools as agents of cultural transmission, arenas of cultural conflict, and sites of potential micro and macro level change (Wilcox, 1988). One of the areas of anthropological study that has proved fruitful for examining the experiences of marginalized students of color in the classroom is the attempt (or lack thereof) of teachers to find ways to match their teaching styles to the culture and home backgrounds of their students.

During the 1980s several terms emerged in the anthropology of education literature that describe these pedagogical strategies used by teachers in an effort to make the schooling experiences of students more compatible with their everyday lives. Those terms include "cultural congruence" (Mohatt & Erickson, 1981), "cultural appropriateness" (Au & Jordan, 1981), "cultural responsiveness" (Cazden & Legett, 1981; Erickson & Mohatt, 1982), "cultural compatibility" (Jordan, 1985; Vogt, Jordan, & Tharp, 1987), and "mitigating cultural discontinuity" (Macias, 1987).

Au and Jordan (1981, p. 139) termed "culturally appropriate" the pedagogy of teachers in a Hawaiian school who incorporated aspects of students' cultural backgrounds into their reading instruction. By permitting students to use "talk-story," a language interaction style common among Native Hawaiian children, teachers were able to help students achieve at higher than predicted levels on standardized reading tests.

Mohatt and Erickson (1981) conducted similar work with Native American students. As they observed teacher–student interactions and participation structures, they found teachers who used language interaction patterns that approximated the students' home cultural patterns were more successful in improving student achievement performance. Improved student achievement also was evident among teachers who used what they termed "mixed forms" (Mohatt & Erickson, p. 117)—a combination of Native American and Anglo language interaction patterns. They termed this instruction "culturally congruent" (Mohatt & Erickson, p. 110).

Cazden and Leggett (1981) and Erickson and Mohatt (1982) used the term "culturally responsive" (p. 167) to describe similar language interactions of teachers with linguistically diverse and Native American students, respectively. Later Jordan (1985, p. 110) and Vogt, Jordan, and Tharp (1987, p. 281) began using the term "culturally compatible" to explain the success of classroom teachers with Hawaiian children.

By observing the students in their home/community environment, teachers were able to include aspects of the students' cultural environment in the organization and instruction of the classroom. More specifically, Jordan (1985) discusses cultural compatibility in this way:

> Educational practices must match with children's culture in ways which ensure the generation of academically important behaviors. It does not mean that all school practices need to be completely congruent with natal cultural practices, in the sense of exactly or even closely matching or agreeing with them. The point of cultural compatibility is that the natal culture is used as a guide in the selection of educational program elements so that academically desired behaviors are produced and undesired behaviors are avoided. (p. 110)

These studies have several common features. Each locates the source of student failure and subsequent achievement within the nexus of speech and language interaction patterns of the teacher and the students. Each suggests that student "success" is represented in achievement within the current social structures extant in schools. Thus, the goal of education becomes how to "fit" students constructed as "other" by virtue of their race/ethnicity, language, or social class into a hierarchical structure that is defined as a "meritocracy." However, it is unclear how these conceptions do more than reproduce the current inequities. Singer (1988, p. 1) suggests that "cultural congruence is an inherently moderate pedagogical strategy that accepts that the goal of educating minority students is to train individuals in those skills needed to succeed in mainstream society."

Three of the terms employed by studies on cultural mismatch between school and home—"culturally appropriate," "culturally congruent," and "culturally compatible"—seem to connote accommodation of student culture to mainstream culture. Only the term "culturally responsive" appears to refer to a more dynamic or synergistic relationship between home/community culture and school culture. Erickson and Mohatt (1982) suggest their notion of culturally responsive teaching can be seen as a beginning step for bridging the gap between home and school:

> It may well be that, by discovering the small differences in social relations which make a big difference in the interactional ways children engage the content of the school curriculum, anthropologists can make practical contributions to the improvement of minority children's school achievement and to the improvement of the everyday school life for such children and their teachers. Making small changes in everyday participation structures may be one of the means by which more culturally responsive pedagogy can be developed. (p. 170)

For the most part, studies of cultural appropriateness, congruence, or compatibility have been conducted within small-scale communities—for example, Native Hawaiians and Native Americans. However, an earlier generation of work considered the mismatch between the language patterns of African Americans and the school in larger, urban settings (Gay & Abrahamson, 1972; Labov, 1969; Piestrup, 1973).

Villegas (1988) challenged the microsocial explanations advanced by sociolinguists by suggesting that the source of cultural mismatch is located in larger social structures and that schools as institutions serve to reproduce social inequalities. She argued that:

> As long as school performs this sorting function in society, it must necessarily produce winners and losers. . . . Therefore, culturally sensitive remedies to educational problems of oppressed minority students that ignore the political aspect of schooling are doomed to failure. (pp. 262–263)

While Villegas' claims add an important dimension to the debate about school achievement for subordinated students, we must be clear that this is not an "either-or" debate. Rather, it is a "both-and" situation that requires that we understand that what is happening to students of color is happening both inside classrooms and outside them. The limitation of this chapter is that it can address only the parameters of the classroom—the role of teachers and teaching.

A number of analyses of successful schooling for African American students (King, 1991; Ladson-Billings, 1992, 1994; Siddle-Walker, 1993) challenge the explanatory power of those who argue that African Americans hold some caste-like status and raise questions about what schools can and should be doing to promote academic success for African American students.

Three examples of scholarship that focus on improving teaching for African American students are found in the work of Irvine (1990), Lee (1994), and Ladson-Billings (1994). Irvine developed the concept of "cultural synchronization" to describe the necessary interpersonal context that must exist between the teacher and African American students to maximize learning. Rather than focusing solely on speech and language interactions, Irvine's work describes the acceptance of students' communication patterns, along with a constellation of cultural mores such as mutuality, reciprocity, spirituality, deference, and responsibility (King & Mitchell, 1990).

Irvine's work on African American students and school failure considers both micro- and macro-analyses, including teacher and student interpersonal societal contexts, teacher and student expectations, institutional contexts, and the societal contexts. This work is important because of its break with the cultural-deficit or cultural-disadvantage explanations that led to compensatory educational interventions. By carefully analyzing each element in the school and social context, Irvine helped to reveal the complexity of the various factors that contribute to school success or failure.

Lee developed a notion of cultural modeling to describe the way that teachers can use African American students' linguistic strengths to build scaffolding that supports literacy learning. More specifically, Lee describes the use of signifying as a linguistic tool for developing literacy. According to Lee (Lee, 1994, p. 302), "Signifying is a form of oral discourse within the African American community that is characterized by innuendo, double meanings, and rhetorical play on meaning and sounds of words." Lee's work underscores the need for teachers to "place value on the learner's culture" (Lee, 1994, p. 299).

Ladson-Billings (1994) developed a theoretical notion of teaching, termed "culturally relevant pedagogy," that describes an approach to teaching that promotes academic and cultural success in settings where student alienation and hostility characterize the school experience. The propositions on which this theory is based are academic achievement, cultural competence, and sociopolitical consciousness.

Rather than focus on the particular "learning styles" of students, this theory argues that teachers have to adopt a particular set of principles about teaching that can be applied in various school and classroom contexts. The focus on academic achievement argues that teachers must place student learning at the center of all classroom activity. Although there have been many explanations offered for why African American students fail to succeed in school, little research has been done to examine academic success among

African American students. The "effective schools" literature (Brookover, 1985; Brookover, Beady, Flood, Schweitzer, & Wisenbaker, 1979; Edmonds, 1979) argued that a group of school-wide correlates were reliable predictors of student success.[1] The basis for judging a school "effective" in this literature was how far above predicted levels students performed on standardized achievement tests. Whether or not scholars can agree on the significance of standardized achievement tests, their meaning in the broader public serves to rank and characterize both schools and individuals. No matter how good a fit develops between a student's home and school cultures, students must achieve. No approach to teaching can escape this reality.

The focus on cultural competence suggests that teachers must help students develop a positive identification with their home culture—an identification that supports student learning. Among the scholarship that has examined academically successful African American students, a disturbing finding has emerged—the students' academic success has come at the expense of their culture and psychosocial well-being (Fine, 1986; Fordham, 1988). Fordham and Ogbu (1986, p. 176) identified a phenomenon entitled "acting white," where African American students who were academically successful were ostracized by their peers. Bacon (1981) found that, among African American high school students identified as gifted in their elementary grades, only about half were continuing to do well at the high school level. A closer examination of the successful students' progress indicated that they were social isolates, with neither African American nor white friends. The students believed that it was necessary for them to separate themselves from other African American students so that teachers would not attribute to them the negative characteristics they may have attributed to low-performing African American students.

Pedagogy must provide a way for students to maintain their cultural integrity while succeeding academically. Many of the self-described African-centered public schools have focused on this notion of cultural competence. To date, little data have been reported on the academic success of students in these school programs.

Finally, teachers must focus on sociopolitical consciousness. This third aspect refers to the kind of civic and social awareness students must develop to work toward equity and justice beyond their own personal advancement, and it has been reflected in successful programs such as Freedom Schools, Citizenship Schools, and Nationalist Schools. This notion of sociopolitical consciousness presumes that teachers themselves recognize social inequities and their causes. However, teacher educators (Grant, 1989; Haberman, 1991; King, 1991; King & Ladson-Billings, 1990; Zeichner, 1992)

---

[1]These correlates include a clear and focused mission, instructional leadership, a safe and orderly environment, regular monitoring of student progress, high expectations, and positive home-school relations.

have demonstrated that many prospective teachers not only lack these understandings but also reject information regarding social inequity. This suggests that more work must be done recruiting particular kinds of students to go into teaching.

Haberman (1995) argues that the best teachers for poor children know how to do a specific set of skills, which include:

1. Protect learners and learning
2. Put ideas into classroom practice
3. Challenge external labels given to students such as "at-risk," "EMR"
4. Develop a professional–personal orientation toward students
5. Know how to satisfy school bureaucracies without comprising teaching quality
6. Recognize their own fallibility
7. Have emotional and physical stamina
8. Have good organizational ability
9. Focus on student effort rather than a vague notion of ability
10. Focus on teaching students rather than sorting them
11. Convince students that they are needed in the classroom
12. Serve as allies *with* students against challenging material

Research by Delpit (1995), Foster (1994, 1995), Irvine (1990), King (1991), Ladson-Billings (1994, 1995), Moll (1988), and Garcia (1988) all suggests that there are some aspects of teaching important to student learning that may be differentially valued and represented in the repertoires of successful teachers in urban, minority contexts.

Foster's (1994, 1995) work identifies cultural solidarity, linking classroom content to students' experiences, a focus on the whole child, a use of familiar cultural patterns, and the incorporation of culturally compatible communication patterns as key elements of success in teaching African American urban students. Irvine's (1990) work has investigated the nested conditions of urban school teaching that require what she terms "cultural synchronization" to produce success.

Ladson-Billings' (1994, 1995) research on successful teachers of African American children found that there is a consensus around how such teachers conceptualize themselves and others (i.e., students, parents, community members), how they conceptualize social relations (both within and outside of the school and classroom), and how they conceptualize knowledge.

Garcia's (1988) work suggests that Latino students benefit from teachers who specify task outcomes and what students must do to accomplish tasks competently, communicate both high expectations and a sense of efficacy about their own ability to teach, exhibit use of "active teaching," communicate clearly, obtain and maintain students' engagement, monitor students' progress, and provide immediate feedback.

Foster (1994, 1995) and Ladson-Billings (1994, 1995) look at specific teacher beliefs and actions. Following are aspects of their work that may be important in understanding the role of teaching in classrooms serving the poor and communities of color.

Cultural Solidarity

Foster (1995, p. 575) argues that although "similar background does not guarantee productive, fluid, or uncomplicated relationships between teacher and student" (Mahiri, 1998), there is evidence that suggests that some of the more successful teaching occurs when teachers do share background and experiences with students (Cazden, 1976, 1988). Siddle-Walker (1993) has demonstrated that a sense of cultural solidarity or connectedness has existed historically, particularly during the era when African Americans were consigned to segregated schools.

The focus on "relationship" in urban schools is particularly important given that urban schools have regularly been described as places where children experience little trust and sense of safety with the adults in the school (Haberman, 1995). But how is a sense of caring and cultural solidarity exhibited in an assessment of teaching? What words, gestures, pieces of evidence can be collected that demonstrate the connection between a teacher and her students? In the case of both Foster and Ladson-Billings, long-term, on-site observations and interviews were used to document this quality. However, nothing in the proposed teacher assessments directly deal with the relationships between teachers and their students. Those relationships are assumed but rarely documented.

Linking Classroom Content with Student Experience

This attribute often relies on how well the previous one (cultural solidarity) is established. The teacher who feels comfortable and has something in common with the students, their community, their language, and their backgrounds has at her disposal a deeper reservoir of skills and abilities on which to draw. For instance, the teacher who attends a church in the community or has had a church experience similar to that of the children in the classroom can more readily make analogues between appropriate behavior at particular times in the school day and appropriate behavior in particular portions of a worship service. These are not necessarily special skills, for indeed we would expect all teachers to be able to provide students with real world examples, but the skills and examples that urban teachers may have can be so familiar to students that their use minimizes conflict and confusion.

Ladson-Billings and Henry (1991), in a look at both African American and Afro-Caribbean-Canadian youngsters and their teachers, demonstrated how the teachers' understanding of the specific situations of students allowed them to better manage and teach in classrooms considered difficult by their peers.

Focus on the Whole Child

Foster (1995) points out that successful teachers of African American children typically concern themselves with much more than the children's cognitive growth. Issues of moral, ethical, and personal development are a part of their pedagogy. However, the proposed standards-driven assessments for teachers focus primarily on student achievement in specific content areas. The relationship between personal, moral, and ethical growth and cognitive growth has not been clearly established, but successful teachers in urban areas seem to believe this more holistic approach to teaching is key to their success.

Use of Familiar Cultural Patterns

Successful urban teachers know (or quickly learn) the cultural norms and patterns of their students. In Ladson-Billings' (1994) study, teachers describe the ways they used cultural knowledge and/or learned from students in order to facilitate the relationship that would subsequently facilitate learning. Rather than attempt to re-socialize students into a dominant paradigm, successful urban teachers soon learn that qualities such as reciprocity, respect, collectivity, and expressive individualism are vital to being able to work with their students. Foster (1995) asserts that routines and rituals are prevalent in the classrooms of African American teachers who are successful with African American students. These cultural patterns mirror aspects of African American life experiences in music, art, dance, religion, speech, and other forms of communication.

Incorporation of Culturally Compatible Communication Patterns

The area of culturally compatible communication patterns has received the most attention in the research literature. Sociolinguists, such as Cazden and Leggett (1981), Erickson and Mohatt (1982), Mohatt and Erickson (1981), Philips (1983), Au (1980), Au and Jordan (1981), and Jordan (1985), all have devoted considerable research time to examining the interactions between teachers and students who are from different linguistic, racial, ethnic, and cultural groups.

Ladson-Billings' (1994, 1995) work uses a related but different rubric by which to assess effective teaching. In a 3-year study of effective teachers of African American students, she was able to discern a set of general principles that characterize such teachers, which she calls cultural relevant teaching.

Conceptions of Self/Other

Culturally relevant teaching constructs a vision of the teacher and student as capable, efficacious human beings. Rather than succumb to the prevailing beliefs about "at-riskness," culturally relevant teachers make demands for academic success from all students. These teachers, like Kleinfeld's (1974) "warm demanders," did not allow students to avoid work because they were poor or came from single-parent households, or had some other personal/social problems. Sometimes these demands for success can appear harsh. Certainly, a snapshot of the teachers in the classroom (such as those that appear in some assessment exercises) may be a distortion of what the teachers actually are trying to accomplish.

Conceptions of Social Relations

In many urban classrooms there is a strict line of demarcation between students and teachers. In fact, some have likened urban schools to prisons with the students as inmates. However, culturally relevant teachers work to deliberately blur the borders between themselves and their students. The erasing of the borders is not acquiescence to a notion that children and adults are peers. Instead, it is an attempt to erase the distance that exists between and among teachers, students, parents, and the community. To an outside viewer this changed set of social relations might appear as if teachers are overstepping their legal authority. A teacher might speak specifically about a student and his parents. On the surface, this interaction may be interpreted as the teacher behaving inappropriately. However, what may lie beneath the surface is a carefully constructed set of social relations that the teacher has worked out with the student's parents and that allows for a degree of informality.

Additionally, culturally relevant teachers work to stretch the boundaries of the classroom so that they extend out into the community. Such teachers may attend students' church services and sporting events and secure personal goods and services from local merchants and business people to make sure that the latter are a presence in the community.

Conceptions of Knowledge

Culturally relevant teachers take as a given the notion that the curriculum is not working in the best interest of urban, poor children of color. Consequently, these teachers help students to develop counterknowledge that challenges the status quo. This subversive strategy is not likely to show up in an assessment because most such teachers are unlikely to share this strategy publicly. In the classrooms of culturally relevant teachers, knowledge is often very tentatively held because students are charged with the responsibility of deconstructing, reconstructing, and constructing knowledge (Shujaa, 1994). From what we have seen of the new teacher assessments, knowledge construction has been more narrowly defined than what the research on effective teachers in urban settings demonstrates.

What We Still Need to Know

The role of culture in schooling is an area that needs much more empirical research and scholarship. Much of what we know thus far is not definitive. Additional work on teachers' belief systems and philosophies of teaching and learning needs to be conducted. We still have no sense of what relationship exists between the racial/ethnic identity of teachers and of students.

We also need to know what is the value-added effect of teachers who have additional subject matter knowledge and experience. This information is critical because more than 50,000 people who lack the training required for their jobs have entered teaching annually on emergency or substandard licenses (National Commission on Teaching & America's Future, 1996). Twenty-three percent of all secondary school teachers do not even have a college minor in their main teaching field. This is true for more than 30 percent of mathematics teachers (*ibid.*). Among teachers who teach a second subject, 36 percent are unlicensed in the field and 50 percent lack a minor. In schools with the highest enrollment of students of color, students have only a 50 percent chance of getting a science or mathematics teacher who holds a license and a degree in the field he or she teaches (*ibid.*).

Currently, much effort and energy are being poured into the development of new forms of assessment for teachers. These assessments have had an adverse impact on African American and Latino teachers, that is, their failure rates have been much higher than those of white teachers. However, we are just beginning to investigate the ways that these assessments might be biased against the instructional styles of teachers of color who teach in urban schools.

Finally, I believe that there needs to be much more research done on pedagogy. Currently, we have naive and ill-formed notions of pedagogy. Unlike other areas of practice—medicine, law, business, theology—pedagogy lacks a sufficient knowledge foundation on which to base sound practice. The old adage, "those who can't, teach" is not so much a dig at teachers as it is emblematic of the low regard we as a society have for teaching. We believe that almost anyone can do it, and we allow almost anyone to do it. However, with growing numbers of poor students and students of color failing to benefit from schooling, we must begin to examine how and why pedagogy works. Ultimately, we must make a decision about whether there is any power in our pedagogy.

REFERENCES

Au, K. (1980). Participation structures in a reading lesson with Hawaiian children: An analysis of a culturally appropriate instructional event. *Anthropology and Education Quarterly, 11,* 91–115.

Au, K., & Jordan, C. (1981). Teaching reading to Hawaiian children: Finding a culturally appropriate solution. In H. Trueba, G. Guthrie, & K. Au (Eds.), *Culture and the bilingual classroom: Studies in classroom ethnography* (pp.139–152). Rowley, MA: Newbury House.

Ausubel, D. P. (1968). *Educational psychology: A cognitive view.* New York: Holt, Rinehart, & Winston.

Bacon, M. H. (1981, May). *High potential children from Ravenswood Elementary School District* (Follow-up study). Redwood City, CA: Sequoia Union High School District.

Brookover, W. (1985). Can we make schools effective for minority students? *The Journal of Negro Education, 54,* 257–268.

Brookover, W., Beady, C., Flood, P., Schweitzer, J., & Wisenbaker, J. (1979). *School social systems and student achievement: Schools can make a difference.* New York: Praeger.

Cazden, C. (1976). How knowledge about language helps the classroom teacher—or does it? A personal account. *Urban Review, 9,* 74–90.

Cazden, C. (1988). *Classroom discourse: The language of teaching and learning.* Portsmouth, NH: Heinemann.

Cazden, C., & Leggett, C. (1981). Culturally responsive education: Recommendations for achieving Lau remedies II. In H. Trueba, G. Guthrie, & K. Au (Eds.), *Culture and the bilingual classroom: Studies in classroom ethnography* (pp. 69–86). Rowley, MA: Newbury House.

Cohen, R. (1976). Conceptual styles, cultural conflict, and non-verbal tests of intelligence. In J. Roberts & S. Akinsanya (Eds.), *Schooling in the cultural context* (pp. 290–322). New York: David McKay Co.

Cronbach, L. J., & Snow, R. (1977). *Aptitudes and instructional methods.* New York: Irvington Publishers.

Delpit, L. (1995). *Other people's children: Cultural conflict in the classroom.* New York: The New Press.

Domino, G. (1971). Interactive effects of achievement orientation and teaching style of academic achievement. *Journal of Educational Psychology, 62,* 427–441.

Edmonds, R. (1979). Effective schools for the urban poor. *Educational Leadership, 37,* 15–24.

Erickson, F., & Mohatt, G. (1982). Cultural organization and participation structures in two classrooms of Indian students. In G. Spindler (Ed.), *Doing the ethnography of schooling* (pp. 131–174). Prospect Heights, IL: Waveland Press.

Fine, M. (1986). Why urban adolescents drop into and out of high school. *Teachers College Record, 87,* 393–409.

Fordham, S. (1988). Racelessness as a factor in Black students' school success: Pragmatic strategy or pyrrhic victory? *Harvard Educational Review, 58,* 54–84.

Fordham, S., & Ogbu, J. (1986). Black students' school success: Coping with the burden of "acting white." *The Urban Review, 18,* 176–206.

Foster, M. (1994). Effective black teachers: A literature review. In E. Hollins, J. King, & W. Hayman (Eds.), *Teaching diverse populations: Formulating a knowledge base* (pp. 225–241). Albany, NY: SUNY Press.

Foster, M. (1995). African American teachers and culturally relevant pedagogy. In J. A. Banks & C. M. Banks (Eds.), *Handbook of research on multicultural education* (pp. 570–581). New York: Macmillan.

Garcia, E. (1988). Attributes of effective schools for language minority students. *Education and Urban Society, 20,* 387–398.

Gay, G., & Abrahamson, R. D. (1972). Talking black in the classroom. In R. D. Abrahamson & R. Troike (Eds.), *Language and cultural diversity in education* (pp. 200–208). Englewood Cliffs, NJ: Prentice-Hall.

Grant, C. A. (1989). Urban teachers: Their new colleagues and curriculum. *Phi Delta Kappan, 70,* 764–770.

Haberman, M. (1991). Can cultural awareness be taught in teacher education programs? *Teaching Education, 4,* 25–32.

Haberman, M. (1995). *Star teachers of children in poverty.* West Lafayette, IN: Kappa Delta Pi.

Hale-Benson, J. (1986). *Black children: Their roots, culture, and learning styles.* Baltimore: Johns Hopkins University Press.

Hilliard, A. (1989). Teachers and cultural style in a pluralistic society. *Issues 89: NEA Today, 7,* 65–69.

Irvine, J. J. (1990). *Black students and school failure.* Westport, CT: Greenwood Press.

Irvine, J. J., & York, D. E. (1995). Learning styles and culturally diverse students: A literature review. In J. A. Banks & C. M. Banks (Eds.), *The handbook of research on multicultural education* (pp. 484–497). New York: Macmillan.

Jordan, C. (1985). Translating culture: From ethnographic information to educational program. *Anthropology and Education Quarterly, 16,* 105–123.

Kagan, J. (1964). American longitudinal research on psychological development. *Child Development, 35,* 1–32.

King, J. E. (1991). Unfinished business: Black student alienation and Black teachers' emancipatory pedagogy. In M. Foster (Ed.), *Readings on Equal Education Vol. 11* (pp. 245–271). New York: AMS.

King, J. E., & Ladson-Billings, G. (1990). The teacher education challenge in elite university settings: Developing critical perspectives for teaching in a democratic and multicultural society. *European Journal of Intercultural Studies, 1,* 15–30.

King, J. E., & Mitchell, C. (1990). *Black mothers to sons: Juxtaposing African American literature with social practice.* New York: Peter Lang.

Klein, G. (1951). The personal world through perception. In R. R. Blake & G. V. Ramsey (Eds.), *Perception: An approach to personality* (pp. 328–335). New York: Ronald Press.

Kleinfeld, J. (1974). Effective teachers of Indian and Eskimo high school students. In J. Orvik & R. Barnhardt (Eds.), *Cultural influences in Alaska Native education.* Fairbanks: Center for Northern Educational Research, University of Alaska.

Labov, W. (1969). The logic of non-standard Negro English. In J. E. Altis (Ed.), *Linguistics and the teaching of standard English* (Monograph Series on Language and Linguistics, No. 22). Washington, DC: Georgetown University Press.

Ladson-Billings, G. (1992). Liberatory consequences of literacy: A case of culturally relevant instruction for African American students. *The Journal of Negro Education, 61,* 378–391.

Ladson-Billings, G. (1994). *The dreamkeepers: Successful teaching for African American students.* San Francisco: Jossey Bass.

Ladson-Billings, G. (1995). Toward a theory of culturally relevant pedagogy. *American Educational Research Journal, 32,* 465–491.

Ladson-Billings, G., & Henry, A. (1991). Blurring the borders: Voices of African liberatory pedagogy. *Journal of Education, 172,* 72–88.

Lee, C. D. (1994). African centered pedagogy: Complexities and possibilities. In M. Shujaa (Ed.), *Too much schooling, too little education: A paradox of black life in white societies* (pp. 295–318). Trenton, NJ: Africa World Press.

Macias, J. (1987). The hidden curriculum of Papago teachers: American Indian strategies for mitigating cultural discontinuity in early schooling. In G. Spindler & L. Spindler (Eds.), *Interpretive ethnography at home and abroad* (pp. 363–380). Hillsdale, NJ: Lawrence Erlbaum Associates.

Mahiri, J. (1998). *Shooting for excellence: African American and youth culture in new century schools.* New York: Teachers College Press and NCTE.

Mohatt, G., & Erickson, F. (1981). Cultural differences in teaching styles in an Odawa school: A sociolinguistic approach. In H. Trueba, G. Guthrie, & K. Au (Eds.), *Culture and the bilingual classroom: Studies in classroom ethnography* (pp.105–119). Rowley, MA: Newbury House.

Moll, L. (1988). Some key aspects in teaching Latino students. *Language Arts, 65,* 465–472.

Philips, S. (1983). *The invisible culture: Communication in the classroom and community on the Warm Springs Indian Reservation.* White Plains, NY: Longman.

Piestrup, A. (1973). *Black dialect interference and accommodation of reading instruction in first grade* (Monograph No. 4). Berkeley, CA: Language Behavior Research Laboratory.

Ramirez, M., & Castaneda, A. (1974). *Cultural democracy, bicognitive development and education.* New York: Academic Press.

Royer, J., & Feldman, R. (1984). *Educational psychology: Applications and theory.* New York: Alfred A Knopf.

Shade, B. J. (1982). Afro-American cognitive style: A variable in school success? *Review of Educational Research, 52,* 219–244.

Shujaa, M. J. (Ed.). (1994). *Too much schooling, too little education: A paradox of black life in white societies.* Trenton, NJ: Africa World Press.

Siddle-Walker, V. (1993). Caswell County Training School, 1933–1969: Relationships between community and school. *Harvard Educational Review, 63,* 161–182.

Singer, E. (1988). What is cultural congruence, and why are they saying such terrible things about it? (Occasional Paper). East Lansing, MI: Institute for Research on Teaching.

Spindler, G. (1988). *Doing the ethnography of schooling.* Prospect Heights, IL: Waveland Press.

Villegas, A. (1988). School failure and cultural mismatch: Another view. *The Urban Review, 20,* 253–265.

Vogt, L., Jordan, C., & Tharp, R. (1987). Explaining school failure, producing school success: Two cases. *Anthropology and Education Quarterly, 18,* 276–286.

Wilcox, K. (1988). Ethnography as a methodology and its applications to the study of schooling. In G. Spindler (Ed.), *Doing the ethnography of schooling* (pp. 457–488). Prospect Heights, IL: Waveland Press.

Witkin, A. H. (1962). Origins of cognitive styles. In C. Scheerer (Ed.), *Cognition: Theory, research and promise* (pp. 127–205). New York: Harper & Row.

Witkin, A. H. (1977). Field-dependent and field-independent cognitive styles and the educational implications. *Review of Educational Research, 47,* 1–64.

Zeichner, K. M. (1992). *Educating teachers for cultural diversity* (Special Report). East Lansing, MI: National Center for Research on Teacher Learning.

6

Comment

Unpacking Culture, Teaching, and Learning: A Response to "The Power of Pedagogy"

Carol D. Lee

Introduction

In Chapter 5, "The Power of Pedagogy: Does Teaching Matter?" Professor Gloria Ladson-Billings provides a comprehensive overview of the research on frameworks through which to conceptualize productive relationships between the culture that students, particularly students of color, bring from their family and community experiences and the nature of teaching that is responsive to those perceptions of culture. One of the major challenges of this work has been how we conceptualize the idea of culture. We also do not have appropriate language with which to talk about the issues on the table. We use terms like "culturally diverse" as synonyms for blacks and others who become affiliated within the political realm of blackness as defined by a European American worldview based on unstated assumptions about race. Such affiliates include Latinos and Native Americans. However, when the term "culturally diverse" gets conflated, as it so often does, with low academic achievement, it becomes problematic as to whether high-achieving Asian American groups fit the colored category. In any case, it is generally implicit in how the term is used that white students are not part of the culturally diverse group. Otherwise the label would simply include all students. We also use the term "students or people of color" to again refer to Blacks, Latinos, Native Americans, and Asian Americans. This term becomes problematic, however, when one sees on census surveys "Hispanic" and "Hispanic–Black." It becomes further problematic when one considers persons who are classified as black whose skin color is the same as that of most whites and persons who are classified as white whose skin color is olive, such as some Sicilians and people of Jewish heritage, for example. As has been aptly pointed out by Asa Hilliard, our constructs of race are a racist fixation and a political and social construction with no basis in phenotype or genetics. And yet, these unstated assumptions about race form the foundation around which our notions of cultural responsivity and the links between culture and achievement rest. Until we de-construct our notions about race, we will remain tethered in ways that limit our vision of the possible.

Instead, Hilliard offers the construct of ethnicity. Unlike race, ethnicity is linked to family and social organization patterns that are both current and connected historically, including language, communal beliefs, values, and everyday practices. The practices associated with ethnicity are observable. Indeed, ethnicity is also a permeable boundary. With race as a pseudobiological concept, one is born into a race and is therefore phenotypically bound to the genetics of that condition. On the other hand, people who are classified as black in western culture sometimes choose to cross ethnic identity borders, and to live—in terms of language, beliefs, and social practices—as members of other ethnic groups than that to which they were born. Within continental African communities (Yoruba, Akan, Zulu, and others) as well as the African American community, what sustained a people across time and adversity were social practices, beliefs, values, family structures, and relationships, not merely the color of their skin. It is the deep influence of these ethnic experiences that help to shape identity formations. In one sense, the United States has both a national culture as well as many ethnic cultures that exist side by side and often interact with and influence one another.

Professor Ladson-Billings describes the history of concepts devised by researchers to frame pedagogy that takes ethnicity into account. In some sense, of the various frames through which to conceptualize the influences of culture on learning, the most comprehensive is that of culturally responsive pedagogy developed by Professor Ladson-Billings herself. I want here to unpack the three core tenets of this culturally responsive framework: (1) a focus on high academic achievement, (2) an emphasis on the development of cultural competence within the students' home culture, and (3) an explicit attention to sociopolitical issues that focus students beyond their personal advancement as individuals. In this chapter I discuss some of the dilemmas of unpacking each of these tenets and will address some of research that systematically addresses such unpacking.

A Focus on High Achievement

Much of the literature on cultural responsivity in teaching dates back many years. None of that literature, to my knowledge, seriously unpacks what we mean by high achievement. The literature that focuses on language considers how knowledge of discourse and interactional patterns of talk can facilitate participation in instructional discourse and yet greater participation of talk around what was rarely addressed (Au, 1980; Cazden, John, & Hymes, 1972; Phillips, 1983; Tharp & Gallimore, 1988). As we move into the twenty-first century (depending on whose calendar you're using), what knowledge is most useful to learn is under scrutiny, and new rigorous standards are being called for. Some have said that the most significant capital of the twenty-first century will be knowledge, and those who are most successful in the marketplace will be those who are able to contribute to the construction of new knowledge. I have great concern that this call for new and more intellectually rigorous standards will only heighten the discrepancies in opportunities to learn between the privileged and the nonprivileged. This concern is heightened by the following observations: (1) the majority of the current teaching force does not know how to teach to these new standards; (2) schools of education, particularly at many of the large public universities where most new teachers receive their preservice education, are not particularly adept at preparing people to teach to these standards; and (3) fewer and fewer African American, Latino, Asian American, and Native American students are choosing to enter the teaching profession. On top of that, neither the veteran teaching force, particularly in large urban and rural districts, nor the schools of education have any real sense of what to make of the cultural backgrounds of students, particularly African American, Latino, Native American, and Asian American students, and especially students among those groups who are poor. Even if we assumed that the propositions put forth in the culturally responsive literature hold true—and for the most part, I think they do—the implications for the incorporation of such orientations into teacher professional development, both preservice and inservice, are enormous. There are policy implications and implications for political action in any attempts to institutionalize an orientation to culture in public schooling. Witness the up-and-down battles in California, as an example. From a research perspective, the challenge is to expand our studies of cultural responsivity to district and multisite levels. The Algebra Project and to some degree the Comer Project are culturally responsive attempts at addressing the question of scale.

The push toward new standards by the professional organizations within academic domains—the National Council of Teachers of English and the National Council of Teachers of Mathematics, for example—and from the massive New Standards Project (1997) calls for

- A focus on complex reasoning
- Application of knowledge in real world settings
- Understanding a few highly generative constructs in a domain
- Learning to reason as experts in a field
- Using technology as a tool through which to construct artifacts as evidence of one's understanding, as a tool through which to explore

complex ideas in a domain in ways that are either impossible, dangerous, or too expensive to carry out in real practice

In subjects like mathematics, these standards call for students to begin to
learn rudimentary concepts in algebra and geometry starting in the primary
grades.

Much of the research focusing on what it means to implement such
standards and to use such technologies has taken place in suburban districts
and in schools serving primarily white, middle-class students. In some instances, when the research moved to schools serving poor and working-class
students of color, the discrepancies in opportunities to learn were not an area
of attention. In many instances, researchers really had little idea how to work
with such schools, because they lacked both a knowledge about teaching and
about schools as organizations and a working knowledge of the dynamics of
culture and how these issues played out in the conduct of instruction. Much
of this research has been carried out in the domains of mathematics and
science. This is, in part, due to the high concentration of federal funding in
these areas in particular.

There is an implicit assumption within the research community and
among educators that mathematics and science are culturally neutral and that
these subjects are about universal facts that are not subject to the whims of
cultural experience. If you look at the New Standards Performance Objectives
(New Standards Project, 1997), at the examples of student work included to
demonstrate what teaching to the standards looks like, or at almost any
state-of-the-art textbooks in mathematics or science, you will see either no
attention to issues of culture or very superficial approaches involving brief
biographies of famous scientists of color or a brief allusion to something like
the Egyptian numbers. Some work by Warren, Rosebery, and Conant (1994)
has looked at Haitian American students' opportunities to learn science, but
this work is largely related to the earlier work on participation structures and
opportunities to participate in instructional conversations. The Algebra Project has the most sustained work in public schools connecting issues of culture
and learning that I know of. In addition, the work of Karen Fuson (1996)
with Latino children in primary mathematics and some work in the QUASAR
Project (Silver, Smith, & Nelson, 1995) from the University of Pittsburgh have
addressed linking culture and mathematics learning in the explicit design of
instruction. Mathematics educators Walter Secada (Secada, Fennema, &
Adajian, 1995) and William Tate (1996) of the University of Wisconsin at
Madison have conducted careful analyses of the need for such an orientation
in mathematics teaching. Mathematicians Marcia Ascher (1991) and Claudia
Zaslavsky (1979) have written useful reference texts on the mathematical
knowledge and practices of many continental African national groups. They
are contributors to an evolving discipline called "ethnomathematics," with a
counterpart in science called "ethnoscience."

The point I am making here is that until we are better able to flesh out how our understandings of culture may productively influence learning in ways that reinforce the intellectual rigor of the new standards now emerging, it is highly unlikely that we will see these cultural connections being made in teaching as a routine practice. This will require, I believe, cross-disciplinary teams of researchers carrying out design experiments and intervention research at multiple school-wide sites across districts as well as at district-wide levels. Such teams need to include (1) researchers in the academic domains—mathematics educators, literacy educators, science educators, and so on; (2) teacher educators; (3) practicing K–12 teachers; (4) researchers who focus on issues of culture and learning; (5) researchers who focus on child, adolescent, and adult development; and (6) policy researchers. Explicit efforts need to be made to include researchers and teachers from diverse ethnic backgrounds within each of these categories, and not just a token black or a token Latina. Such teams need to be made up of people with explicit and long histories of working productively in urban and/or rural schools serving children who are poor. Such research teams need to include political activists and community organizers.

Teaching in ways that are responsive to culture is problematic, in part because we operate out of impoverished views of culture and because policy makers and often teacher educators do not fully understand the complexity of teaching as a practice. Many of our efforts to improve teaching are based on limited behaviorist models (punish the teachers or reward them with money [not a bad idea]). We give teachers a totally prescribed curriculum or set of objectives to follow slavishly. We subject them to professional development where they listen to people tell them what to do, or we assume that a prescribed set of strategies will do the trick. We do this without any real investment in understanding what the trick is that we're trying to perform—is the trick to raise test scores, or to socialize young people into being productive citizens who support the development of the communities from which they come? Such community development may sometimes require that the students learn to resist the politics and policies that currently operate school systems. It may require that we socialize young people into being competent members of their cultural communities.

Toward a Framework for Analyzing Culture to Support Learning and Teaching

Once we have moved beyond the more spurious construct of race to one of ethnicity, we begin to consider the language and routine social practices within a community that are stable across generations. We also consider cultural models (D'Andrade, 1987) or stable beliefs within a community about learning and self-efficacy. For example, Stevenson and Stigler (1992) have argued that in the Japanese national culture, people believe that learning is a result of hard work and effort. By contrast, in what Stevenson and Stigler call U.S. culture (which is sometimes synonymous with middle-class Euro-American culture[1]), people tend to believe that learning is a result of native talent or native intelligence. These cultural models of learning influence the nature of schooling in this country and can work adversely against populations who are presumed to be less "intelligent" (bell curve) (Herrnstein & Murray). Thus, there is substantive research documenting how some teachers have low expectations for students of color and subsequently engage in practices that do not support learning for certain populations (Anyon, 1980; Knapp & Shields, 1990; McDermott, 1987; Oakes, 1990).

I have developed a framework for conceptualizing a productive relationship between learning and culture called "Cultural Modeling" (Lee, 1993, 1995, 1996, 1997). In the Cultural Modeling framework, we focus on learning within specific subject matters. We first conduct a careful analysis of problem solving within the subject matter and then a careful analysis of routine everyday practices within the family and community experiences of a target audience of students. We look for everyday practices in which the students routinely engage in the reasoning processes that are comparable to those expected for problem solving in the subject matter. Our work to date has focused on African American students and literacy, specifically their response to literature. Through careful ethnographic analyses and review of sociolinguistic literature on African American vernacular English (AAVE) (Smitherman, 1977), we concluded that speakers of AAVE routinely interpret figurative language and tropes, including satire, irony, and use of unreliable narrators (Lee, 1997). AAVE speakers across generations participate in the oral genre of signifying (Mitchell-Kernan, 1981). Signifying is a form of talk that often involves ritual insult—although not necessarily—in which participants play with language. Double entendre is a hallmark of signifying. AAVE speakers produce and interpret tropes but are not conscious of the strategies they invoke in such language practices (Lee, 1993, 1995). In a similar vein, young people who are deeply involved in African American youth culture, in particular hip hop, routinely and tacitly interpret all the classic interpretive problems of literature. For example, young people who listen to "The Mask" by the Fugees understand that the mask is symbolic and not literal. They may

---

[1]It is important that we are sensitive to the slippery slope of stereotyping that attention to culture can sometimes invite. While there are clearly differences between national ethnicities from Western Europe, from Eastern Europe, from Southern Europe, the extent to which each cultural tradition is manifested in the everyday practices and language use in the United States depends on immigrant status (first generation, second, etc.), socioeconomic standing, and geographical location. Admitting these differences, there are still macro-level belief systems and social practices that characterize long-term living within the United States. These macro-level commonalities, however, do not eliminate ethnic differences within the United States.

not have the language of literacy to say that the mask is a symbol. They may not on their own articulate the reasoning strategies they use to determine that the mask is symbolic. However, there is no question that they interpret the tropes meaningfully.

Through Cultural Modeling, we design curriculum in which teachers first organize meta-cognitive instructional conversations (Lee, 1998) in which students analyze cultural data sets such as signifying dialogues or the lyrics of "The Mask." The point of such instructional conversations is not merely to engage the students in analyzing the cultural text. More importantly, the point is to help them make public, to themselves and to other students, the reasoning processes they invoke to solve the interpretive problem, as well as to learn the domain-specific language to talk about the nature of the problem (i.e., a problem of symbolism) and the reasoning processes they use. From such experiences, the curriculum progresses to canonical texts that pose the same category of problems the students attacked in the cultural texts. So, for example, students might explore how to attack problems of symbolism by starting with "The Mask" by the Fugees and a series of similar lyrics, videos, and so on and then move to short stories, novels, poems, and/or plays in which symbolism plays a central role. With African American students, for example, we begin with canonical African American literary texts. We work from the assumption that as designers we are streamlining the nature of the problems students will meet as they progress through an apprenticeship in literary reasoning. We choose texts to which students bring significant prior knowledge of the social world, the social codes of the subjunctive world of the fictional text, while they are still novices in attacking the technical problems of, say, symbolism. We later move to texts where the social world of the text is further from the students' experiences, but at a time when they have become more expert at attacking problems, of say, symbolism.

We have a second reason for choosing texts in which the social world of the text is closer to the experiences of the students. A second tenet of culturally responsive pedagogy according to Ladson-Billings is to emphasize the development of cultural competence within the students' home cultures and an explicit attention to sociopolitical issues that focus students beyond their personal advancement as individuals. A preponderance (although certainly not all) of African American literature invites reflection of what it means to be an African American and struggles with some of the major tensions within African American historical and cultural experiences. We believe that by inviting African American students to engage such texts and to empower them with the technical tools (similar to what Delpit [1995] calls the language of power) to attack classic interpretive problems of canonical literature, these students both learn to engage with high academic standards and experience cultural development at the same time.

While our work centers on literacy, a similar approach has been developed by civil rights activist Bob Moses (Moses, Kamii, Swap, & Howard, 1989;

Silva, Moses, Rivers, & Johnson, 1990) in The Algebra Project. Moses determined that a central problem in the transition from arithmetic to algebra was understanding the nature of rational numbers, that is, positive and negative numbers. Algebra, he argued, was a gatekeeper to opportunities to learn advanced mathematics. Inspired by a political commitment to community activism, Moses reasoned that the African American middle-school children who were his original target audience had already developed a mental model of the urban train transit system. This model of the train transit as a system shared sufficient attributes with the target aspect of rationale numbers as to serve as a generative analogy on which a curriculum could be built. Moses also respected the language practices of the target community of students, realizing that as humans we reason in and through language. Thus in the protocols of The Algebra Project, students take a trip on the transit system. They return and construct algebraic problems: You're at point A and wish to go to Point J; how many stations must you traverse and in what direction? Students first construct a graphic representation of the problem, then translate that graphic representation into the home or community language of the student—for example, African American vernacular English, Spanish, or Hmong. Students then translate from their home/community language to a mathematical representation of the problem. The Algebra Project has been very successful in developing a curriculum model that connects culture and learning on a larger scale than almost any other interventions.

I use these two examples to make the case that there are existing examples of research programs that design curricula and learning environments that take into account all three of the tenets of a culturally responsive framework as described by Ladson-Billings. Both Cultural Modeling and The Algebra Project focus on high achievement by addressing rigorous intellectual performance objectives. Each strategically draws on cultural models that students develop from their home and community experiences (related to Moll's conception of cultural funds of knowledge [Moll and Greenberg, 1990]), experiences that in the traditional academy have been viewed more as deficits than assets. In addition, both programs have agendas that focus on empowering communities through education and in apprenticing students to become responsible members who contribute to their communities. These two projects take up the mantle of cultural responsivity from the earlier work on cultural difference (Cazden, John, & Hymes, 1972). These earlier attempts to attend to culture in the design of curricula and learning environments emphasized congruence between classroom and community discourses. It was argued that by minimizing discrepencies in discourse patterns that students from minority language communities would have greater opportunities to productively participate in instructional conversations (Cazden, John, & Hymes, 1975). A series of studies documented both the discrepancies and their consequences for language minority students (Au, 1980; Philips, 1983; Tharp & Gallimore, 1988). The more recent work of projects like the

Cultural Modeling Project and The Algebra Project explore the cognitive consequences of social and linguistic practices of communities that have not been adequately served by public education in this country (see also Ball, 1992; Boykin, 1994; Foster, 1997; Smitherman, 1994).

Deconstructing What We Know—Using the Lens of Culture

The statistics on educational achievement by any measure show two stable trends. "Minority" or students of color have been steadily achieving over the past two decades. At the same time, whether in integrated and more affluent schools, in large urban systems, or in rural systems, these students score substantively below their white counterparts and below those Asian American ethnic groups who have been labeled as "model minorities." Therefore, it is absolutely crucial that we consider what lessons are available to improve educational opportunities for these students. Professor Ladson-Billings and I agree that attention to culture in the design of learning environments offers meaningful contributions to solving this dilemma.

REFERENCES

Anyon, J. (1980). Social class and the hidden curriculum of work. *Journal of Education, 162,* 67–92.

Ascher, M. (1991). *Ethnomathematics: A multicultural view of mathematics ideas.* Pacific Grove, CA: Brooks/Cole Publishing Company.

Au, K. H. (1980). Participation structures in a reading lesson with Hawaiian children: Analysis of a culturally appropriate instructional event. *Anthropology and Education, 11*(2), 91–115.

Ball, A. F. (1992). Cultural preferences and the expository writing of African-American adolescents. *Written Communication, 9*(4), 501–532.

Boykin, A. W. (1994). Harvesting culture and talent: African American children and educational reform. In R. Rossi (Ed.), *Educational reform and at risk students.* New York: Teachers College Press.

Cazden, C., John, V. P., & Hymes, D. (1972). *Functions of language in the classroom.* New York: Teachers College Press.

D'Andrade, R. (1987). A folk model of the mind. In D. Holland & N. Quinn (Eds.), *Cultural models in language and thought* (pp. 112–147). New York: Cambridge University Press.

Delpit, L. (1995). *Other people's children: Cultural conflict in the classroom.* New York: The New Press.

Foster, M. (1997). *Black teachers on teaching.* New York: The New Press.

Fuson, K. C. (1996). Latino children's construction of arithmetic understanding in urban classrooms that support thinking. Paper presented at the Annual Meeting of the American Educational Research Association.

Hernstein, R. J., & Murray, C. (1994). *The bell curve: Intelligence and class structure in American life.* New York: Free Press.

Knapp, M., & Shields, P. (1990). Reconceiving academic instruction for the children of poverty. *Phi Delta Kappan, 71*(10), 752–758.

Ladson-Billings, G. (1994). *The dreamkeepers.* San Francisco: Jossey-Bass.

Lee, C. D. (1993). *Signifying as a scaffold for literary interpretation: The pedagogical implications of an African American discourse genre* (Research Report Series). Urbana, IL: National Council of Teachers of English.

Lee, C. D. (1995). A culturally based cognitive apprenticeship: Teaching African American high school students' skills in literary interpretation. *Reading Research Quarterly, 30*(4), 608–631.

Lee, C. D. (1997). Bridging home and school literacies: A model of culturally responsive teaching. In J. Flood, S. B. Heath, & D. Lapp (Eds.), *A handbook for literacy educators: Research on teaching the communicative and visual arts* (pp. 330–341). New York: Macmillan.

Lee, C. D. (1998). Supporting the development of interpretive communities through metacognitive instructional conversations in culturally diverse classrooms. Paper presented at the Annual Conference of the American Educational Research Association.

Lee, C. D. (unpublished, under review). Cultural modeling in reading comprehension: An analysis of African American students' responses to culturally familiar and culturally less familiar fiction.

McDermott, R. (1987). Achieving school failure: An anthropological approach to illiteracy and social stratification. In G. Spindler (Ed.), *Education and cultural process* (2nd ed.) (pp. 173–209). Prospect Heights, IL: Waveland Press.

Mitchell-Kernan, C. (1981). Signifying, loud-talking and marking. In A. Dundes (Ed.), *Mother wit from the laughing barrel* (pp. 310–328). Englewood Cliffs, NJ: Prentice-Hall.

Moll, L., & Greenberg, J. B. (1990). Creating zones of possibilities: Combining social contexts for instruction. In L. Moll (Ed.), *Vygotsky and education: Instructional implications and applications of sociohistorical psychology* (pp. 319–348). New York: Cambridge University Press.

Moses, R. P., Kamii, M., Swap, S. M., & Howard, J. (1989). The Algebra Project: Organizing in the spirit of Ella. *Harvard Educational Review, 59*(4), 423–443.

New Standards Project. (1997). *Performance standards.* Washington, DC: National Center on Education and the Economy & the University of Pittsburgh.

Oakes, J. (1990). *Multiplying inequalities: The effects of race, social class and teaching.* Santa Monica, CA: Rand.

Phillips, S. U. (1983). *The invisible culture: Communication in classroom and community on the Warm Springs Indian Reservation.* New York: Longman.

Secada, W., Fennema, E., & Adajian, L. B. (1995). *New directions for equity in mathematics education.* New York: Cambridge University Press.

Silva, C. M., Moses, R. P., Rivers, J., & Johnson, P. (1990). The algebra project: Making middle school mathematics count. *Journal of Negro Education, 59*(3), 375–392.

Silver, E., Smith, M. S., & Nelson, B. S. (1995). The QUASAR Project: Equity concerns meet mathematics education reform in the middle school. In W. Secada, E. Fennema, & L. B. Adajian (Eds.), *New directions for equity mathematics education* (pp. 9–56). New York: Cambridge University Press.

Smitherman, G. (1977). *Talkin and testifyin: The language of Black America.* Boston: Houghton Mifflin.

Smitherman, G. (1994). The blacker the berry, the sweeter the juice: African American student writers. In A. Dyson & C. Genishi (Eds.), *The need for story: Cultural diversity in classroom and community* (pp. 80–101). Urbana, IL: National Council of Teachers of English.

Stevenson, H. W., & Stigler, J. W. (1992). *The learning gap: Why our schools are failing and what we can learn from Japanese and Chinese education.* New York: Simon & Schuster.

Tate, W. (1996). Urban schools and mathematical reform: Implementing new standards. *Urban Education, 30*(4).

Tharp, R., & Gallimore, R. (1988). *Rousing minds to life: Teaching, learning, and schooling in social context.* New York: Cambridge University Press.

Warren, B., Rosebery, A., & Conant, F. (1994). Discourse and social practice: Learning science in language minority classrooms. In D. Spencer (Ed.), *Adult biliteracy in the United States* (pp. 191–210). Washington, DC: The Center for Applied Linguistics and Delta Systems Co., Inc. Prepared by the National Clearinghouse on Literacy Education, an adjunct ERIC Clearinghouse.

Zaslavsky, C. (1979). *Africa counts.* New York: Lawrence Hill Books.

7 Identity, Achievement Orientation, and Race

"Lessons Learned" about the Normative Developmental Experiences of African American Males

Margaret Beale Spencer

Significant conceptual, empirical, and methodological "lessons learned" have been achieved during the preceding fifty years about identity processes and correlates of achievement for African American youth. However, a focus on African American male youth from a culturally sensitive and contextual perspective that utilizes a normative *developmental* framework continues to experience significant resistance (Spencer; 1983, 1995; Spencer & Dornbusch, 1990; Spencer & Markstrom-Adams, 1990; Swanson, Spencer, & Petersen, 1998; Dupree, Spencer & Bell, 1997; Cunningham, 1994; Cunningham & Spencer, 1996, in-press). The preferred perspective continues to be the relegation of minority male experiences to the pathology and deviancy literatures in psychiatry, sociology, and criminal justice (specifically for the latter), rather than the traditional developmental literature that continues to document the experiences of whites, middle-income people, and, too frequently, male participants. In his psychological review of the field, Gutherie (1976) laments the narrowly focused literature by observing that "even the rat was white (and male!)."

In fact, developmental theory more generally depended on sampling and assumptions concerning this "narrow band of the human experience." A litany of developmental reviews generally do not mention (i.e., as an index item) the experiences and unique developmental challenges of identifiable minorities; most must certainly overlook the specific experiences of African American males, *except* when noting studies of problem behaviors and deviance in the text itself. However, textbooks published in the 1990s, for example, *Children, Adolescent Development* and *Life-span Development* by John Santrock, represent evident strides in correcting the significant omission in the textbook trade.

In general, a significant contribution to this "developmental oversight" has been a failure or reluctance to understand, integrate, and *critique* the myriad contributions from *normative* developmental psychology theorizing, cultural psychology insights, context and relational themes from sociology, and persistent *a priori* psychopathology assumptions from the counseling, clinical, and psychiatric literatures. The shortsightedness continues to limit our understanding of the special context-linked experiences of black boys and, more generally, the necessary supports required for maximizing the life course development of African American males. The current volume presents an important opportunity to explore assumptions and interpretations about identity, achievement patterns, and outcomes of a particularly vulnerable group in twenty-first-century America: African American adolescent males.

The programmatic research findings and current theorizing have been organized as a chapter with specific goals in mind. *First,* as an introduction, the introductory section describes several overall issues and concerns. The importance of emphasizing and integrating the meaning and experience of culture is highlighted as a core and context-linked view of human development. Thus, the first section examines the exacerbating influence of urban character on contemporary and historical thinking about culture; highlights the more general conduct of psychological science, particularly in the case of twentieth-century American minorities; and notes the more general educational praxis and life course human development experiences had by diverse American minorities.

In response to some of the dilemmas examined in the introduction, the *second* section of this chapter introduces a theoretical framework (Phenomenological Variant of Ecological Systems Theory [PVEST]) (Spencer, 1995, 1999). The theory's undergirding and dynamic identity-focused cultural ecological (ICE) perspective evolves from fifteen years of resiliency-focused programmatic research and drives our recent (i.e., PAC [Promotion of Academic Competence] Project), current (ALPHA [Achievement Linked Programming and Health Advocacy] Initiative), and longitudinal research efforts. *Third,* a synthesis of longitudinal patterns of male adolescents' hypermasculinity is also presented. Exacerbating school and neighborhood high-risk experiences are integrated as part of a gender-intensification analysis of African American males' special adolescent experiences. *Fourth,* in concluding the chapter, several poignant issues are described that still require serious and programmatic study. In addition, policy and program recommendations are described that should encourage better societal-level practices and ultimately significantly improve life-course outcomes, particularly for African American male adolescents.

Introduction

As a place to start an introductory analysis of the contribution of social science assumptions to the literature, it is important to trace the history of psychological science and the alternative advent of cultural-historical-psychology. Also salient is the highlighting and integrating of the actual meaning and experience of culture in the consideration of human development. It is commonly agreed on that identity development during adolescence involves coming to understand one's self as a member of a society within a particular ethnic, cultural, religious, or political tradition. In addition, we agree that an orientation to *habitual right action* (i.e., whether or not we're referring to neighborhood experiences with peers or achievement-oriented behavior in school) is fundamental to identity processes insofar as *defining oneself* entails becoming part of a *normative cultural tradition* (see Steinberg, 1999). Members of devalued and unique culturally defined groups may have very different experiences from those considered more "mainstream." Such groups are usually socially constructed and their societal position based on assumptions of inferior versus superior social status.

In fact, from a normal human development perspective that includes assumptions about stage-linked cognitive maturation, society's youth engage in unavoidable shifts in "meaning making processes" and, thus, respond to such social constructions in particular ways. Youths from devalued groups may infer the need *to react against broader societal traditions,* such as the construction of social roles based, for example, on ethnicity, race, or gender. Importantly, although knowing that one lacks an equitable access formally provided "first-class" citizens, a response may represent an unconscious consideration of societal expectations for appropriate behaviors. Referred to as "oppositional" by Ogbu (1985), the response style may be most probable for young people who generally remain outside the mainstream of American life. Accordingly, one's "orientation to habitual right action" may represent somewhat of a conundrum of competing allegiance to dual contexts of socialization. One set of expectations is uniquely cultural and evolves from within the socially defined cultural niche. The attendant set of responsive values frequently provides an integrated or "reference group self" that affords its members mental health and a sense of "we-ness" or "collective identity." On the other hand, the set of broadly held values and expectations for all societal members, independent of resources provided, are not only constructed and imposed from without, but require the use of a double consciousness for survival (DuBois, 1903). In fact, Boykin (1985) suggests the competing sets of values and expectations leave African American youth with a "triple quandary"—a sense of self and values representing dominant norms, cultural norms and values, and those values that are unique to the individual.

African American Male Adolescents

In the particular case of African American boys who are generally viewed with some degree of dissonance and trepidation by the larger society (see Cunningham, 1994; Spencer & Cunningham, in press), the task of managing an ego-supporting identity while coping with generalized negative imagery is, at best, daunting. In some respects, the dilemma may be parallel to the situation of male adolescents more generally. However, African American males specifically are expected to shoulder the traditional negative stereotypes associated with male adolescence in general, along with the *added burden* of enhanced and often unacknowledged negative imagery linked with minority status. Although often formally unacknowledged, negative stereotypes frequently influence character and reactions to socialization efforts, such as those extended both in and out of school. The fact that these conditions and experiences are not formally *recognized* (although part of the youths' daily experiences) makes the individual's management of normative developmental tasks more challenging at best. Specifically, those tasks associated with establishing a *moral identity or academic (achievement-linked) identity* are particularly salient with attendant outcomes potentially more diverse and open to misinterpretation. Accordingly, African American male adolescents, in their efforts to cope with normative developmental tasks with few resources and supports, may deploy coping methods that prove to be less than constructive. The responsive methods deployed (i.e., what we generally term as "coping methods") may be experienced as emotionally comfortable "in the short run." Too frequently, however, they further exacerbate an already challenging situation in the "long run." For males the reactive responses or unconstructive coping methods are often linked to risky behavior gender-identity themes.

Gender-Intensification Assumptions: Autonomy Needs

The linking of expected developmental and socialization tasks to gender themes is not novel. As noted in Steinberg's (1985) review, Hill and Lynch (1983) have speculated about a *gender-intensification hypothesis.* They suggest that many of the sex differences observed between adolescent males and females are due not to biological differences, but to an acceleration in the degree to which youngsters are socialized to act in stereotypically masculine and feminine ways (Steinberg, 1985, p. 267). They suggest that with adolescence "girls become more self-conscious and experience more disruption in the self-image than boys." Of course, they do not rule out contributions of biology but indicate that "some areas of sex role socialization show *intensification*. For example, it may be more important to act in ways that are consistent with sex-role expectations and that meet with approval in *the peer group*" (p. 267). We suggest that in the case of members of devalued minority groups, particularly its youth, individual adolescents of specific subgroups (e.g., African American males) similarly experience heightened self-consciousness and demonstrate *potential* for more disrupted self-images than nonminority youth. Specifically, more often than not, youths infer a lack of *respect* often accorded others as they pursue an orientation of *"habitual right action."* As noted, these efforts frequently occur in hostile environments or minimally supportive environments. Unfortunately, American schools *"fill the bill"* in both cases when it comes to African American youth (see Spencer, 1999).

Importantly, in the quest for more general identity-formation pursuits and those specifically linked to achievement and gender-linked social expectations, such as instrumentality for males, the development of *autonomy* becomes a particularly critical issue. It is at adolescence that youths find themselves moving into positions that demand *responsible* and *independent behavior.* One aspect of independence suggests *value autonomy.* As described by Steinberg (1985, p. 277), value autonomy refers to "more than simply being able to resist pressures to go along with the demands of others; it means having a self of principles about what is right and what is wrong, about what is important and what is not." Although Steinberg generally ignores non-mainstream youth, the ideas are salient and poignant when considered for African American males in that they involve changes in youths' views about moral, political, ideological, and religious (spirituality) issues. Specifically, in the case of African American male adolescents, we suggest that the three aspects of autonomy, as described by Steinberg, are particularly salient.

First, independent of how youth are "objectively performing in school," adolescents become increasingly abstract in their thinking. Accordingly, youths may decide that they are *not* interested in adhering to dress codes, achievement expectations, and aspirations for success and music preferences or language styles promulgated by society. Instead, young people generally show resistance to imitate values modeled by a society that treats their *referent identity group* unfairly. *Second,* their beliefs are increasingly connected to general principles that represent ideological positions; thus, when the behavior of youths' own referent group for racial group identification is not ordinarily accorded (and assumed *earned*) respect, a *reactive coping response* may be the taking on of an interpersonal style or (non)achievement orientation that "demands" respect, such as a hypermasculinity persona or bravado orientation. Thus, male youths' exaggerated sex-role orientation is assumed to be "okay" and, in fact, *principled behavior* if youths infer that the response style is the only method for obtaining *"earned"* or *"owed"* respect. Finally, the *third* aspect of autonomy suggests that beliefs become nested in youths' own values as opposed to becoming a system of values passively handed from parents, teachers, administrators, and other socializing adults. Unavoidable cognitive maturation, particularly during adolescence, makes the adoption of such a simplistic and passive system less than probable.

Theorists suggest that growth in value autonomy is linked to expected cognitive changes (Steinberg, 1985, pp. 297–298). We suggest that these changes, although infrequently considered for African American youths, particularly males, in fact require a sensitive synthesis of context character. Necessary for consideration in this synthesis are the process and product of individuals' evolving understanding of the world as they struggle with inequitable conditions, normative stage-specific processes, growth in value autonomy, and expected positive outcomes in response to normative developmental tasks. Irrespective of societal status, expectations are generic, and an equivalent level of competence and resiliency is expected for all, independent of degree of special challenges experienced by specific groups. That is, both entitlements and extra challenges are ignored, although similar outcomes of competence, health, and achievement are expected for all. Generally lacking in our thinking, as we consider achievement-linked outcomes like the achievement gap between black and white academic performance, is an appreciation of youths' interpretive framework and perceptions concerning *context risk, attendant stress and accessible supports, available coping methods* for reactive deployment (used for guaranteeing psychological health and physical survival), and a variety of *stable coping processes (identities)* and *patterned coping outcomes* (e.g., including both achievement-linked and *moral identity-linked*.)

This dilemma of competing allegiances or "triple quandary" (see Boykin, 1986) and competing socialization contexts (see Allen, 1985; Boykin & Toms, 1985; Boykin & Ellison, 1995; Brookins, 1988; Hare & Castenell, 1985) is infrequently more poignant than in the consideration of African American males. For such youth, the growth of value autonomy may be represented by urban youths' pursuit and acquisition of *"respect."* For many boys growing up in low-resource communities, the demand and demonstration of independence and responsibility occur early (see Holliday, 1985). The value and recognition of both of these character qualities are evident in particular microsystems such as family, community, and church. In fact, it is not only the recognition, but also the quite early characterization of African American boys that is interesting. Although generally reported anecdotally, there is a penchant to refer to a male baby or toddler as "little man." Of course, the motivation for the term's frequent usage is linked to an expressed and global valuing of "maleness" and does not represent a conscious effort "to adultify children." Instead, the evident widespread use of the term, particularly by African American men, suggests an effort "to short-circuit" the use of the slavery-associated penchant of white Americans to *refuse adulthood status to black men by referring to them as boys.* Thus, from an African American adult male's perspective regarding the use of "little man language for his son," his motivation may be solely one of endearment. The particular language used connotes *pride in his son and expectations for future role performance.* However, young children are developmentally egocentric (i.e., appropriately self-centered in regard to perception) and remain so until about 6 or 7 years of age (see Spencer, 1976, 1982). Being able to take the perspective of another is dependent on evolving cognitive maturation coupled with social experience. As a consequence, children hear, use, and understand language and interpret its content from their own (appropriately) limited cognitive perspective. Accordingly, in the case of African American men and boys, use of "little man language" may unavoidably result in children's inferring a set of expectations to behave and take on the responsibilities of manhood while still a youngster and, clearly, unprepared for such burdens. Again, specific socialization tasks by parents serve to "short circuit" the misinterpretation. Of course, this "added task" is in addition to the other traditional socialization tasks for which *all parents* are responsible. Thus, adult males' responsive coping to a historical fact (i.e., under slavery the attempt to render adult African American men to child status) ultimately makes child-rearing responsibilities particularly challenging for African American parents (see Spencer 1983, 1990).

African American male adolescents' pursuit of respect from others (e.g., teachers, police officers) can be problematic at best. Teachers uniformly expect "student-like" behavior from children irrespective of the problematic affective school climate experienced by many African American children and the group's unique historical conditions in America. Gender would appear to be an exacerbating factor for African American students. It results in a heightened salience of respect as a pursuit and often takes on more importance than the highly shared and valued *acquisition of academic achievement* (Spencer, 1999). As suggested, if generalized respect from the broader society and *the school* are not forthcoming, adolescent males' "reactive or less constructive" coping response may be the taking on of "habitual right actions," which are polar opposite to those generally valued by society and anticipated by schools.

Specifically, gender-intensified behavior, such as *hypermasculinity,* may be seen by youth as potentially more effective in generating "respect" than the instrumentality- and future-linked outcomes associated with academic achievement. Of course, given that, the relatively late acquisition of a "time-perspective" or a true sense of the future, as linked to the present and past as a cognitive construction and acquisition, is usually reserved until mid or late adolescence. Before then, young people require *significant aid* in understanding and implementing the links between current behavioral investments (e.g., studying and school engagement) and long-term valued outcomes (e.g., secondary school graduation and successful career preparation). It is *not surprising* that many young men do not understand that the 12 years of primary and secondary school preparation and academic engagement provide an important opportunity. It increases (not guarantees) the probability of acquiring the *very long-term respect* that hypermasculine behavior connotes and that black boys and adolescents desperately seek and need.

In sum, given the growth in autonomy and the unavoidable cognition-dependent changes in youths' understanding of moral, political, and ideological issues, our programmatic research efforts and theoretical synthesis suggest a particular perspective. The theoretical approach represents a view that acknowledges the importance of the individual's own *perceptions and experience,* which together represent the hallmark and implicit assumption of phenomenology (Rogers, 1961, 1963). As suggested by Figure 7.1, the synthesis perspective represents multiple theories and models. Figure 7.2 depicts the five-component processes of PVEST and indicates that the theory's five bidirectional components together suggest a dynamic set of processes. The hypothesized dynamic character of the framework is depicted in Figure 7.3

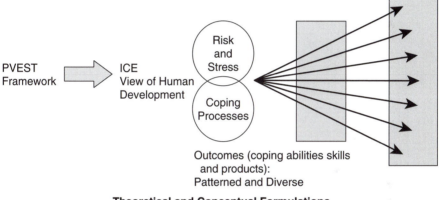

PVEST Framework → ICE View of Human Development

Risk and Stress

Coping Processes

Outcomes (coping abilities skills and products): Patterned and Diverse

Theoretical and Conceptual Formulations

- Obgu's notions concerning minority status
- Eriksonian theorizing about ego identity processes
- Du Bois's notion of double consciousness
- Symbolic interactionists theorizing about phenomenological processes, (e.g., Sullivan and Mead)
- Competence and socialization perspectives (e.g., Robert White and Brewster Smith)
- Resiliency and vulnerability (e.g., J. Anthony)

- Chestang's views of character formation
- Spencer's notions about the social cognition/culture cognition interface
- Ecological psychology and Bronfenbrenner's views about context
- Boykins's notions cornering the "triple quandary"
- Normal human development life-course theorizing (e.g., Brim's notions about continuity *and* change)
- Historical perspectives (e.g., V. P. Franklin, John Hope Franklin, and Glen Elder)

FIGURE 7.1 Significant contributors to a Phenomenological Variant of Ecological Systems Theory (PVEST)

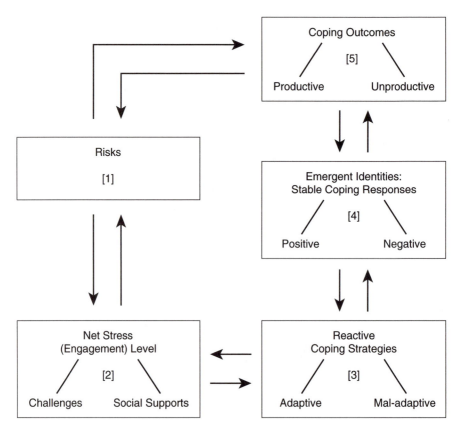

FIGURE 7.2 Phenomenological Variant of Ecological Systems Theory (PVEST)

as a "life course spiral." It is hypothesized to represent the system's dynamism and the linked nature of the theory's five-component structure and its recursive and evolving nature as lives unfold across the life course. Depicted is that particular outcomes at one stage serve as a major contributor to the character and quality of risk experienced by the individual at the subsequent stage of life. Specifically, the model links the relationship between *risks* with associated *stress engagement* (i.e., net effect between challenges experienced and support afforded) literally from "the cradle" (i.e., beginning at conception) "to the coffin" or to the end of the life course (i.e., death) (refer to Figure 7.2). Specifically, the net level of stress requires *reactive coping* that may be adaptive or maladaptive. When deployed consistently, the reactive coping becomes firmly internalized with stability across context as *emergent identities*. It is the stability of the identities (e.g., as a learner, parent, worker, or member of a particular racial group or religious institution) across settings that contributes to the salience of *coping outcomes*. As a life-course model of human development, the outcomes at one stage have bidirectional significance and

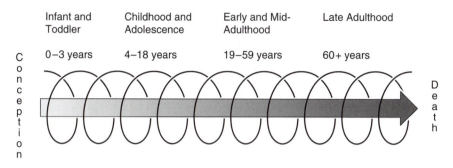

FIGURE 7.3   Spiraling, recursive, bidirectional, and interactive PVEST typology across the life course

implications for the next. We call the framework a *Phenomenological Variant of Ecological Systems Theory* (*PVEST*) (Spencer, 1995, 1999; Spencer, DuPree, & Hartman, 1997; Swanson, Spencer, & Petersen, 1998). Additionally, as indicated by Figure 7.4, patterned outcomes through the nature of contextual experiences have subsequent implications for subsequent risks and stress to be coped with. Said another way, the context also includes individuals who are recipients *and* providers of feedback. Thus, Figure 7.5 presents an interactional rendering of the individual bidirectionally influenced and influencing others in cultural and embedded ecologies.

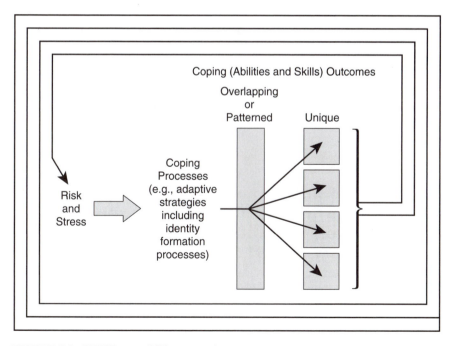

FIGURE 7.4   PVEST as an ICE perspective

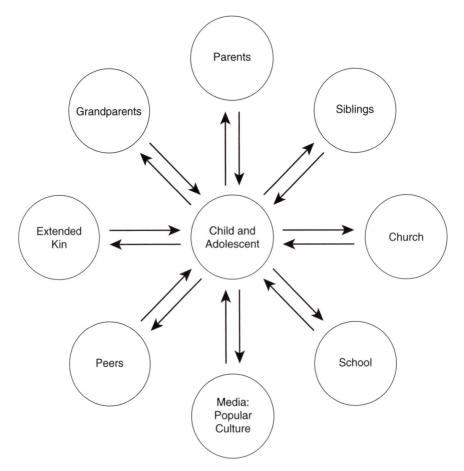

FIGURE 7.5 An interactional perspective of the individual bidirectionally influenced and influencing others in cultural and embedded ecologies

A Culturally Sensitive and Context-Integrated Theory of Life Course Human Development: A Phenomenological Variant of Ecological Systems Theory (PVEST)

As listed in Figure 7.1 and suggested by Figures 7.2 to 7.5, the Phenomenological Variant of Ecological Systems Theory (PVEST) borrows and integrates context issues, as described by Bronfenbrenner (1989) and the ecological psychologists, while also emphasizing the life-course salience of identity processes. Accordingly, PVEST affords an identity-focused cultural ecological (ICE) perspective of human development. Critical to the perspective is an acknowledgment of the person's lived experience considered in cultural context. As noted and illustrated in Figure 7.2, the perspective links the experience of risks (e.g., chronic poverty, race, ethnicity), stress engagement (e.g., available supports or threats, such as unpopularity with peers, inferred negative teacher perceptions), coping methods (i.e., both adaptive and maladaptive [e.g., aggressive attitudes]), patterned identity processes (e.g., hypermasculinity or sense of efficacy), and coping outcomes (e.g., school success, health, resiliency, steady employment, incarceration). Demonstrations of resiliency—success and competence displayed by youth in spite of adverse living conditions—often go unrecognized, thus denying individuals a sense of efficacy, success, and accomplishment. A lack of understanding of normative developmental processes and the character and impact of diverse cultural contexts leads to a misinterpretation of urban youths' behavior and development. When successes are acknowledged, the factors that lead to subsequent resilience in high-risk settings are often neither identified nor considered. A conceptual framework that assists in the unpacking and identifying of these factors, along with their implementation within intervention and prevention programming efforts, is crucial to promoting instrumentality and life-course competence of youth in high-risk settings. PVEST considers and supports an analysis of how individuals traverse multiple and sequentially experienced contexts in light of their diverse levels of unique risks, stresses, and coping requirements. It is a contextual, process-oriented approach that considers not only structural obstacles to healthy coping and community integrity, but also *individual differences* in the perception of those obstacles and the resultant effects on responsive coping styles and identity processes. Particularly when applied to the community level, PVEST provides an option as a *theory of change* (Weiss, 1995) in that it can be used in the design, implementation, and evaluation of intervention programs for all youth and families, including *comprehensive community initiatives* (Kubish, Weiss, Schorr, & Connell, 1995). PVEST also provides a basis for examining interactions between various contexts, including families, schools, and neighborhoods; in relation to this, the theory demonstrates utility in its ability to analyze the relationship between these interactions and individual outcomes, with coping and identity processes mediating the relationship between contextual factors and outcomes.

From the perspective of developmental psychology, PVEST is an ideal framework for *theory-based evaluation* (Weiss, 1995)—it can be used to test the effects of identity processes on outcomes and yield suggestions for promoting positive, resilient identities, irrespective of ethnicity, race, developmental status, or social class. Therefore, this framework is especially helpful for interpreting the experiences and identity-based outcomes of those living under specific conditions of risk.

An Overview of the PVEST Framework

How individuals and groups make meaning of family, peer, and societal expectations and their prospects for competence and success is central to understanding resiliency and for devising interventions that promote and revitalize communities. Given this complex reality, PVEST consists of five components linked by bidirectional processes (refer to Figure 7.2). It is a cyclic, recursive model that describes identity development as a core aspect of coping processes across the life course (refer to Figure 7.3). Thus, when considered at the community level as a context for adolescent development, the framework identifies processes for all members of communities from the community's inception to its demise.

As indicated by Figure 7.2, the first component, *risk contributors*, consists of factors that may predispose individuals to experience adverse outcomes. For urban youth, these outcomes include socioeconomic conditions, such as poverty; sociocultural expectations, such as race and gender stereotypes; biological predispositions, such as temperament and cardiovascular reactivity; and sociohistorical processes, including immigration status, group subordination, and discrimination. For many white middle-class youths, risk may also include the loss of secure jobs (which is often expected within this population) as linked with the redistribution of wealth in the United States (see Darity & Myers, 1998; Wilson, 1987). Indeed, any unacknowledged shift of resources has exacerbating implications for working and low-economic status individuals, regardless of ethnicity and race. Furthermore, perceptions, diverse experiences, and self-appraisal are key factors in how individuals view themselves, including their inferred expectations and related cognitive and affective processes.

Stress engagement represents the net outcomes of perceived challenges versus available supports. It refers to the actual (perceived) experience of situations that challenge one's psychosocial identity and sense of well-being given available support. For urban youth, violence, negative stereotyping, and a lack of resources may be examples of challenges confronting certain adolescents. On the other hand, available programming supports and individual assistance may offset the negative impact of systemic challenges. For example, buffering supports, such as parental monitoring and cultural socialization efforts, aid in diminishing the experience of stress (e.g., see Spencer, 1990; Spencer & Markstrom-Adams, 1990). Stress engagement, then, may be viewed as the "net effect" of stress experienced according to inferred individual differences, manifested supports available, and the significance of challenges confronted. In response to the net effect of stress, *reactive coping methods* are deployed. Figure 7.2 indicates that reactive coping methods represent two coping processes: specific *coping strategies* and *coping responses* (i.e., stable identity processes).

Reactive coping methods are employed to resolve dissonance-producing situations and the net level of stress experienced. These include the mobilization of specific coping strategies to solve problems that may be either adaptive (e.g., heightened school engagement) or maladaptive (e.g., hypermasculinity by males in particularly dangerous settings), and both can have long-term implications. In addition, a solution may be adaptive in one context, such as hypermasculinity in a dangerous neighborhood, and maladaptive in another, such as in school settings. In fact, in the latter case, the response of context may be to further stereotype and neglect the individual's actual needs, thereby further exacerbating the situation. For example, a youth's response to inferred disrespect from teachers may be to invoke a negative learning attitude. As coping strategies are employed, self-appraisal processes continue, and those strategies yielding desirable results for the ego may be preserved and become stable coping responses. When such coping strategies and self-appraisal processes are coupled repetitively over time, they often yield stable *emergent identities.*

Such emergent identities define how individuals view themselves within and between their various contextual experiences. That is, these thematic responsive patterns frequently show stability across settings, and not just within families and neighborhoods. Individuals' sense of identity then lays the foundation for future perceptions and behavior, yielding adverse or productive *life-stage outcomes* manifested across settings for particular developmental periods. Productive outcomes include good health, positive and supportive relationships with neighbors and friends, school completion, academic achievement, and effective motivation. Importantly, the quality of the current life-stage outcomes (i.e., either productive or adverse) serves to reinforce the degree of risk to which that one is vulnerable during subsequent life-stage transitions as individuals cycle across the life course and as suggested by Figures 7.3 and 7.4. Without an understanding of these linked components and processes, it becomes easy to label a person as a victim and subsequently blame that person for the problematic character of an unfolding life course. On the other hand, without the recursive and sociocultural contextual analysis that PVEST provides, it may be just as tempting to conclude that persons who enjoy significant privileges may solely credit their own efforts in experiencing cumulative life-course successes.

As illustrated in Figures 7.3 and 7.4, the PVEST framework recycles as one transitions across the life course (i.e., across multiple settings, including community and school). Individuals encounter new risks and stressors, try different coping strategies, and redefine how they (and others) perceive themselves. Particularly for more visibly identifiable groups, such as minorities and low-status individuals, the presence of certain structural conditions poses severe and chronic risk conditions for the learning of adaptive coping strategies and positive outcomes, such as competence and instrumentality.

Our program of research implemented over several decades specifically explores the prediction of resilient outcomes in the case of urban youth and families. Males link perceptions of dangers and physical aggression to their sex role and efficacy assumptions, and these remain important challenges that are responded to differentially—particularly by adolescents and also more generally.

For youth who live in high-risk environments, the PVEST framework affords an opportunity for understanding value autonomy as a process that *identifies and intensifies* the character of competing coping methods and attendant moral identities that may represent the same set of shared values and beliefs (e.g., school achievement and completion) but are coupled with behaviors that suggest a need for respect as a consequence of early demonstrated independence and responsibility. Such behaviors are often neither understood (regarding etiology and ego functioning) nor easily tolerated in a system where the socializing agents themselves (i.e., teachers, staff, and administrators) frequently lack an understanding of the actual American cultural environment as it is experienced by identifiable minorities and represents the socialization context of many urban children; this includes the necessary and unique "double consciousness" experiences of African American males.

Accordingly, in addition to gender themes, when issues of racial identity formation are also factored in and considered, the identity processes that occur in multiple contexts, most significantly in the school, are unavoidably complex and linked to achievement outcomes, particularly when considered for African American males.

As noted by the 1964 UNESCO proposal and signed by leading scientists throughout the world: "All humans living today belong to a single species, *Homo sapiens,* and are derived from a common stock" (Nanda, 1980, p. 12). The remaining scientific questions have to do with how and when different groups diverged from this common stock. However, this common understanding does not aid or correct the effects of an extreme sense of ethnocentrism, which continues to plague American life and the conduct of behavioral science and its interpretation. Anthropological reports have made it quite evident that ethnocentrism, the tendency to view the world through the narrow lens of one's own culture or social position, is universal. People tend to see things from their own culturally patterned point of view, to value what they have been *taught to value,* to see the meaning of life in their own culturally defined purposes. To illustrate, the American tourist who, when presented with a handful of Italian *lira,* asks, "How much is this in *real money?*" is ethnocentric. On the other hand, members of the Diribi society in New Guinea may have great difficulty understanding what kind of "work" a visiting anthropologist is doing since the writing down of "stories" about other peoples' lives appears quite foreign to their notion of "work" (Nanda, 1980, p. 12–13).

Of course, the critical point here is that ethnocentrism is much more than just the biases of perception and knowledge (i.e., racial and ethnic attitudes and stereotypes). It is also the practice of judging other cultures by the standards of one's own (Nanda, 1980, p. 11). Although all peoples are ethnocentric, the ethnocentricity of Western societies has had significantly greater consequences than that of smaller, less technologically advanced, and geographically isolated peoples. The historical circumstances that led to the spread of Western civilization have given us a very strong belief in its rightness and superiority (Nanda, 1980, p. 11). It has been possible to impose strong Western beliefs on others given the various Western technological advancements and abundance of consumer goods that others have quickly learned to desire. Importantly, others' acceptance of our vast products have led Americans to believe that, in fact, our values and other social institutions are also superior.

However, since America is quite diverse, the nation's race and color-based biases hold sway both "at home" and abroad, strongly influencing intergroup relations. The critical paradox associated with ethnocentrism illustrates the issue's complexity. That is, "although ethnocentrism gets in the way of understanding, some ethnocentrism seems necessary as a kind of glue to hold a society together. When a people's culture loses value for them, they may experience great emotional stress and even lose interest in living. To the extent that ethnocentrism *prevents building bridges* between cultures, in fact, it becomes maladaptive. Where one culture is motivated by ethnocentrism to trespass on another, the harm done can be enormous. Of importance to our discussion is the fact that this kind of ethnocentrism to *racism transition* is but a short step that has been made in both popular and scientific thought in the West" (Nanda, 1980, p. 12). It is important to understand how young children and youth are effected by and inadvertently participate in this transition, specifically, from healthy ethnocentrism to racism. It is also very important to note the role of social and political institutions in process. In fact, W. E. B. DuBois (1903), the first African American Harvard-graduated social scientist, at the start of the twentieth century, pronounced that the heavy burden of that century for America would be the issue of the color line. The UNESCO's 1964 pronouncement concerning humankind's shared *racial history* continues "to enjoy" minimal impact on both the quality of life for this country's minority members and the quality of intergroup relationships between members of diverse groups. Along these same lines, although retired from the federal bench, A. Leon Higginbotham, Jr., in a recent interview suggested critical and parallel societal tasks that parallel the challenge identified 100 years ago by W. E. B. DuBois. Higginbotham noted, ". . . the problem with the twenty-first century is *not recognizing* the consequences of racism. The real test of the twenty-first century is our being able to move from equality in the abstract to equality in significant results." Higginbotham's pronouncement (Odom, 1998, E-1) is important since it forces us to consider the complexity of racial issues. His perspective foreshadows the continuing and difficult period ahead and emphasizes the need to approach extreme ethnocentrism and its expression and consequence to racial attitudes, bias, symbolic racism (Bobo, 1983), and racial identity, from a coordinated multidisciplinary perspective. A critical part of the process, from an interventionist and programming perspective, is to understand *its developmental character* from "the cradle to the coffin." The direction set by DuBois and added to by Higginbotham is instructive and affords a more enlightened analysis of the exacerbating impact of race on developmental tasks and normative processes for youth of color, particularly for males given their added (gender stereotype–linked) vulnerability. The gender fragility of males has been suggested by several theorists, although most analyses have been nondevelopmental. Accordingly, the treatment of gender by reviewers has been nondevelopmental and decontextual in character, and thus appears similar—as a perspective—to the views concerning race and attendant identity processes.

Gender Themes and Perspectives on Hypermasculinity: An Overview

Regardless of exacerbating influences of ethnicity and race, it is well established that the traditional ideals of masculinity encourage the devaluation and rejection of typically feminine characteristics, such as empathy and domestic responsibility.

Deficit Perspectives and Limited Views of Context and Culture

It is generally agreed on that traditional ideals of masculinity involve issues of dominance, expressed in acts of aggression or violence. In discussing hysterical personality disorders as a natural manifestation from the culturally bolstered feminine ideal, Chodoff (1982) ends his discussion by proposing a corresponding model of perverted masculinity, wherein qualities of bravery, coolness, risk-taking, assertiveness, and logicality are escalated into brashness, haughtiness, overcompetitiveness, belligerence, and vengefulness. His term for this distortion is the "macho personality." The personification of these exaggerated ideals is commonly referred to as hypermasculinity. Males striving toward this inflated form of male gender definition invite great stress and, ultimately, damage to intrapsychic and interpersonal development. Adler's idea of the "masculine protest" describes this behavior as a result of male overcompensation for feelings of inferiority (Hall & Lindzey, 1978). Various forms of compensatory masculine behavior may originate from feelings of failure in males to accomplish the socially sculpted criteria of the masculine role. Thus their behavior becomes an attempt to validate or prove their masculinity. Without attention to the underlying developmental themes and actual character of impact, theorists generally suggest the applicability of their perspectives to the African American male adolescent experience.

African American Male Assumptions

Staples (1986) maintains that manhood is very closely tied to power and the control of others and that black male youth learn rather early that power over and control of others are direct functions of economic resources. His perspective suggests that for many urban black male youths the acquisition of these resources is most accessible through illegal means. This only serves to foster the risk-taking and dominant posturing promoted in hypermasculine, or hard, behavior, further endangering the well-being of these youths and enhancing their level of social dysfunction.

As suggested, race and racism continue to represent a major focal point in the identification of African American male youth. African Americans are burdened with chronic aspects of social dislocations, such as poverty, inadequate educational opportunities, and racism among others, that frequently translate within the individual as social deficit and dysfunction (Wilson, 1987; Gibbs, 1988). These factors, including more general societal changes, have implications for the stability of marital relationships. The situation is worsened for some chronically stressed family systems that have consequently contributed to the growing number of single-parent household structures. The situation has important implications for the character of socializing environments in that it leaves fewer men prepared and available to contribute to child-rearing.

Reports show that "the share of Black children living with two parents declined from 58 percent in 1970 to 38 percent in 1990" (O'Hare, Pollard, Mann, & Kent, 1991). The Population Bureau reported in 1990 that 55 percent of all African American youth lived in single-parent households and 51 percent were living with single mothers. Of course, in these same reports, the experiences of the 45 percent living in dual-parenting households are infrequently described. It is the design of these "resiliency-oriented" studies, which should aid in better understanding of the independent factors, that contribute to the macho personality style described by Chodoff (1982) and the unique contributions to neighborhood character from other factors independent of father-presence or socioeconomic status.

Adler's model of masculine protest has its origin in an infantile weakness and fear of women that develops into neurotic fantasizing. It is to these fantasies that the protest is activated to respond. In Glass's (1984) discussion of hypermasculinity, he describes its manifestation in two distinct types, which he terms the "Man's Man" and the "Lady's Man." He found that the Man's Man typically experiences a compelling and powerful mother figure coupled with a weak or absent father figure. The Lady's Man, on the other hand, usually experiences a young, attractive mother subject to repeated seductions and a father whose behavior ranges from "ethical slipperiness to outright criminality." The Man's Man usually creates a he-man ideal to emulate as a substitute for the absent father or acts in rivalry with the weak example provided, in spite of the dominant mother (Ross, 1977, 1979, 1982). Like other perspectives, these views assume a passive individual and uniformly experienced familial and social context. The very deficit-oriented and psychodynamically passive perspectives are very similar to the 1940s' and 1950s' "culture of poverty" and "deficit-oriented" perspectives that were current during the first seventy to eighty years of the twentieth century in regard to the effects of race and racism.

Implicit and Negative Assumptions about Women and Their Social Status

Brown (1940, p. 319) suggested that attachment to the phallic mother would constitute an intensely conflicted passivity that is subsequently "resented and rebelled against" by total masculinity. Fenichel (1945) also found ties between male passivity to the feminine and overcompensations of active and masculine behaviors in males. Horney (quoted in Ross, 1975, p. 792) cited misogyny as an ominous reversal of a wish to be a woman. Freud (1937) also suggested that male passivity in response to the mother could manifest neurotic overcompensations. Kleeman (1976) reassessed Freud's findings and supported his conclusion that family psychodynamics are of greater importance than biology in these regards. Freud's model (1925) describes a boy with a strong mother reacting in one of two ways once he "rediscovers" the differentiation of their sexes: (1) he reacts with horror at the mutilated creature and is compelled to disassociate from it; or (2) he reacts with triumphant contempt and views her as inferior. The boy, regardless of which response he adopts, turns against all that he perceives to be expressions of the feminine within himself. He sees the female as vulnerable and riddled with bloody holes, and himself as an intact and total being.

Glass (1984) explains that, at its most fundamental level, the male's lack of empathy for the feminine relies on his inability to imagine himself, not only without a penis, but with female genitals. He maintains masculine anxiety consists of a stalwart defense against fears of penetration in connection with issues of control. Much of this fear for males is then focused on their anus and translates into a massive anxiety concerning homosexuality. Glass (1980) also notes that cultural structures can create "package solutions" to homosexual anxiety. These behavioral "packages" are typically hypermasculine, promoting the neglect of feminine character aspects in both the self and women, stereotypes of intergender relationships, and the rationalized degradation of homosexuals. Ovesey, who has written much of the literature available on the topic, describes dependent men, in a culture whose idea of masculinity is tightly connected to the idea of ambition and self-assertion, as overcompensating for their homosexual anxieties by habitually striving for power and dominance over other males. Pleck (1981b) attributes homosexual anxieties as the most influential factor keeping men from straying off the path of traditional masculinity (1981a).

Developmental Implications and Consequences of Gendered Stereotypes

As suggested by the dire and negative stereotyping concerning the preferred male role and extreme negativity associated with femaleness, it is not surprising that gender-identity themes are extremely salient and ever-present for boys. In fact, it is generally understood in the developmental literature that gender constancy occurs early and that boys show gender preference between 18 months and 2 years of age. When coupled with the need to manage racial stereotypes, the dynamic suggests a much greater fragility of the more significant child-rearing tasks and responsibilities for parents of African American boys. Given the later adulthood difficulties and challenges associated with the need to show instrumentality, it appears that a very special form of life course "male fragility" is experienced by African American men. Of course, Caucasian males are also burdened with their own quality of life course "male fragility." They are burdened with life course expectations for significant success and plagued with insecurities having to do with the assumptions of privilege and entitlement, although these stresses are infrequently unacknowledged and have been discussed quite recently in the "whiteness literature" (e.g., Ignatiev, 1995; Roediger, 1994). However, independent of differences in ethnicity, race, and socioeconomic status, these issues are seldom considered from a developmental perspective. The oversight leaves policy-makers "short" on what to do and for whom and how to do it and when best to introduce supportive changes. Equally important is the fact that few perspectives implement the physical or neighborhood environment as an added source of risk.

Adolescent Hypermasculinity Longitudinal Research Findings

Recent and more developmentally sensitive research findings by Cunningham (1994, 1999) and by Spencer, Cunningham, and Swanson (1995) indicate that the neighborhood and context character matter more broadly in the socialization experiences and academic pursuits of African American male youths. The pattern of findings has important implications for parental socialization efforts (see Spencer, 1983, 1990), teaching context, teacher training (see Spencer, 1999), and social policy (see Swanson, Spencer, & Petersen, 1998).

Study Background and Overview

The Promoting Academic Competence (PAC) Project database represents a large longitudinal study of 562 African American urban youths. It explores the relationship between neighborhood and family characteristics, perceived context experiences, and achievement, focusing specifically on the development of competence and resiliency in African American boys. Theory-driven analyses (i.e., PVEST) examine adolescent coping methods and competence outcomes. Some of the analyses predict productive coping methods (e.g., learning responsibility behavior, academic self-esteem) versus maladaptive coping methods (e.g., negative learning attitudes, hypermasculinity). Participants consisted of 394 adolescent males and 168 adolescent females randomly selected from sixth, seventh, and eighth grade classrooms of participating public middle schools in a metropolitan southeastern American city. As part of their participation, all adolescents filled out several scales and completed an interview schedule.

Subjects. The African American sample was randomly selected from four middle school populations. Signed consent rates by school ranged from 55 to 80 percent. For three of the four schools, 80 to 90 percent of the students received free or reduced lunch support. For the fourth school, the rate was approximately 70 percent. It is evident from the parental self-report information that 58 percent of the subjects' families met federal poverty guidelines (i.e., for a family size of four, the criterion for poverty used was annual family income of $13,395).

Procedures and Measures

As part of their participation in the larger longitudinal study, subjects were seen in small groups at their respective schools; females were included to offset the possible impression by boys of their focal import to the project. All participants completed survey instruments during three sessions. The majority of the small-group testers were the same race as the participants. All testers were well-trained graduate, undergraduate, or older adult interviewers who were hired especially to serve as adolescent interviewers.

Findings: Hypermasculinity (Machismo) Prediction

The most consistent predictor of machismo for boys was the perception of neighborhood-level violence and aggression. The relationships to context and developmental implications for machismo-like behavior have been carefully described as a dissertation project by Cunningham (1994), published and referred to in several forms (e.g., Cunningham 1993; Cunningham & Spencer, 1996; in press; Spencer, 1999; Spencer, Cunningham, & Swanson, 1995).

Presented are longitudinal data for years 1 thru 3 for the three hypermasculine subscales when the majority of male students were initially expected to be 11 to 15 years of age and in the sixth, seventh, or eighth grades of their respective middle schools. In exception to this, there was one 10-year-old and approximately seven 16-year-olds. They were combined with the two proximal age groups, ages 11 and 15, respectively. On average, youths were generally older than expected by grade because many had been "retained in grade" either once, twice, or, as was often the case, three times by grade six! The three subscale scores that comprise the Hypermasculinity Scale include Violence as Manly and Callousness Towards Women and Danger as Exciting and are presented in Figures 7.6, 7.7, and 7.8, respectively, as three years of longitudinal findings.

It is evident from Figure 7.6 that only the youngest group of students at Time 1 show an increase in their Attitudes Toward Violence, indicating somewhat of a male pubertal increase that decreases by the third year. The oldest age group (i.e., 15-year-olds), although somewhat higher at year 1, decreased steadily during the second and third years. Callousness Towards Women were highest for the oldest students (i.e., 15-year-olds) at Time 1 but decreased significantly by Year 3, suggesting somewhat of a "reality check" experienced by boys with age and over time.

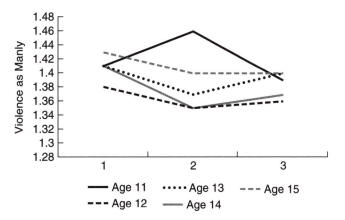

FIGURE 7.6 Attitudes about violence across time

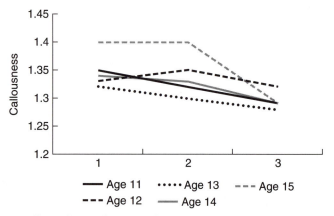

FIGURE 7.7 Calloused attitudes toward women across time

Similar to the subscale measure of Violence as Manly, the attitude that Danger is Exciting was initially low for the youngest age group but increased dramatically during the subsequent year, after which it plummeted. Generally, the data pattern suggested an apparent attitudinal vulnerability for the youngest boys; responses suggest strong stereotypic attitudes that increase at 12 to 13 years and then significantly decrease afterward. Since this is also the developmental period when the majority of boys are reaching puberty, it suggests a "fragile" developmental period because of the apparent "trial-and-error" experimentation apparently occurring at this time. It is also a period when youth are engaged in an identity crisis that suggests a significant level of psychological vulnerability as youngsters begin the search for a healthy identity.

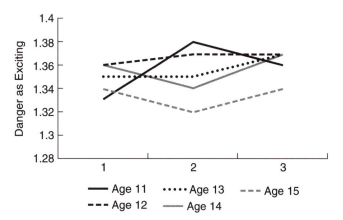

FIGURE 7.8 Attitudes about danger across time

Conclusions

The literature reviewed on hypermasculinity theorizing suggested a quite negative picture concerning the correlates of hypermasculine behavior. Both a PVEST perspective and pattern of findings suggest that the phenomenon does not imply a static process, but instead, more dynamic processes that connote correlates with normative adolescent processes. Specifically, for boys at the height of puberty onset, the degree of espoused problematic attitudes is worth noting. However, implicit in the pattern over time is a "reality testing" and "attitude readjustment." There is a need to examine these patterned findings conjoined with an analysis of racial attitudes and reactive coping responses. Both hypermasculine gender-linked responses appear not unlike the reactive and racially stereotypic attitudes that adolescents have been reported as using under conditions of racial dissonance. For example, we suggest that the hypermasculine or racial attitudes and cultural styles adopted by adolescents in particular settings indicate an adaptive response to perceived high-risk environments.

Educational settings represent an environment potentially attentive to both maladaptive gender and ethnicity/race coping responses. Helping parents, teachers, and administrators to understand what the coping responses do and do not mean may aid in a diminished maladaptive response pattern for youth. The support is necessary for helping male youth to focus on their self-conceptions as learners first, as opposed to a preoccupation with structuring scenarios that aid the reaffirmation of a fragile view of self "as a man." Providing proactive opportunities for affirming self-beliefs of more positive aspects of manhood supports beneficial coping and more transparent transitioning between contexts. In addition, providing productive opportunities for "re-defining" manhood decreases male youths' problematic contribution to contexts of risk for girls. In sum, such programming directly impacts adolescent males while impacting the contextual experiences of female adolescents, thus maximizing the use of available resources and supports. In sum, PVEST provides insights for informed programming that acknowledges the unavoidable normative developmental contributions to psychological discontinuities that accompany normal adolescent transitions. Accordingly, through the utilization of supportive "theory of change" perspectives (see Weiss, 1995), theory-driven interventions not only ensure the maximization of youth outcomes as social capital but demonstrate that the problem may not be "in the child." It suggests, instead, that the problem may be in the way we conceptualize young people and define and support contexts of normal development.

REFERENCES

Allen, W. R. (1985). Race, income and family dynamics: A study of adolescent male socialization processes and outcomes. In M. B. Spencer, G. K. Brookins, & W. R. Allen (Eds.), *Beginnings: The social and affective development of black children* (pp. 273–292). Hillsdale, NJ: Lawrence Erlbaum Associates.

Bobo, L. (1983, December). Whites' opposition to busing: Symbolic racism or realistic group conflict? *Journal of Personality & Social Psychology, 45*(6), 1196–1210.

Boykin, A. W. (1986). The triple quandary and the schooling of Afro-American children. In U. Neisser (Ed.), *The school achievement of minority children* (pp. 57–92). Hillsdale, NJ: Lawrence Erlbaum Associates.

Boykin, A. W., & Ellison, C. M. (1995). The multiple ecologies of Black youth socialization: An Afrographic analysis. In R. L. Taylor (Ed.), *African-American youth: Prospectives on their status in the United States* (pp. 93–128). Westport, CT: Praeger.

Boykin, A. W., & Toms, F. D. (1985). Black child socialization: A conceptual framework. In H. P. McAdoo & J. L. McAdoo (Eds.), *Black children: Social, educational, and parental environments.* Newbury Park, CA: Sage.

Bronfenbrenner, U. (1989). Ecological systems theory. In R. Vasta (Ed.), *Annals of Child Development, Vol. 6. Six theories of child development* (pp. 187–249). Greenwich, CT: JAI Press.

Brookins, G. K. (1988). Making the honor roll: A black parent's perspective on private education. In D. T. Slaughter & D. J. Johnson (Eds.), *Visible now: Blacks in private schools.* New York: Greenwood Press.

Brown, R. N. (1940). The preoedipal phase of the libido development. *Psychoanalytic Quarterly, 9,* 293–319.

Chodoff, P. (1982). Hysteria and women. *American Journal of Psychiatry, 139,* 545–551.

Cunningham, M. (1993). African American adolescent males' sex role development: A literature review. *Journal of African American Males Studies, 1*(1), 30–37.

Cunningham, M. (1994). *Expressions of manhood: Predictors of educational achievement and African American adolescent males.* (Unpublished) Dissertation submitted for the Ph.D., Emory University, Atlanta.

Cunningham, M. (1999). African-American adolescent males' perceptions of their community resources and constraints: A longitudinal analysis. *Journal of Community Psychology, 27*(5), 569–588.

Cunningham, M., & Spencer, M. B. (1996). The Black male experiences measure. In R. L. Jones (Ed.), *Handbook of tests and measurements for Black populations* (pp. 1–6). Hampton, VA: Cobb and Henry Publishers.

Cunningham, M., & Spencer, M. B. (submitted). Peer influences on African American adolescent boys' exaggerated male gender identity. *Developmental Psychology.*

Darity, W. A., Jr., & Myers, S. L. (1998). *Persistent disparity: Race and economic inequality in the United States since 1945.* Cheltenham, UK; Northampton, MA: Edward Elgar.

DuBois, W. E. B. (1903). *The souls of Black folk.* Greenwich, CT: Fawcett Publications.

Dupree, D., Spencer, M. B., & Bell, S. (1997). The ecology of African-American child development: Normative and non-normative outcomes. In G. Johnson-Powell, J. Yamamoto, G. E. Wyatt, & W. Arroyo (Eds.), *Transcultural child development: Psychological assessment and treatment* (pp. 237–268). New York: John Wiley & Sons, Inc.

Fenichel, O. (1945). *The psychoanalytic theory of neurosis.* New York: Norton.

Freud, S. (1925). Some psychical consequences of the anatomical distinction between the sexes. In Stansard Edition of the *Complete psychological works.* Hogarth, 1953–1974, Vol. 19.

Freud, S. (1937). Analysis terminable and interminable, Vol. 23 of *Standard edition of the complete psychological works.* London: Hogarth, 1953–1974.

Gibbs, J. T. (1988). Conceptual, methodological, and sociocultural issues in Black youth suicide: Implications for assessment and early intervention. *Suicide & Life-Threatening Behavior, 18*(1), 73–89.

Glass, L. L. (1980a). The Dartmouth animal and the hypermasculine myth. *Dartmouth Alumni Magazine, 73,* 34–46.

Glass, L. L. (1984). Man's man/ladies' man: Motifs of hypermasculinity. *Psychiatry, 47*(3), 260–278.

Gutherie, R. (1976). *Even the rat was white: A historical view of psychology.* New York: Harper & Row.

Hall, C. S., & Lindzey, G. (1978). *Theories of personality.* (3rd ed). New York: John Wiley & Sons.

Hare, B. R., & Castenell, L. A. (1985). No place to run, no place to hide: Comparative status and future prospects of Black boys. In M. B. Spencer, G. K. Brookins, & W. R. Allen (Eds.), *Beginnings: The social and affective development of Black children* (pp. 185–200). New York: Lawrence Erlbaum Associates.

Hill, J., & Lynch, M. (1983). The intensification of gender-related role expectations during early adolescence. In J. Broules-Gans & A. Petersen (Eds.), *Female puberty.* New York: Plenum Press.

Holliday, B. G. (1985). Towards a model of teacher-child transactional processes affecting Black children's academic achievement. In M. B. Spencer, G. K. Brookins, & W. R. Allen (Eds.), *Beginnings: The social and affective development of Black children* (pp. 117–131). New York: Erlbaum Publishing Company.

Ignatiev, N. (1995). *How the Irish became white.* New York: Routledge.

Kleeman, J. A. (1976). Freud's views on early female sexuality in the light of direct child observation. *Journal of the American Psychoanalytic Association* (Supplement), *24,* 3–28.

Kubish, A. C., Weiss, C. H., Schorr, L. B., & Connell, J. P. (Eds.). (1995). *New approaches to evaluating community initiatives: Concepts, methods, and contexts.* Washington, DC: The Aspen Institute.

Nanda, S. (1980). *Cultural anthropology.* New York: Van Nostrand.

Odom, M. (1988, March 17). Judge decries growing gap between races. *The Philadelphia Inquirer.* p. E-1.

Ogbu, J. U. (1985). A cultural ecology of competence among inner-city Blacks. In M. B. Spencer, G. K. Brookins, & W. R. Allen (Eds.), *Beginnings: Social and affective development of Black children* (pp. 45–66). New York: Lawrence Erlbaum Associates.

O'Hare, W. P., Pollard, K. M., Mann, T. L., & Kent, M. M. (1991). African Americans in the 1990s. *Population Bulletin, 46,*(1).

Ovesey, L. (1969). *Homosexuality and pseudohomosexuality.* Science House.

Pleck, J. (1981a). How psychology constructed masculinity: The theory of male sex role identity. In D. David & R. Brannon (Eds.), *The 49% majority: The male sex role* (2nd ed.). New York: Addison-Wesley.

Pleck, J. (1981b). *The myth of masculinity.* Cambridge, MA: MIT Press.

Roediger, D. R. (1994). *Towards the abolition of whiteness.* New York: Verso.

Rogers, C. R. (1961). *On becoming a person.* Boston: Houghton Mifflin.

Rogers, C. R. (1963). Actualizing tendency in relation to "motives" and to consciousness. In M. R. Jones (Ed.), *Nebraska symposium on motivation.* Lincoln: University of Nebraska Press.

Ross, J. M. (1975). The development of paternal identity: A critical review of the literature on nurturance and generativity in boys and men. *Journal of American Psychoanalytic Association, 23,* 783–817.

Ross, J. M. (1977). Towards fatherhood: The epigenesis of paternal identity during a boy's first decade. *International Review of Psychoanalysis, 4,* 327–347.

Ross, J. M. (1979). Paternal identity: The equation of fatherhood and manhood. In T. B. Karasu & C. W. Socarides (Eds.), *On sexuality.* New York: International Universities Press.

Ross, J. M. (1982). Oedipus revisited: Laius and the "Laius Complex." *Psychoanalytic Study of the Child, 37,* 169–200.

Santrock, J. W. (1992). *Children.* (3rd ed.). Madison, WS: Brown & Benchmark.

Santrock, J. W. (1995). *Life-span development.* (5th ed.). Madison, WI: Brown & Benchmark.

Spencer, M. B. (1976). *The social-cognitive and personality development of the black preschool child: An exploratory study of developmental process.* Unpublished doctoral dissertation, University of Chicago.

Spencer, M. B. (1982). Preschool children's social cognition and cultural cognition: A cognitive developmental interpretation of race dissonance findings. *Journal of Psychology, 112,* 275–296.

Spencer, M. B. (1983). Children's cultural values and parental child rearing strategies. *Developmental Review, 3,* 351–370.

Spencer, M. B. (1990). Parental values transmission: Implications for black child development. In J. B. Stewart & H. Cheatham (Eds.), *Interdisciplinary perspectives on black families* (pp. 111–130). New Brunswick, NJ: Transactions Press.

Spencer, M. B. (1995). Old issues and new theorizing about African American youth: A phenomenological variant of ecological systems theory. In R. L. Taylor (Ed.), *Black youth: Perspectives on their status in the United States* (pp. 37–69). Westport, CT: Praeger.

Spencer, M. B. (1999). Social and cultural influences on school adjustment: The application of an identity-focused cultural ecological perspective. *Educational Psychologist, 34*(1), 43–57.

Spencer, M. B., & Cunningham, M. (in press). Patterns of resilience and vulnerability: Examining diversity within African-American youth. In G. K. Brookins & M. B. Spencer (Eds.), *Ethnicity and diversity: Minorities no more.* Hillsdale, NJ: Lawrence Erlbaum Associates.

Spencer, M. B., Cunningham, M., & Swanson, D. P. (1995). Identity as coping: Adolescent African American males' adaptive responses to high risk environments. In H. W. Harris, H. C. Blue, & E. H. Griffith (Eds.), *Racial and ethnic identity* (pp. 31–52). New York: Routledge.

Spencer, M. B., & Dornbusch, S. (1990). Challenges in studying minority youth. In S. Feldman & G. Elliot (Eds.), *At the threshold: The developing adolescent* (pp. 123–146). Cambridge, MA: Harvard University Press.

Spencer, M. B., Dupree, D., & Hartmann, T. (1997). A phenomenological variant of ecological systems theory (PVEST): A self-organization perspective in context. *Development and Psychopathology, 9,* 817–833.

Spencer, M.B., & Markstrom-Adams, C. (1990). Identity processes among racial and ethnic minority children in America. *Child Development, 61*(2), 290–310.

Staples, R. (1986). *The black family: Essays and studies.* Belmont, CA: Wadsworth Publishing Company.

Steinberg, L. (1999). *Adolescence.* New York: McGraw-Hill.

Steinberg, L. (1985). *Adolescence.* New York: Knopf.

Swanson, D. P., Spencer, M. B., & Petersen, A. (1998). Identity formation in adolescence. In K. Borman & B. Schneider (Eds.), *The adolescent years: Social influences and educational challenges.* Ninety-seventh Yearbook of the National Society for the Study of Education, Part 1 (pp. 18–41). Chicago: University of Chicago Press.

Weiss, C. H. (1995). Nothing as practical as good theory: Exploring theory-based evaluation for comprehensive community initiatives for children and families. In J. P. Connell, A. C. Kubish, L. B. Schorr, & C. H. Weiss (Eds.), *New approaches to evaluating community initiatives: Concepts, methods, and contexts.* Washington: The Aspen Institute.

Wilson, W. J. (1987). *The truly disadvantaged: The inner city, the underclass and public policy.* Chicago: University of Chicago Press.

8

Comment

Human Development and the Social Structure

Enora R. Brown

Introduction

> . . . Black male identities have been historically and culturally constructed through complex dialectics of power and subordination. (Mercer, 1994, p. 137)

> A discourse on black masculinity . . . constructs black men as both sources of pleasure and sources of danger . . . (Gilroy, 1993, p. 228)

African American male youth are faced with the normative challenge of constructing coherent, self-affirmative identities, while negotiating a system of social inequality and attendant depreciatory societal meanings ascribed to the black male (Mercer, 1994; Spencer, 1999). Two cover stories in *Newsweek* magazine provide illustrative examples of this social reality. The cover of the November 29, 1993 issue bore the title, "When Is Rap 2 Violent?" and featured a head shot of the rap artist Snoop Doggy Dog. He was adorned in a knit cap, with his head turned to the side, mouth upturned, and eyes fixed in a penetrating stare, i.e., "hard look" (Hall, 1997). In stark contrast, two years earlier, the June 24, 1991 issue, entitled "What Do Men Really Want?" displayed the full-body picture of a tanned, lean, white, married man, adorned in jeans and tie, wedding band, and a smile, with his baby on one hip and a drum on the other. *Newsweek*'s cover stories present a graphic depiction of the interdependence of race and gender (Winant, 1994) and simultaneous co-construction of the "responsible, nurturant white male" and the "dangerous, irreverent Black male."

These images and other discursive practices in the larger society reflect the relative sociohistorical/economic positions of black and white masculinity within societal hierarchies of power (Hall, 1997). They represent African

American males as hypermasculine identities, with a penchant for aggression, sex, misogyny, and violence, juxtaposed against the image of the successful, clean-cut, middle-class European American male who values women, intimate relationships, marital responsibilities, and mutual resolution of differences. Further, these images are buttressed by the dominant discourse in developmental literature, which legitimates educational policies and practices that normalize the development and life choices of European American youth and pathologize those of African American and other youth of color. As such, they *represent* an *authentic* picture of the range of possibilities and class-based life outcomes for black and white male youth (Kelley, 1997).

Spencer's chapter, "Identity, Achievement Orientation, and Race: 'Lessons Learned' About the Normative Developmental Experiences of African American Males," investigates the complexity of the normative identity formation and achievement correlates for African American male youth. She explores "hypermasculinity" and the culturally and contextually induced "quest for respect" as a reactive coping mechanism that may jeopardize school adjustment and achievement, relational competence, and healthy gender-identity formation of African American males.

In this response, I will discuss Spencer's work and the implications of her theory and research for the study of human development and for ongoing intervention efforts with African American males and other youth of color. In addition, I will pose some questions that were raised by her work, through which I will explore the role of human agency and social structures of power in forging the aspirations and identificatory life choices of African American and other marginalized males.

Spencer's PVEST Model and African American Male Youth

Spencer's PVEST Model (Phenomenological Variant of Ecological Systems Theory) (1995a, 1999) provides a comprehensive, integrative framework to examine the complex interdependent relationships between the subjective experiences, stressors/supports, coping strategies, and emergent identities and life outcomes of these youth within the context of the family, peer relations, community, school, and societal race/class relationships (Spencer, 1994, 1995b). In contrast to unidimensional approaches that locate the source of development "inside" and/or "outside" of the individual, Spencer's *identity-focused, cultural ecological* (ICE) model reflects the interplay of both psychological and social processes that occur within multiple embedded contexts, and highlights the significance of sociostructural and cultural realities, as well as relationships with adults and peers in adolescents' identificatory processes of *meaning-making*. As such it is anchored in the Eriksonian view that identity resides both "in the core of the individual and the core of the common culture" (Erikson, 1968).

The PVEST model is marked by (1) its cross-disciplinary nature (e.g., psychology, history, sociology, anthropology, and philosophy), its grounding in the theoretical works of Bronfenbrenner, Sullivan, Mead-Chestang, V. P. Franklin, DuBois, Elder, and others, and its broad-based applicability to human development across the life span; (2) its conceptual and empirical grounding in an understanding of the normalcy of development processes for youth of color, despite the pervasiveness of deficit-models; (3) the pivotal role of self-appraisal and other perceptual processes in interpreting and responding to/coping with life experiences; (4) its unerring attention to history and the role of social inequity and racism in shaping the development of youth of color; (5) the interdependent relationship that exists between the individual's social, emotional, intellectual, and physiological processes and interpersonal relations across a range of cultural and social contexts; and (6) the link drawn between coping responses, emergent identities, and life outcomes (Spencer, 1999).

Spencer's PVEST model frames her longitudinal research and current inquiry on "hypermasculinity" and achievement orientation in African American working-class male youth. She posits that as African American boys are subjected to and become increasingly aware of racism and related institutional and societal inequities that affect their lives, they seek to gain the right-to-respect that they have been denied through gender-intensified behaviors, that is, hypermasculinity. Spencer suggests that this psychic need for respect is a reactive coping response that also grows out of the early cultivation of independence and assumption of responsibility that characterizes the lives of children in poor white and working-class communities of color. Further, she attributes this response to the ongoing efforts of youth to combat pervasive racial stereotypes that promote disrupted self-images in African American males and other marginalized groups. This demand for respect is reinforced within familial/community contexts, in which African American men use the term "little man" in reference to young African American males to counter the historical significance of the term "boy" in reference to black men. Thus, Spencer poignantly links the history of slavery and current objective realities in poor resource communities to African American males' embrace of hypermasculinity (Staples, 1982) and renunciation of academic achievement.

In addition, Spencer discusses the ways in which normal adolescent growth in value autonomy (Steinberg, 1985), abstract thinking, and ideological orientation becomes operative for youth of color in challenging contexts. She suggests that as African American males begin to forge a deeper understanding of and commitment to what is important and what is right or wrong and to stand by those beliefs in the face of opposition or adverse pressure, they may righteously resist adherence to the dress codes, language styles, and academic expectations of institutions that stigmatize them and marginalize other members of their racial group. Thus, hypermasculinity becomes a form of principled opposition to social inequity and a means to garner the respect deserved.

Spencer states further that, although the youthful embrace of hyper-masculinity may serve the short-term need of black males to attain immediate respect and cope with racial and other societally induced stressors, this coping response is not sanctioned by the dominant culture and is not conducive to the attainment of societally valued life outcomes or the long-term respect so desired. African American male youth are thus faced with the daunting task of employing mutually exclusive "habitual right actions" that are valued in one context, for example, among peers, and stigamatized in another, for example, in school. She suggests that the conflictual and often mutually exclusive nature of the values and outcomes that emerge from dual residence in oppositional contexts present youth with the difficulty of sustaining a double consciousness and of choosing to align with one's peers and referent racial group and/or the dominant culture.

Spencer notes that for African American male youth, the culturally and contextually framed developmental press to forge a coherent identity is characterized by a "triple quandary." These youth must try to reconcile their own values and expectations with those of their referent group and those of the dominant society. If in the process hypermasculinity, rather than achieve-ment orientation, becomes the enduring "coping response of choice" for male youth, their habitual and principled use of these macho behaviors will forge an emergent identity with related life outcomes. This presents an ongoing challenge for parents and other adults to support youth in making choices that will foster resilience and competence in navigating their own develop-mental processes across competing and often inhibitory contexts.

Finally, Spencer substantiates her conceptual and theoretically grounded claims with a discussion of empirical data from her comprehensive longitudinal study on African American youth. She refers to Cunningham's work (1994), documenting a link between school outcomes and hypermas-culinity, and the relationship between perceived neighborhood violence/ag-gression and machismo in youth. Her longitudinal data, cited elsewhere (Spencer, 1999), also show significant correlations between hypermasculinity and unpopularity with peers, negative teacher perceptions, and parental monitoring.

Spencer concludes with data from her sample of 394 predominantly poor, African American male youth. Based on three subscales of hypermas-culinity—callousness toward women, danger as exciting, and violence as manly—the overarching pattern that emerges for these 11- to 15-year-old youths is that they embrace macho-like behavior at the onset of puberty in their developmental quest to "try out" new identities. Over time, however, as the fragility of early adolescence passes, the boys' negative attitudes toward women and positive attitudes toward violence and danger abate considerably.

Spencer suggests that this overall renunciation of hypermasculinity reflects a reassessment by youth of the relative value or effectiveness of this coping response and recommends coordinated analysis of racial attitudes and coping responses of these youth. She discusses their shift in attitude as an indicator of the fluidity and contextually driven nature of hypermasculinity as a coping response, and suggests that the locus of the "problem" with youth may reside in adult conceptualizations of them and in the range of supports provided for youth across the varying social contexts in which they develop.

Emergent Issues: Aspirations, Human Agency, and Structures of Choice

Spencer's conceptual model and extensive research have major implications for ongoing intervention efforts that facilitate the achievement outcomes and healthy sense of self for African American males and other youth of color. Her work promotes a comprehensive examination of the complexity of human development, in light of cultural, contextual, and psychological realities that inform the ways in which people grow and change. While her work is unique in its ability to systematically address the lived experiences of youth of color and other marginalized groups, it has the broad-based capacity to capture the processes of growth and change for middle-class white children and youth who, in contrast, experience relative privilege in society.

Spencer's present inquiry raises three questions that are worth posing as we consider hypermasculinity, gender-identity formation, and achievement orientation for African American males. MacLeod's statement on the interdependent relationship that exists between human agency and social structure frames the questions posed. Each question addresses the intersection of race, class, and gender formations as framed in the quote by Kincheloe, Slattery, and Steinberg (2000):

> Structure and agency are inseparable. Individual agents . . . are always structurally situated, and thus human agency is itself socially structured. (MacLeod, 1995, p. 255)

> The forces of class, gender and race create a multilevel playing field on which students gain a sense of their options and to some extent negotiate their academic and vocational possibilities. (Kincheloe, Slattery, & Steinberg, 2000, p. 352)

First question: *Does the social class position of middle-class African American male youth create differential gender and racially induced stressors that contribute to self-appraisal processes, coping responses, and potential life outcomes than those experienced by working-class male youth? Specifically, are "hypermasculine" behaviors embraced by middle-class youth, and if so, are they interpreted as such by others?*

Spencer's current findings on working-class youth prompted these questions. It would be valuable to examine the nature of the stressors and supports that are experienced by middle-class African American male youth in racially mixed communities. Middle-class African American youth have more material and social resources to navigate educational and other institutional contexts. In addition, the ideological orientation, values, and beliefs that often characterize middle-class status may forge racial and gendered realities that differentially inform the self-appraisal processes of these youth, mediate others' interpretative evaluations of their adaptive/maladaptive coping responses, and thus foster related life outcomes.

Brantlinger's (1993) research in schools has shown differences in the lived and intersubjective experiences of middle-class and working-class youth. Similarly, MacLeod's (1985/1995) ethnographic study of poor European and African American males in an urban housing development illustrates the significance of social class in his examination of the familial and ideological differences that shape achievement efforts. Thus, social class structure may inform individual youth's agency and efficacy in traversing developmental processes and future goal attainment. For middle-class African American male youth, the "need for respect" and achievement outcomes may be mediated by compensatory economic and social resources related to one's relative racial/class status in the local community and dominant culture. Various sets of relations of power along racial, economic, and gendered lines may produce differential youth identities.

Second question: *In light of the history of the dominant culture's negative ascriptions to "black masculinity," who determines what behavioral or attitudinal patterns are normal, pathological, adaptive, or maladaptive. Specifically, is there an organic relationship (mutually exclusive or mutually coexistent) between hypermasculinity and achievement orientation?*

Spencer addressed the sociohistorical and economic context from which hypermasculinity emerged as a response to slavery, racism, and the pervasive denial of rights to African American men. Thus, particular meanings have been forged about the identity of the black male that reflect the history of social inequity and continue to reinforce exploitation and oppression in different forms. Hence, this poses us with the dilemma of trying to tease out (1) socially constructed meanings that have been used to pathologize African men and women and thus justify racism, economic subjugation, and other social inequities; (2) those positive meanings forged out of this same history; and (3) those meanings that reflect the debilitating effects of this history. This dilemma engenders the question of who "decides" which gendered identificatory meanings foster social equity and which meanings will instantiate the dominant social order, and how youth and adults of color may contest social relations of power and privilege to forge new identificatory meanings.

Embedded in this discussion is the issue of whose meanings are authenticated and what social and ideological function the ascribed meanings from the dominant culture serve. Attitudes and observed behaviors in working-class communities of color that are foreign to white middle-class communities are discursively positioned as indicators of deviance. By normalizing and privileging white, middle-class ways of being, poor youth of color are constructed as deviants from the dominant culture, that is, they are *structured out.* The marginalization of members of the working class, racial and ethnic groups, and others by sex and gender, characterizes work across academic disciplines and reflects daily life within educational and other institutions. Kelley (1994) suggests that the assumption underlying this exclusionary practice/policy is the new culture of poverty theory that "the lifestyles of the so-called black 'underclass'. . . constitute a significant deviation from mainstream values . . . ," even though they may epitomize the values of America in different form (p. 201). Through historical relations of power based on gender, class, and race, society has constructed the "normal male" to be one who is tough, independent, in control, powerful, and dominating (Mercer, 1994; Kelley, 1997). Despite the "normalcy" of these masculine attributes, they are, ironically, stigmatized in African American men. Again the intersection of race, class, and gendered identity formation is apparent.

If the behaviors and attitudes of black men are automatically constructed as deviant and pathological, even if they mirror society's values, then it is possible that behaviors and attitudes of African American males are not, in fact, hypermasculine, but rather perceived that way through the lens of racism or class bias. The stigmatization of particular behaviors and attitudes of African American youth may position them in opposition to academic achievement, and thus sustain racial and class-based relations of privilege and power.

This highlights the need to access the actual voices of youth and the meanings that they co-construct in their daily interactions. Kelley (1994, 1997) asserts that the embedded meanings in working-class youth culture are not unidimensional, static, essentialist constructs, representing a "core black culture." Multiple-layered meanings may emerge that represent varying ideological stances, psychological needs, and interpersonal/social relationships. For example, ideologically, hypermasculinity may represent a healthy resistance to oppressive social structures or may embody one's nihilistic resignation to limited life options. Similarly, macho-like behaviors may serve divergent social functions. On the one hand, they may represent an aesthetic "style" of interaction that creates a common, pleasurable way of being with one's peers; on the other hand, the behaviors and attitudes may be ideologically grounded in emergent misogyny and social violence (Kelley, 1994; Rose, 1994). The structural legitimization of particular meanings and interpretations has implications for the validation of the perspectives of youth and their efficacy in managing their social world.

This discussion is not intended to excuse the degradation, subjugation, or domination of women, but to consider the range of meanings that may be forged for youth as they negotiate their identities and places in the world.

Finally, violence is a dimension of the hypermasculinity construct. A plethora of images and institutional practices equate violence with race as a black problem (Giroux, 1996; Hall, 1997), and represent black youth as the source rather than as the victims of systemic violence of poverty, racism, and other social inequities. As exemplified in the *Newsweek* cover stories discussed earlier, written, visual, and other forms of discourse make identificatory statements about who is normal and who is not. In turn, these representations of the violent, dangerous, black youth justify state violence, current loitering laws, and the ways in which black youth are policed, while pathologizing their resistance to this oppression. By obscuring the violence of poverty, devastating effects of racism and unemployment, and inhumanity of poor education, the violence in poor, black, and other communities of color is seen as the cause, rather than the toxic effect, of systemic social inequity (Giroux, 1996). Simultaneously, other forms of political, recreational, and economic violence are widely sanctioned, nationally and internationally, and are justified under the banner of personal and national freedom (Foner, 1998). Again, this discussion is not to suggest that violence in the African American community is a good thing. It is, however, to point out the presence of multiple meanings and their significance in the construction of African American male identities.

These issues may undergird our ongoing scholarly inquiry as well as related intervention initiatives and social action endeavors. At each juncture, it is important to attend to the source and the function of the co-constructed meanings embodied in black and white masculine identities and the implications of privileging certain racially and class-based masculinities over others.

Third question: *To what degree do institutional and social hierarchies of power shape the aspirations, sense of agency, and probable life outcomes for marginalized youth and simultaneously thwart their efforts to create new future possibilities?*

This question emerges as I consider the importance of intervention in the daily efforts of African American male youth to attain desired life outcomes. It is clear from Spencer's theoretical and empirical work that the role of supportive parents, educators, and other adults is pivotal in fostering the child's healthy sense of self, despite the negative racial messages conveyed in the broader society (Spencer, 1982, 1983). In addition, adult intervention may facilitate resilient responses in youth and buffer them from deleterious effects of gender, racial, or class-based inequities. Complementarily, Jay MacLeod's (1987/1995) ethnography, *Ain't No Making It: Aspirations and Attainment in a Low-Income Neighborhood,* on working-class African American and European American male youth, poses an issue that has implications for the identity formation of African American males and for ongoing research, intervention, and social action. His work persistently raises the question of the source of the aspirations of youth and the probability of success in contexts of social and economic inequity. MacLeod states:

> Aspirations reflect an individual's view of his or her own chances for getting ahead and are an internalization of objective probabilities. (p. 15)

Guided by social reproduction theory (Bourdieu, 1977), MacLeod conducts a longitudinal study to examine the role of aspirations and the achievement ideology on the educational and career outcomes of a group of African American working-class youth, the Brothers, and a group of European American working-class youth, the Hallway Hangers, in a low-income housing development. His study and follow-up span a 10-year period during which he documents their aspirations; their stated beliefs on race, social class, and women; and their explanations for personal success/failure. MacLeod also describes their familial relations, ideological stances, and ultimate outcomes for these youth as adults. The Brothers embraced the achievement ideology, achieved in school, and believed that "If you work hard, you will make it," whereas the Hallway Hangers did not believe in the equality of opportunity or social mobility and did not invest in academic outcomes.

When MacLeod followed-up eight years later, he found that despite the valiant efforts of the Brothers, they fared no better than the Hallway Hangers. The Brothers had aspirations and believed in the American dream, and some had supportive families to guide the way. Although they recognized that the economy and lack of professional connections and other resources had inhibited their overall success in "making it," the Brothers blamed themselves for their failure. This inquiry poses the simple question of whether aspirations are enough and simultaneously debunks the myth of the achievement ideology . . . for all.

MacLeod's study illustrates the intricate link that exists between aspirations, human agency, and social structures and underscores the profound impact of race and social class on the educational and career outcomes of white and black working-class youth. Fueled by a belief in social mobility, the Brothers' aspirations catalyzed a sense of agency to attain educational and career goals. However, their aspirations were leveled as social structural realities thwarted their goal attainment. The Hallway Hangers did not have achievement aspirations based on their assessment that success was improbable and not worth the effort. The daunting specter of social structures defused their agency and goal pursuit. In different ways, structural inequities leveled the aspirations of both groups and contributed to the reproduction of their class positions. Impinging structural inequities included poverty, pervasive institutional racism, poor public education, school tracking systems, racial and class-based ideologies of teachers, downturn of the economy, and absence of financial and professional resources.

Through their inquiries, both Spencer and MacLeod link the psychological and the social in their analyses of achievement outcomes for youth of color. Both highlight the pivotal role of youth self-appraisal processes and their assessment of the immediate and broader socio-structural contexts. Both authors also illustrate the significance of differential coping responses employed by youth in hostile or challenging environments.

In different ways, Spencer and MacLeod address the synergy between aspirations, human agency, and social structure. On the one hand, Spencer's theory and research highlights the contextualized meaning-making processes of African American youth and illustrates the need for educators and other adults to intervene with youth in ways that facilitate their immediate and long-term management of the processes of growth and change across many contexts. On the other hand, MacLeod illustrates the need to simultaneously address social change at the systemic level. Intervention at this level is crucial to support the development of youth. Work must be done in educational institutions to challenge inequitable policies and practices that limit the identificatory possibilities for African American youth. Work must also be done around white educators' and administrators' racial identity formations along with examinations of the dominant discourse in curricular texts that reproduce and contribute to the marginalization of youth of color (Brown, in press). As work continues with youth within their multiple contexts of work and play, social systems of inequity must be central sites for social change. The pivotal role of social and economic structures and societal relations of power and privilege in the process of identity construction make them requisite sites for such change.

Efforts are necessary at every level—the psychological and the social—to support youth in their day-to-day survival to cope with contextual stressors in their pursuit of individual life goals and to provide long-term relief from social and economic structures of inequity that prevent the masses of working-class youth and youth of color from envisioning and attaining a broad range of life possibilities. In our efforts to leverage the range of choices that African American male youth have in constructing identities and attaining life goals, Dyson's (1995) quote captures the breadth of the task:

> . . . Choice itself is not a property of autonomous moral agents acting in an existential vacuum, but rather something that is created and exercised within the interaction of social, psychic, political, and economic forces of everyday experiences. (Dyson, 1991, p. 75)

REFERENCES

Bourdieu, P. (1977). *Reproduction in education, society, and culture.* London: Sage Publications.

Brantlinger, E. (1993). *The politics of social class in secondary schools: Views of affluent and impoverished youth.* New York: Teachers College Press.

Brown, E. (in press). Intersection of the individual and the social: White pre-service teachers' narrative constructions of identity. In M. B. Spencer. *Identity and education.*

Dyson, M. (1991). Growing up under fire: Boyz N the hood and the agony of the Black man in America. *Tikkun, 6*(5) (November/December), pp. 74–78.

Epstein, D. (1998). *Failing boys? Issues in gender and achievement.* London: Taylor & Francis.

Erikson, E. (1968). *Identity, youth and crisis.* New York: W. W. Norton.

Foner, E. (1998). *The story of American freedom.* New York: W. W. Norton.

Gilroy, P. (1993). *Small acts: Thoughts on the politics of black cultures.* New York: Serpent's Tail.

Gilroy, P. (1994). *Small acts.* London: Serpent's Tail.

Giroux, H. (1996). *Fugitive cultures: Race, violence, and youth.* New York: Routledge.

Hall, S. (1997). The spectacle of the "Other". In S. Hall (Ed.), *Representation: Cultural representations and signifying practices* (pp. 223–290). Thousand Oaks, CA: Sage Publications.

Hall, S. (Ed.). (1997). *Representation: Cultural representations and signifying practices.* Thousand Oaks, CA: Sage Publications.

Kelley, R. D. G. (1994). *Race rebels: Culture, politics, and the Black working class.* New York: Free Press.

Kelley, R. D. G. (1997). *Yo' Mama's disfunktional! Fighting the culture wars in America.* Boston: Beacon Press.

Kincheloe, J., Slattery, P., & Steinberg, S. (2000). *Contextualizing teaching.* New York: Longman.

MacLeod, J. (1987/1995). *Ain't no makin' it: Aspirations and attainment in a low-income neighborhood.* Boulder, CO: Westview Press.

McDowell, D. (1997). Pecs and reps: Muscling in on race and the subject of masculinities. In H. Stecopoulos & M. Uebel, *Race and the subject of masculinities* (pp. 361–365). Durham, SC: Duke University Press.

Mercer, K. (1994). Black masculinity and the sexual politics of race. In K. Mercer (Ed.), *Welcome to the jungle* (pp. 131–170). New York: Routledge.

Mercer, K. (1994). *Welcome to the jungle.* New York: Routledge.

Nixon, S. (1997). Exhibiting masculinity. In S. Hall (Ed.), *Representation: Cultural representations and signifying practices* (pp. 291–336). Thousand Oaks, CA: Sage Publications.

Rose, T. (1994). *Black noise: Rap music and Black culture in contemporary America.* Hanover, NH: Wesleyan University Press.

Spencer, M. B. (1982). Personal and group identity of Black children: An alternative synthesis. *Genetic Psychology Monographs, 106,* 59–84.

Spencer, M. B. (1983). Children's cultural values and parental child rearing strategies. *Developmental Review, 3,* 351–370.

Spencer, M. B. (1995). Old issues and new theorizing about African-American youth: A phenomenological variant of ecological systems theory. In R. L. Taylor (Ed.), *African-American youth: Their social and economic status in the United States* (pp. 37–70). Westport, CT: Praeger.

Spencer, M. B. (1999). Social and cultural influences on school adjustment: The application of an identity-focused cultural ecological perspective. *Educational Psychologist, 34*(1), 43–57.

Spencer, M. B. (in press). Identity, achievement orientation and race: Lessons learned about the normative developmental experiences of African American males. In W. Watkins, J. Lewis, & V. Chou, *Race and Education.* Allyn & Bacon.

Staples, R. (1982). *Black masculinity: The Black man's role in American society.* San Francisco: Black Scholar Press.

Stecopoulos, H., & Uebel, M. (1997). *Race and the subject of masculinities.* Durham, SC: Duke University Press.

Steinberg, L. (1985). *Adolescence.* New York: Knopf.

Uebel, M. (1997). Men in color: Introducing race and the subject of masculinities. In Stecopoulos, H., & Uebel, M. *Race and the subject of masculinities* (pp. 1–14). Durham, SC: Duke University Press.

Winant, H. (1994). *Racial conditions: Politics, theory, comparisons.* Minneapolis: University of Minnesota Press.

9 Why Can't Sonya (and Kwame) Fail Math?

Signithia Fordham

Introduction

Several years ago I read an article about a young black woman named Sonya who was not permitted to take an advanced mathematics class. Why? Because her performance on the requisite placement exam indicated that she did not have the aptitude for the subject matter. Sonya was devastated. Her life's flight plan was contingent on her ability to display and demonstrate ownership of high-level math skills. Her motive: she wanted to become an astronaut. Her counselor and other school officials were unanimous in their expert advice: Don't let that girl take an advanced placement mathematics course because of her low score on the math placement exam.

Sonya, however, was persistent. She begged her counselor and the teachers at the school to permit her to take the course, to no avail. Fortunately, her father—unlike many parents who send their children to public school—was not afraid of or intimidated by the school experts. He went to the school, met with the principal, and asked the following elegant but simple question: "Why can't Sonya fail math?"

Sonya's father recognized that the opportunity to fail is essential to success; that risk is the primary prerequisite to academic achievement. Deprive the individual of this challenge, of the opportunity to fail, and you also divest her of the possibility of success. Sonya's father's question convinced the principal to allow Sonya to take the desired course. Her performance in that course, and in all the subsequent math courses she took during high school and college, enabled her to achieve her life's flight plan: to become an astronaut. Had Sonya not been allowed to risk failing advanced placement math—had her father been unwilling to challenge the school experts—she would not have been able to realize her dream; she would not have been given the opportunity to fail. Ironically, because girls are enmeshed in an ethos of loss in a patriarchal system, protecting them from success and the attendant access to economic power is a major component of what is widely understood as male dominance.

Thus, in the case of African American females, it is the intersecting and hemorrhaging of blackness and femaleness that undermine academic achievement. As in the case of African American males, black females' legacy of enslavement has led to the construction of a female identity that is ambiguous, somewhere between male and female, that is, a little female but not quite male. In a convoluted attempt to validate their femaleness while minimizing their blackness, adolescent black girls often eschew advanced placement courses and other markers of academic acumen. More on this below.

Viewed primarily as sexual beings, transforming their sexual identity appears to be one of the primary goals of African American female schooling. Indeed, research tends to show that black girls are rewarded not for their academic performance but for their willingness to assume policing, helping, and care-taking roles (Grant, 1984, 1994; Schofield, 1989). Moreover, because contemporary black girls are the descendants of females whose social history was profoundly shaped by the sexualized nature of their enslavement, one might ask the following question: Is there something other than the possession of breasts that makes black girls female, particularly in the school context? This is an important question because in most popular representations, "'[B]lack . . .' is usually imagined as an exclusively male domain." The convergence of maleness and blackness makes performing femaleness a far more difficult task. For example, in her book *Black Ice*, Lorene Cary (1991) notes that in the exclusive private school she attended, she was only episodically female. She writes:

> Black girls were only really girls within the Afro-Am [club] . . . In the school at large, where more than 300 of the 500 students were still white boys, we [Black females] were more black than girls [emphasis added] . . . Race had a neutering effect. In class, I was not subjected to the special girlie putdowns in which teen-age boys delight. On student council I was not obliged to champion the "girls' issues," not compelled to worry about striking the perfect balance of assertiveness and femininity. Humiliating asides were aimed elsewhere, and no one would have expected me to play a dumb blond. (pp. 18–19)

As Cary's text suggests, her blackness, not her femaleness, was a "master status," so powerfully marking her body that it allowed her to perform her female identity only intermittently. In fact, her academic "success" neutered her, marking her as unpretty and not feminine, and therefore undesired as a possible date or potential mate. Her academic "success," as Weitz and Gordon (1993) empirically demonstrates, was held against her, marking her an inappropriate female.

It is against this background that I offer the following argument for why Sonya (and other black girls [and boys]) ". . . can't fail math . . .": This is an inappropriate gender space for females and an inappropriate race space for students identified as black, regardless of gender.

So how is the Sonya vignette either instructive and/or typical vis-à-vis African American students' academic performance? What can it teach us about African American females' (and males') academic performance? As the Sonya narrative suggests, achieving academic success is a struggle for African American girls (and boys), but, if the Capital High findings are generalizable, there are gender-specific routes to this social destination that are often blurred under the general racial label "black." Here I begin the process of unraveling this tightly constructed argument, highlighting the saliency of gender in academic performance.

In the following section of this analysis, I offer the reader an overview of the research site and a brief review of the major findings emerging from that study. I do this as a way of preparing the reader for the analysis that follows. A discussion of fictive kinship, the theoretical frame that shaped the larger study on which this analysis is based, is presented in the next section of this chapter. The third section interrogates race passing, that is, it examines what "give[s] voice" to black Americans' culturally and politically inventive and contested visions of blackness and group identity and the more traditional ethnographic practice of seeing blackness—and to a lesser degree whiteness—as a seamless whole. Empirical data on female academic performance—success and failure—are presented from the research site in the fourth section of this analysis. The final section offers some possible implications.

Background/Cultural Context

Several years ago, I completed a multiyear study at a high school in Washington, DC, that is chronicled in several sources but most notably in my book, *Blacked Out: Dilemmas of Race, Identity and Success at Capital High* (Fordham, 1996). The most prevalent discontinuities I describe in the Capital High study can be subsumed under the rubric of resistance, both as conformity and avoidance. Embedded in an oppositional identity, resistance—both as conformity and avoidance—to the hegemony of whiteness was a primary finding of the study. Moreover, I found that this resistance was the common response among both the high-achieving and underachieving students, male and female, albeit it took different shapes and forms, as the above vignette suggests.

The first question that cries out for an answer might be stated as follows: How and why have resistance and other discontinuities become so central in the academic practices of the children of postintegration African-descended Americans? Why, despite improved social and economic conditions, are so few contemporary African American students succeeding in school? Why are the sons and daughters of upper- and middle-income African Americans performing in school in ways that closely parallel their more economically disadvantaged peers? Why is socioeconomic class not a distinction in the academic performance of contemporary African-descended adolescents? In other words, why are the black children whose parents own homes in Cleveland's Shaker Heights (and other middle- and upper-income areas) and the black children whose parents qualify for subsidized housing in East Baltimore, for example, performing at about the same level on standardized examinations? In fact, in a recent announcement from the Shriver Center at the university where I was then employed, the following claim was made: "On average, only three percent of Baltimore City's third and fourth graders read on grade level. . . ." The writer goes on to claim that she is sharing this shocking statistic in order to convince her readers of the desperate need for reading tutors at the identified elementary school. Let us put aside, for the moment at least, doubts about the accuracy of the writer's claim. If on average 97 percent of Baltimore City's public school students (who are primarily African American) are failing to read on grade level, are cultural discontinuities the explanation or at least a critical component of the explanation? Moreover, aren't there students from other social groups who are doing well academically but who are also experiencing cultural discontinuities in school?

The answer to the latter question is an unequivocal yes. There are many students from different social groups who are doing well in school, despite the existence of cultural discontinuities. However, as John Ogbu (1988) notes, there are at least two kinds of discontinuities critical to academic success: primary and secondary. According to Ogbu, these primary discontinuities predate contact with a dominating population, e.g., language; in striking contrast, secondary discontinuities evolve out of the shared experiences of a particular social group and a dominating population, e.g., the oppositional identity of African Americans. It is, in fact, then, researchers' failure to historicize the school behaviors and practices of different social groups that weakens the explanatory potential of their analyses.

Secondary discontinuities were implicated in the academic performance of the students I studied at Capital High. The first and most prominent was resistance. As noted above, this ubiquitous response pattern was found among both males and females, high-achieving and underachieving. Time does not permit me to offer in-depth examples but, as I have noted elsewhere (Fordham, 1996), resistance was manifested in both the conformity of the high-achieving students and the avoidance of the underachievers. Since resistance as avoidance is less familiar and less likely to be thought of as a secondary discontinuity, the most prevalent examples offered in this paper are intended to illuminate what I found at Capital High and how resistance as conformity evolved out of the historical relationship between black and white Americans. First, a brief reference to the conceptual frame.

The Conceptual Frame: Fictive Kinship[1]

Among African-descended Americans, kinship is socially constructed broadly to embrace all members of the community.[2] While fictive kinship is a term used by anthropologists to describe the relationship between people in a society who are not related by blood or marriage, but who nonetheless have some social or economic relationship, among African Americans, it has a much broader meaning. Within this community, the term conveys "brotherhood" or "sisterhood" of all black Americans. This collective social identity is evident in numerous kinship-like terms that black Americans use to refer to one another. Examples of the kinship and pseudo kinship terms most commonly used by adolescents and adults are "brother," "sister," "blood," "folk," and "my people" (Folb, 1980; Liebow, 1967; Stack, 1974). Here, fictive kinship is used to denote a cultural symbol of collective identity of black Americans, the term used to describe the particular mindset, that is, the specific worldview of those persons who are appropriately labeled "black." Since "blackness" is more than a skin color, fictive kinship is the concept used to denote the moral judgment the group makes on its members (Brain, 1972). Essentially the concept suggests that the mere possession of African features and/or being of African descent does not automatically make one a black person, nor does it suggest that one is a member in good standing of the group. One can be black in color but choose not to seek membership in the fictive kinship system and/or be denied membership by the group because one's behavior, activities, and lack of manifest loyalty are at variance with those thought to be appropriate and group specific.

Because fictive kinship symbolizes a black American sense of peoplehood in opposition to white American social identity, it is closely tied to their various boundary-maintaining behaviors and attitudes toward whites. An example is the tendency for black Americans to emphasize group loyalty in situations involving conflict or competition with whites. Furthermore, black people have a tendency to negatively sanction behaviors and attitudes they consider to be at variance with their group-identity symbols and criteria of membership. And, since only black Americans are involved in the evaluation of group members' eligibility for membership in the fictive kinship system, they control the criteria used to judge one's worthiness for membership, and the criteria are totally group-specific. That is, the determination and control of the criteria for membership in the fictive kinship system are in contrast to

[1] Most of this section and the case studies are taken from my book, *Blacked Out: Dilemmas of Race, Identity and Success at Capital High* (Chicago: University of Chicago Press).

[2] A detailed discussion of the meaning of fictive kinship in the African American community can be found in my book, *Blacked out: Dilemmas of Race, Identity and Success at Capital High* (Chicago: University of Chicago Press). (Fordham, 1996).

the determination and control of the criteria for earning grades in school or promotion in the mainstream workplace by white people. Fictive kinship means a lot to black people because they regard it as the ideal by which members of the group are judged; it is also the medium through which black people distinguish "real" from "spurious" members.

Black children learn the meaning of fictive kinship from their parents and peers while they are growing up. And it appears that the children learn it early and well enough so that they more or less unconsciously but strongly tend to associate their life changes and "success" potential with those of their peers and members of their community. Group membership is important in black peer relationships; as a result, when it comes to dealing with whites and white institutions, the unexpressed assumption guiding behaviors seems to be that "my brother is my brother regardless of what he does or has done" (Haskins, 1975). The important question is how fictive kinship enters into and affects the schooling of black females—and males—in a school system where white hegemony reigns.

Race Passing: Acting White

The setting of the study, Capital High School and its surrounding community, has been described in detail elsewhere (Fordham, 1996). Suffice it to say here that Capital High is a predominantly African American high school (some 99 percent African American, or 1,868 out of 1,886 students at the start of the research effort in 1982). It is located in a historically African American section of Washington, DC, in a relatively low-income area.

While the pervasiveness and influence of fictive kinship are extensive among African American students, both male and female, it is not the primary reason for the widely noted underperformance of the students at the research site. Rather, it is their way of coping with the reign of whiteness in the curriculum and organizational structure of the school. Fictive kinship is evident not only in conflicts between blacks and whites and between black students and black teachers, who are often perceived to be "functionaries" of the dominant society, but also in the students' constant need to reassure one another of the primacy of black loyalty and identity. They appear to achieve this group loyalty by defining certain attitudes and behaviors as "white" and therefore unacceptable, and then employing numerous devices to discourage one another from engaging in those behaviors and attitudes, that is, from "acting white, when it is not absolutely necessary."

Within the African American community, "acting white" is generally used as an epithet to convey the response of African Americans to the institutionalization of norms that are generated, imposed, and maintained by the larger, dominant community. As the students at the research site defined it, "acting white" entailed passing for the "Other" in the presence of black people. Capital students marked this response as acceptance of the dominance of whiteness, a political statement about whose views and ideas are to be promulgated. Most Capital students are consciously or unconsciously attempting to avoid dominating the black Other and evading domination by the black Other. The idea of dominating other black people is both a powerful conundrum for these students and a deterrent to academic excellence because they generally, albeit often unconsciously, construct the school's core curriculum as "racial text" (Castenell & Pinar, 1993), inevitably compelling undesired alterations and transformations in their perceptions of an appropriate black self. Moreover, since, as Michelle Wallace (1990, p. 41) asserts, "schooling has always been, first and foremost, a means of transmitting social values, not knowledge or power," black students' reluctance to embrace the values reflected in school-sanctioned practices undermines their teachers' confidence in their ability to master the proscribed knowledge and power. Indeed, the individualistic, capitalistic values sanctioned by the school are often in conflict with the idealized collective, egalitarian values attributed both to the African American community generally and the Capital community in particular. At the school, students had an inordinately long list of ways by which it was possible to act white, many of them directly related to behaviors in and outside the school and some directly related to the pursuit of academic achievement.

Interestingly, because black Washingtonians are both African and American, the Other is not totally *other*. The notion of a pristine or authentic racialized identity, uncontaminated by contact with another culture, is both not possible and a non-issue here. Acting white presupposes contact with an Other. It is therefore more than a set of behaviors; it is even more than the reluctance to act in ways that mimic white people. Central to the idea of "acting white" is Gramsci's (1971) notion of hegemony, that is, the maintenance of the existing system of power and domination through the celebration of practices and an ethic put in place by people who migrated primarily from Europe. While these powerful people may have, for example, appropriated and incorporated a black or an African ethic in their stories and texts (see, for example, Fishkin, 1993), their failure to publicly acknowledge a "multiplicity of voices" in either the "public transcript[s]" (Scott, 1990) or the footnotes of these transcripts negates the idea of a multiple ethic that includes the black self.

"Acting white" then is both unavoidable and inevitable, the inescapable outcome of American citizenship, American schooling, employment in America, and, as Scott (1990, p. 4) asserts, the embodiment of "the dialectic of disguise and surveillance that pervades relations between the weak and the strong . . . domination and subordination." While becoming white or the Other is not literally possible, that is not the issue. Rather, the issue is how the black self is symbolically dissolved and reconstituted (Kondo, 1986,

1990) as an Other in the ideological celebration of what is known as an American ethic, in the daily practices of living in America (see Gramsci, 1971; Castenell & Pinar, 1993). For many African Americans, acting white implies (1) acceptance of an ethic that is normed and nurtured by the dominant society and inevitably and unavoidably practiced by African Americans in the process of living in America; (2) tacit endorsement of what is written (text) as embodying African Americans' social realities; and (3) unwitting practice of the dominating ideology (Foucault, 1980) by controlling and dominating an Other, possibly including the domination of other black people. Many African Americans find this last possibility particularly abhorrent.

Accordingly, this inquiry migrates between an analysis that seeks to "give voice" to black Americans' culturally and politically inventive and contested visions of blackness and group identity and the more traditional ethnographic practice of seeing blackness—and, to a lesser degree, whiteness—as a seamless whole. It examines how female (and male) students who are doing well academically are able to do so and how other females (and males) who are underachieving manage to avoid academic success. More specifically, this analysis looks at how black adolescents achieve school success in a setting where the latent, though dominant, socially sanctioned ethos—at least as constructed by the black students at Capital High—seeks to reconstruct them to minimize their perceived connectedness to blackness and the African component of their hyphenated, hybridized identity.

While it is possible to argue, quite convincingly, that it is virtually impossible to avoid acting white in America, the students at this particular research site do not bring that level of sophistication to the chronicling of their everyday practices. Among the attitudes and behaviors the students at the school identify as "acting white" and therefore unacceptable include: (1) speaking standard English; (2) listening to white music and white radio stations; (3) spending a lot of time in the library studying; (4) getting good grades in school (those who get good grades are labeled "brainiacs"); (5) going to the opera or ballet; (6) going camping, hiking, or mountain climbing; (7) being on time; (8) reading and writing poetry; (9) putting on "airs"; and so forth. This partial listing indicates the kinds of attitudes and behaviors likely to be negatively sanctioned and therefore avoided by a large number of students at the school. Under these circumstances, students who want to do well in school must find some strategy to resolve the attendant tension. This tension, along with the extra responsibility it places on students who choose to pursue academic success and its effects on the performance of those who resolve the tension successfully and those who do not, constitute "the burden of 'acting white'." High-achieving students have learned to cope more successfully with the burden of acting white, whereas the underachieving students have not succeeded in a manner that enhances academic success. The following cases are intended to illuminate this point.

Achieving Successful Failure: The Female Students

Female Achievement: Losing by Winning

Blackness and femaleness are often constructed as mutually exclusive categories. Indeed, because blackness is routinely constructed as masculine, breasts on a black body are primarily viewed as symbols of sexuality and not necessarily femaleness or its analogue, goodness. Many writers explicitly or obliquely render the street a masculine social space, the site where impoverished bodies are compelled to live and where what is constructed as the most culturally "authentic" prevails in many black communities. The street as a masculine (black) cultural space is largely unchallenged even though its construction entombs black female bodies in an inappropriate gender aesthetic. Thus, while the problems confronting black females are different from those confronting black males, the impact is similar.

It is widely acknowledged that American women—regardless of race or class—are socially rewarded more for suffering than for achievement (Brown, 1998). Indeed, suffering and success are inextricably interwoven in an essentialist, female-specific reward system that, ironically, compels girls to find prestige in losing, not winning. Indeed, because suffering is generally affiliated with loss and losing, in most socially competitive situations, American females win by losing. Among American women of African descent, this normalized female-specific mantra is both imposed and resisted, its social impact intensified and exacerbated by their racialized identity. Hence African-descended females' resistance, revealed in their self-reported high self-esteem ratings and their prepubescent voice, visibility, poise, and confidence, is reframed by the larger society as loudness and/or aggression—inappropriate qualities for (adult) female bodies.

Not surprisingly, then, in the classroom context, adolescent black girls' connection to a stigmatized racial status—blackness—and an inappropriate femaleness (i.e., confidence and high self-esteem), jeopardize their academic achievement goals. For example, "Mychild," the daughter of the only teacher who allowed her child to attend Capital High, was severely punished by her teacher for her confidence and academic performance and, at least in her mother's perception, for being an African American female. Ms. Costen, a physics teacher at Capital High, was the doting mother of Mychild, an early-admission student who was in tenth grade at the age of fourteen. Like two of the high-achieving students in my sample, Paul and Katrina, Mychild won first place in her chosen category at the science fair. This was a very prestigious honor and reflective of the commitment she and her mother made to gender-specific border crossings. Ms. Costen worked hard to help her daughter—Mychild—win the first place prize at the science fair and the border crossings her winning conveyed. For example, on a daily basis for more than a month, she took Mychild to Georgetown University during the school's one lunch hour so that she could obtain one-on-one instruction from the appropriate professors there.

> [Ms. Costen shared with me] . . . the problems she [encountered] obtaining excuses from her daughter's [female] German teacher during the last week [in order] to work on her [science] project. Her German teacher, Ms. O'Brian, demanded that before she could be readmitted to class after having been absent the previous day, she had to obtain a signed excuse. [In her role as a teacher at the school] Ms. Costen . . . wrote Ms. O'Brian a note telling her why her daughter had been absent from class: she was working on her science project. This did not satisfy Ms. O'Brian; she [insisted on] an excuse from Ms. Aster, the teacher-sponsor of the [science] fair [at Capital]. . . . Ms. O'Brian's behavior annoyed Ms. Costen because, as she saw it, [Mychild] had one of the best averages in [Ms. O'Brian's] German class. . . . Ms. Costen perceived Ms. O'Brian's behavior as harassment of her daughter [as well as competition between the two of them], and she is determined to see that Ms. O'Brian teach "Mychild" well. [Ms. Costen's] daughter does extremely well in [Ms. O'Brian's German] class. . . . "Mychild" has an A average in the class and [ironically] that [appears to] annoy Ms. O'Brian. . . . [O]ne day when the class took an exam, ["Mychild"] finished well in advance of the other students, put her pencil down, lay her head on her desk and closed her eyes as if she were asleep. . . . Ms. O'Brian (who apparently read her behavior to mean that she found the test too easy and was bored) was not amused! she insisted that ["Mychild"] sit up. She did. Ms. Costen went to talk with her [about the incident] and told her that she was going to have to "teach 'Mychild'" because [according to Ms. Costen, she] was going to be on [Ms. O'Brian's] case like "white on rice." (Fieldnotes, March 8, 1983)

Mychild's mother's investment in her daughter's scientific training produced the desired outcome in that she won first prize in her category at the science fair, propelling her to exceed the general expectations for all students at Capital but especially the female students in this male-dominated area of study. At the same time, however, it was counterproductive in that her efforts to cross the gender-specific limitations imposed on the black female adolescent's body severely altered her relationship with her German teacher and, through the grapevine, other teachers at the school. Ironically, it was Mychild's mother's support—her efforts to help her daughter win—that both transformed and subverted her success.

At Capital High, the female students—both high-achieving and underachieving—were generally outperforming their male peers academically. While their higher grades and more acceptable deportment were widely noted, this knowledge did not result in either a concerted effort to understand why a larger percentage of the female students were doing better than the male students or a collective effort to expand the number of female achievers.

Rather, the typical response was to mourn the lower male achievement. For example, Ms. Yanmon, the counselor for the advanced placement or high-achieving students, did not give me Katrina's name for several weeks even after she had identified several high-achieving males and, to be fair, a few high-achieving female students. Clearly annoyed by her own son's less than stellar performance at an exclusive private school in suburban Maryland and the higher academic performance of the female students at Capital (Katrina would graduate valedictorian of the class), Ms. Yanmon succumbed to her ambiguity regarding female academic achievement by mourning:

> Capital has not had a male [valedictorian] in about 10 years. . . . The girls do better [academically than the boys]. . . . (Fieldnotes, 1983)

Like the Sonya example cited earlier, the high-achieving female students' academic success was often viewed as a threat to the male students' survival—as males. Ms. Yanmon's response to Katrina's academic success suggested a belief that the female students' higher academic performance was in some unarticulated way harming the male students. And, indeed, the female students were often forced to pay an enormous price for outperforming their male peers. This was clearly evident in many aspects of the discourse styles and practices of the students and the adults. For example, that Katrina would graduate valedictorian of her class annoyed her male classmates tremendously. Two of them, Paul and Norris, noted how this aggravated them and jokingly indicated that they should "throw her from the train" in order to eliminate her as a competitor.

Katrina felt the stranglehold of this perception in most of the cavities of her life but most notably at home.

> [Katrina] . . . lamented the fact that her mother and father never praise her for her work in school. When she showed her mother her report card last advisory, she said her mother's only comment was, "I see you changed the B's to A's" (she received two B's the first advisory). When I suggested that perhaps her mother was also behaving as she (Katrina) claims she is behaving (trying to minimize the disappointment associated with the inability to keep up the track record as well as the negative consequences associated with boasting), she noted how differently her mother reacted to her [younger] brother's grade improvement last advisory. She said her mother gave him lots of compliments, telling him how proud she was of him, etc. I suggested that perhaps it was because he was younger. That, too, did not go over very well. She refused to believe anything other than that her parents were not proud of her performance. (Fieldnotes, February 22, 1983).

Katrina's parents are concerned about her and want to be supportive of her development as a proper young lady. Hence, they emphasize conformity as the way to resist the low expectations for African American females. At the same time, however, they are fearful of her desire to leave home—both metaphorically and literally. Most of their fear relates to her developing sexuality. Interestingly, she does not read their strict constraints and curfews as evidence of both support and fear; rather, she perceives these unilateral limitations as unmitigated lack of support.

Katrina acknowledges that she has put brakes on her school achievement both because she "reads" her parents' practices as not caring and because she fears alienating her peers. This double-barrel perceived threat has led to a sense of alienation or "affective dissonance" between her and the larger black community. She has come to view most black Americans as not desiring to "make it," as being too lazy to persevere for upward mobility. Her lack of a diachronic perspective regarding African Americans' pre-enslavement history reinforces this perception, which is then reinforced by her belief that black females are too dependent on black men for their sense of identity, a position she seeks to avoid. While she considers being female a burden, she does not make the same judgment regarding blackness, attributing the massive poverty in the black community, for example, to black people's lack of desire to change their social and economic conditions and not necessarily the result of a racist social system.

While at some level the female informants, regardless of academic performance, consider black Americans responsible for their impoverished social status, it is the high-achieving females who dissociate themselves more behaviorally from the black community, deliberately avoiding black music, rock concerts by black stars, and TV programs that focus on the "lifeways of black people." Consequently, these high-achieving female students' knowledge of black life and culture is rudimentary at best.

Female Underachievement: Winning by Losing

In striking contrast, the underachieving female students appear to be much more involved in what is generally described as black life and culture. They belong to predominantly black churches, or at least the congregation of their particular church is black; and they enjoy black music and other forms of black entertainment. Indeed, in many ways they tend to avoid activities and entertainment forms that could conceivably be described as non-black activities, activities that might put one at risk of being described as "acting white."

An underachieving female at Capital, Sakay experienced inordinate conflict around race, gender, and academic success: she could not do well in school without seeing that performance as a violation of the intersection of these multiple identities. It was not until she reached the age of puberty that this conflict arose. However, her official excuse for why her grades began to fall does not reflect this conundrum. At the conscious level, Sakay is only aware that her academic performance began to decline when she was in the ninth grade.

Sakay's performance on the administered standardized exams—PSAT, CTBS, and LSE—was so high that she was one of only five students at Capital selected for possible designation as an Outstanding Negro Merit Scholar. But although her scores demonstrate unqualified mastery of the subject matter, her grade point average indicates that she is failing or almost failing most of the courses she is taking as an eleventh-grade student.

Sakay's performance on standardized measures of school success were virtually ignored at Capital because her grades were so low. Her contradictory performance led many of her peers as well as her teachers and other adults to describe her as being "lazy," a euphemism for an unwillingness on her part to put forth the effort necessary to perform well in class on a day-to-day basis. This is not a valid explanation or assessment.

When asked to explain the discrepancy between her exceptional performance on standardized measures of school success and her dismal GPA, Sakay implied that avoidance is the key:

> I figure that I do better on the standardized tests because it just goes over general stuff—you know, stuff that I think tenth- and eleventh-graders are supposed to know. And in my classes, it's—when I go over the work or something, like, if I do work in class, I have the examples right there before me, and I get lazy, because, okay, I have the formula—maybe A equals 7X squared or something like that—I have the formula sitting right in front of me, so if I forget it, I can just refer back to it. But when I take a test for my class, it's like, "Oh-oh, you forgot the formula. You should have remembered it, you should have went over it." And then I start panicking, and then I know I'm not going to remember it. So I just say, "Well, I'll just do it the next time." And after a while I'll start trying to improve, but by then it's affected my grade already. (Interview, February 4, 1983)

Like most of the underachieving students, Sakay admits that the primary reason for her unacceptably low grades is a lack of effort, or time she devotes to a task. She attends most of her classes most of the time. The time she devotes to homework and studying, however, is severely limited.

> I hate studying. It's just going home, and opening your book—I think the problem is, not just with me, but with a lot of [Black] kids—they need lot of . . . somebody looking over their shoulder all the time, saying you know, you know, pushing to make sure you do your homework, and you do your classwork . . . In classwork, I feel my classwork is pretty good. But the homework brings it down—or not doing the homework brings it down. And, I don't know, I'm just going to have to work with it. (Interview, February 4, 1983)

There is more than mere abhorrence of the idea of studying involved here. Sakay does not believe that her performance on school measures of success will lead to rewards commensurate with that effort. She also asserts that other African American adolescents share her perception. This implies either that they doubt the avoidance or disbelieve the efficacy of potential academic accomplishments to erase a stigmatized Self, or it implies that they choose to avoid erasing the Self and accepting Otherness. Kaela admits that most Capital students are not self-starters in the academic arena; many have to be literally "compelled" to perform academically assigned tasks. This suggests resistance. Sakay is only partially conscious of why she and the other black students at Capital do not put forth the effort necessary to achieve academic distinction. But her lack of awareness in no way diminishes her involvement in the conflict between white and black worldviews operating at Capital High.

Failing Academic Success: The High-Achieving Males

Like the underachieving black students in the sample, who appear to have the ability to do well in school or at least better than their present records show, the male students at Capital High who are relatively successful academically also face the problem of coping with the "burden of acting white." But they have usually adopted strategies that enable them to succeed. These students decide more or less conspicuously (1) to pursue academic success and (2) to use specific strategies to cope with the burden of acting white.

Norris is a high-achieving male student who has developed specific strategies for coping with the burden of acting white. His performance results on the verbal and math sections of the PSAT were at the 85th and 96th percentiles, respectively. His scores on the CTBS were similarly impressive. His overall grade equivalent in every section—reading, language, math, reference skills, science, and social studies, as well as in every subsection—is at the college level (13.6 overall grade equivalent [OGE]).

Norris has maintained an outstanding academic record since elementary school, where he was recommended to skip the fifth grade. He graduated from Garden Junior High as the valedictorian of his class. He also received several ancillary awards, including the "most improved student" and "the most likely to succeed." He earned all As in his first semester at Capital High, taking advanced placement courses. His cumulative grade average is A.

How does Norris do so well in school and still engage in resistance? Norris has faced the problem of resistance since his elementary school days, when he discovered that he was academically ahead of other students, and that these students did not like anyone like himself doing well academically. He says that what has been critically important in his acceptance by his peers, even though he is a good student, is his appearance of not putting forth much academic effort. At the elementary and junior high school levels, where his peers thought that Norris got good grades without studying, they attributed his academic success to his "natural talent" or special gift. Therefore they did not view him as a pervert "brainiac."

The public elementary school he attended was "filled with hoodlums, thugs, and the dregs of society," in his own words. Fighting was a frequent pastime among the students. Under these circumstances Norris's strategy was to choose friends who would protect him in exchange for his helping them with homework assignments and tests. He explains the strategy as follows:

> I didn't want to—you know—be with anybody that was like me, cause I didn't want to get beat up. The school I went to, Berkeley, was really rough, see? It was really tough, you know. Lived in the projects and everything, and known tough and everything. So I used to hang with them. If anybody ever came in my face and wanted to pick on me, they'd always be there to help me. So I always made sure I had at least two or three bullies to be my friends. Even though if it does mean I had to give up answers in class . . . I was willing to give up a little to get a lot. So I did that for elementary school. Then, by the time I got to junior high school, I said, "Forget it. If people don't tend to accept me the way I am, that's too bad. I don't need any friends, I have myself."

His alliance with "bullies" and "hoodlums" worked in elementary school. At the junior high level, he had a second factor in his favor, namely, his growing athletic prowess. This helped to lessen the image of him as a brainiac. But he also deliberately employed another strategy, this time acting as a clown or comedian. He explains it this way:

> [In junior high school] I had to act crazy then . . . you know, nutty, kind of loony, they say . . . [the students would then say], "He's crazy," not a class clown, to get on the teachers' nerves, I never did that to them -around them. I'd be crazy. As soon as I hit that class, it was serious business . . . Only the people who knew me knew my crazy side, when they found out I was smart, they wouldn't believe it. And [t]he people that knew that I was smart, wouldn't believe it if they were told that I was crazy. So I went through that. I'm still like that now, though.

Norris continues his comedian strategy at Capital High. He says that it is important for him to employ this strategy because he wants to do well in order to go to college on scholarships. All the high-achieving students wrestle with the conflict inherent in the unique relationship of black people with the dominant institution: the struggle to achieve success while retaining group support and approval. In school, the immediate issue is how to obtain good grades and meet the expectations of school authorities without being rejected by peers for acting white.

Conclusions/Implications

I have argued that African American female (and male) students wrestle with the conflict inherent in the unique relationship of black people with dominant American institutions: the struggle to achieve success while retaining group support and approval. This is especially problematic for African American girls who are doubly burdened with the desire to have both race-specific and within-group males' approval. As is the case with racial isolation, male disapproval is a strong deterrent to independent actions/reactions. In what passes for male domination within the African American community, black females are compelled to either live by the patriarchal rules or self-select themselves out of the dating and mating and the procreating game. In school, the immediate issue is how to obtain good grades while meeting the expectations of school authorities without being rejected by peers for acting white.

In the case of the female students, one might ask how their response pattern is a mirror reflection of the Sonya story I offered at the beginning of this analysis. How are black girls routinely eliminated from the highest echelons of the adult economic game by their high school course selections? How are their parents', particularly their mothers', economic status and gendered worlds implicated in their daughters' school performance?

Well, first there are so many females at the research site whose distorted and/or limited views of their futures are reinforced by school officials. They are denied the opportunity to fail because teachers and other school officials will not permit them to take the advanced placement courses at the school, not because they lack the academic ability but because they have displayed behaviors considered inappropriate for females. Most often, these officials will attempt to absolve themselves of the irresponsibility in the resulting failure of these students by insisting that, unlike Sonya, who insisted on being given an opportunity to fail, most of the female (and male) students at the school do not want to take the advanced placement courses. When I was a kid and did not want to do something, I remember my mother's constant advice that her adult status and experience had taught her: "It's good for you." Regrettably, so many teachers at this school permit these preadult females to act as if they are making informed decisions when they say "I don't want to do that" or "I won't do that." So many girls at Capital need the unwanted advice that my mother and adults in general give adolescents: "It's good for you." This is an important orientation because it compels adults to do what they have always been expected to do: protect the young. The fact that black girls (and boys) do not seek to take the advanced placement courses and that their parents do not come to the school to challenge the school experts is no excuse. At some point, *in loco parentis* has to mean something.

At the same, it must be acknowledged that the data presented here suggest that even when black girls do well academically, their success is essentially a phyrric victory, a victory so costly, in fact, that many girls opt not to seek it in order to avoid the viciousness of the pain.

Among the black males at Capital High, the challenge of academic success is defined by how one resists the dominating practices of the school and, by extension, the larger society. Underachieving males cope by avoiding academic success, while high-achieving males cope by conforming to the academic standards necessary for success. Both groups resist being labeled "acting white" by adopting behaviors and attitudes that enable them to retain a highly valued marker of success: their link to peers and the black community. It is around this link that black male identity is constructed and maintained. Like John Wideman (1984), black males at Capital High endure their link to the dominant culture by adopting a series of masquerades to guide them through varied definitions of success.

What do these gender-specific academic responses teach us? First, like all human groups, African American females (and males) are strongly connected to their social and economic histories. Having been either totally excluded from publicly supported schooling both during enslavement and for approximately one hundred years thereafter, African American students who were born and schooled during the Second Emancipation[3] resist their recent inclusion—as internalization—in the American school system. While a few African American students resist by conforming to school-sanctioned norms and practices, in striking contrast, the vast majority resist through avoidance of the schooling process. In addition, even though the strategies are different, the high-achieving and underachieving students at Capital are marginalized vis-a-vis the central social space. Consequently, when as researchers we fail to historicize African Americans' contemporary practices and responses, we do them a disservice by subjecting them to a continuation of what produced their initial degradation. Second, in the case of African American males, they appear to be, albeit largely unconscious, engaged in "ritualized warfare" with dominant American males, with each group of males seeking to (re)claim ownership of specific public and private social spaces. The American system of public education appears to be one such space dominated by the norms and values of the male Other. In order to avoid being subordinated in that context, African American males fail academically primarily through lack of effort, inappropriate behaviors, and so on. The tethering of this response—the predominant response—to the structures of knowledge sanctioned and con-

[3]Elsewhere (Fordham 1996), I have identified African-Americans, as having lived through two emancipations. For a more detailed discussion of these two manumissions, see *Blacked Out: Dilemmas of Race, Identity and Success at Capital High* (Chicago: University of Chicago Press).

trolled by the male Other in the school context, ensures the survival of black maleness. Ironically, however, achieving successful failure in the academy reproduces subordination and continuous degradation, not social transformation. While it is important to consider other options—if there are others—we certainly have to ask ourselves if this is all there is.

REFERENCES

Brain, J. J. (1972). Kinship terms. *Man* 7(1), 137–138.

Brown, L. (1998). *Raising their voices: The politics of girls' anger.* Cambridge, MA: Harvard University Press.

Cary, L. (1991). *Black ice.* New York: Alfred A. Knopf.

Castenell, L. A., & Pinar, W. F. (1993). Introduction. In L. A. Castenell & W. F. Pinar (Eds.), *Understanding curriculum as racial text: Representations of identity and difference in education.* Albany: State University of New York Press.

Fishkin, S. F. (1993). *Was Huck black? Mark Twain and African-American voices.* New York: Oxford University Press.

Folb, E. A. (1980). *Runnin' down some lines: The language and culture of black teenagers.* Cambridge, MA: Harvard University Press.

Fordham, S. (1991). Racelessness in private schools: Should we deconstruct the racial and cultural identity of African-American adolescents? *Teachers College Record, 92*(3), 470–484.

Fordham, S. (1996). *Blacked Out: Dilemmas of Race, Identity and Success at Capital High.* Chicago: University of Chicago Press.

Fordham, S. (1997). A low score wins: Is high self-esteem compromising Black girls' academic achievement. Paper presented at the RISE Conference Proceedings. New Brunswick, NJ: Rutgers University, October 1999.

Foucault, M. (1977). *Intellectuals and power. Language, counter-memory, practice.* In D. F. Bouchard (Ed. and Tran.). Ithaca: Cornell University Press.

Gramsci, A. (1971). On intellectuals: Selections from the prison notebooks. Q. Hoare & G. N. Smith (Eds.), *Selections from the prison notebooks of Antonio Gramsci.* New York: International.

Grant, L. (1984). Black females' 'place' in desegregated classrooms. *Sociology of Education, 57,* 98–111.

Grant, L. (1994). Helpers, enforcers, and go-betweens: Black females in elementary school classrooms. In M. B. Zinn & B. T. Dill (Eds.), *Women of color in U.S. Society.* Philadelphia: Temple University.

Haskins, K. (1975). You have no right to put a kid out of school. In A. Tobier, Four conversations: The intersection of private and public. *The Urban Review, 8*(4), 273–287.

Kondo, D. K. (1986). Dissolution and reconstitution of self: Implications for anthropological epistemology. *Cultural Anthropology, 1*(1), 74–88.

Kondo, D. K. (1990). *Crafting selves: Power, gender, and discourses of identity in a Japanese workplace.* Chicago: University of Chicago Press.

Liebow, E. (1967). *Tally's corner: A study of negro street-corner men.* Boston: Little, Brown.

Ogbu, J. U. (1988). Understanding cultural diversity and learning. *Educational Researcher, 21*(8), 5–14.

Schofield, J. W. (1989). *Black and white in school: Trust, tension, or tolerance?* New York: Praeger.

Scott, J. (1990). *Domination and the arts of resistance: Hidden transcripts.* New Haven: Yale University Press.

Stack, C. (1974). *All our kin: Strategies for survival in a black community.* New York: Harper & Row.

Wallace, M. (1990). Modernism, postmodernism, and the problem of the visual in Afro-American culture. In R. Ferguson, M. Gever, T. T. Minh-ha, & C. West (Eds.), *Out there: Marginalization and contemporary cultures.* Cambridge, MA: MIT Press.

Weitz, R., & Gordon, L. (1993). Images of black women among Anglo college students. *Sex Roles, 28*(1/2), 19–33.

Wideman, J. E. (1984). *Brothers and keepers.* New York: Holt, Rinehart and Winston.

10 Comment

Cultural Discontinuity, Race, Gender, and the School Experiences of Children

Vivian L. Gadsden

Any cursory glance at the literature on African American children reveals the salience of cultural and social discontinuities between home and school and between the needs of African American children and the ability of schools to respond in effective and appropriate ways. Only within the past few years, however, have we attempted to examine critically the gendered experiences of African American children within schools and the complexity of the relationships around gender. In addition, we are just beginning to explore, despite considerable public and scholarly discussions, the connectedness existing between the expectations that schools and families hold for African American boys and girls and that these children hold for themselves and the ways in which these expectations are valued and supported by teachers, family members, and children's own peer groups.

This chapter was developed initially in response to Chapter 9, by Signithia Fordham, for the conference from which this volume is derived. It focuses, in part, on the work that Fordham has contributed to this volume, using her work as a lens to engage a critical discourse about the nature of African American boys' and girls' gendered experiences and relationships within school, home, and community settings.

This chapter is situated within the discussion of cultural continuities, not only as a response to Fordham's chapter but also for three additional reasons. The first is that the study of African American children has focused historically on their culture and racial identities, rather than on other personal and developmental dimensions. Their experiences have largely demonstrated the ways in which they manipulate and negotiate the discontinuities between home and school, not how society has prepared for their academic achievement. The second is that the gendered experiences of children in schools often represent a subset of cultural discontinuity, one in which the cultural expectations and valuing of male and female students are mapped onto ethnic and cultural history, tradition, beliefs, and practices. The third is that children's experiences are as likely, if not more likely, to be embedded within their home and community lives as within their school lives.

An initial premise around which this chapter is developed is that families and communities are amalgams of multiple cultural and ethnic beliefs and practices. Parents and other adults negotiate these beliefs and practices across different generations and transfer interpretations of them to their children. Whether children carry the practices and interpretations of cultural expectations across the boundaries of home into school influences their performance and may disrupt the cultural continuum to which they are exposed out of school. A second premise is that what is needed is greater understanding of the degree to which schools accommodate or integrate the gendered and cultural experiences of children and the degree to which they engage them in co-constructing a continuum of learning. This continuum is both based upon and combines the separate and shared social contexts and cultural expectations of home and school. However, as Fordham reminds us, the intragroup problems around cultural discontinuity are as great as, if not greater than, the intergroup concerns.

I include families in this discussion not simply because they are the context of much of my own research but primarily because families influence children's development and schooling in ways that we have yet to understand fully. Moreover, the schooling and education of children are family matters as much as they are school-based issues. How children acquire, understand, and value schooling, persistence, and culture may not reflect patterns of family knowledge entirely, but they contribute knowledge to and reflect the cultures of families, that is, the cumulative effect of history, experiences, and beliefs with which families identify from one generation to another.

This chapter is divided into four sections. The first focuses on broad issues of gender within schools. The second focuses on issues of race. The third provides two case studies, intended to focus on the degree to which race may engulf issues of gender. The fourth discusses gender, culture, and male and female learners in school based upon Fordham's analysis.

Gender Within School

Considerable research has focused on gender within educational and social science research over the past 30 years. Although the term, gender, and the practices and policies associated with it are a part of the national discourse, gender has been defined in relatively narrow ways. Citations on gender and its relationship to achievement, for example, typically focus on two primary domains: (1) comparative constructs of differences in behavior, cognitive ability, and achievement; and (2) feminist analyses, which point to the social inequities and historical subjugation and mistreatment of women and girls in schools and society. The focus on these two areas is neither inappropriate nor surprising. However, only recently have conceptualizations of gender moved past restrictive practices such as sex-typing or enabled us to understand the issues outside simplistic references to *female* and *male* as categorical variables.

Research on gender and school over the past ten years has aimed to expand traditional conceptualizations and analyses of gender issues. Such work focuses on a broader range of populations—i.e., cultural and ethnic groups, age ranges, developmental frameworks, and life-course issues. It has examined the definitions and interpretations of gender and learning and of gender ideology; it has explored the assessment of gender differences within diverse social and cultural contexts (Cole, 1997; Sadker & Sadker, 1994). It has highlighted a range of other issues such as gender development and gender effects (Eisenberg et al., 1996), including questions about the development of gender identity, knowledge, preferences, social behaviors, and emotional responses; gender and developmental differences in the academic study of elementary students (Hancock et al., 1996); gender attitudes, e.g., among talented and gifted students; and access to information, knowledge, and structures that promote mathematical and science ability, athletic ability, and social status among and for girls and women (Meece & Jones, 1996; Updegraff et al., 1996).

Despite changes in the conceptualizations and the range of research, gender studies continue to be limited in their ability to deepen our understanding of the nature and intensity of gender as an asset or detractor within and outside of racial categories. For example, most of the research over the past thirty years has focused on girls, and typically on white girls. Critical analyses of male behaviors, in relationship to and separate from female behaviors, opportunities, and changing perceptions, are still conspicuously absent. Perhaps the issue of greatest interest and concern, however, to many researchers of color is the absence of a rigorous discourse about students of color, e.g., African American girls or Latinas or African American boys that is not based upon deficit models of behaviors and indictments of their cognitive ability and performance (Gadsden & Smith, 1994; Gadsden & Bowman, 1999; Myers & Dugan, 1996).

Two other limitations appear to exist. The first addresses the complex relationships among gender, sexual preferences, and the effects and implications of labels such as "lesbian" and "gay," as adapted by and imposed upon students, not only because of the acknowledgment by growing numbers of students of their same-sex preferences but also because of the physical threat and intellectual obstacles that such acknowledgment creates for these students.

The second concerns gender and its impact over the life course, within and outside of educational structures. Although there are some studies that focus on college-age students, graduate students, and university faculty, they are few and usually focused on women (see Hawkins, 1995, for example). Not even for women, however, do we have a good portrait of what the problems are, what changes have resulted in what options, and what the effects have been for women with diverse cultural and ethnic backgrounds (Hill-Collins, 2000).

Related Issues of Race

Three decades after the passage of the Civil Rights Act and four decades after school desegregation, Americans still struggle with issues of race and racism and the practices, beliefs, and attitudes associated with this reality in society. The persistence of this struggle may be attributed to a variety of factors but may emanate from the sense that race is deeply entrenched in society, has intergenerational impact, and has complex roots. How people construct race often dictates how they look at the world and has functioned historically to the advantage of particular individuals and groups. Smedley (1993) notes that the ideological components of race persist as part of a fixed conception of the world. This conception is as likely to serve the needs of scientists as of lay persons.

Over the past decade, analyses and discussions about race have become notably visible and significant within educational and social science research. They are rooted in discourses carrying the banner of " race, class, and gender," to denote their relationship to other factors that have been used historically to oppress students in schools and individuals within society. The focus on race demonstrates the ways in which schools mirror society—both the problems and the submersions of possibility. Whether through quiet or subtle rejections of race and racism as salient issues or through vocal denouncements of their significance, the mere mention of the words "race" and "racism" either captivates or evokes discomfort. Attempts to move beneath surface references and examples are often replaced by terms more likely to reduce discomfort and to increase the engagement of non-minority audiences of students and professionals. Within these discussions, for example, culture is a more palatable concept than race, and race is preferred to racism.

Attitudes toward race and the effects of racism influence the lives of all people, both those who are affected negatively by discriminatory and racist practices and those who perpetrate the practices themselves. Racism is often described as a modern idea, associated with western culture and beginning after the seventeenth century (Smedley, 1993). As Smedley notes, contemporary social scientists "deplore" racism, seeing it as an "abominable product of the lay person's confused misconception of the 'true' or 'real' meaning of race" (Smedley, 1993, p. 291). She asserts that if people were made cognizant of the actual scientific understandings of biological differences, then the irrational prejudice associated with racism would disappear. Similarly, proponents of desegregation suggest that the greater a child's familiarity with the values and lifestyles of others, the greater will be his or her potential appreciation of racial differences (Gadsden, Smith, & Jordan, 1997).

Race Over Gender? Two African American Students Placed At-Risk

Fordham's analysis of the treatment of African American girls asks us to examine the problems that these girls face at the same time that we recognize the uniqueness of children in each gender group and the risks to which they are exposed, irrespective of gender. These risks exist largely because of what may be considered the inextricability of gender and race for African American students, boys and girls, and the salience of race in African American students' school lives. Race then may be seen as a definer of both the school and life experiences of African American students, the perceptions that they and their teachers hold of their ability, and the way that African American boys' experiences in schools approximate those of African American girls. Consider, for example, the school lives of two African American boys, one living and attending school in a low-income, urban community and the other in an upper-income, suburban community.[1] What are the ways in which their experiences converge with or differ from each other's experiences, from those of other African American male students such as the students described by Fordham, and from those of African American girls? Equally important is how are they similar to or different from those of white boys and girls?

Tommy

Tommy is a seventh grader who attends middle school in a severely low-income community in Philadelphia. His school is 95 percent African American and 5 percent Latino. The school has approximately 530 students in grades six through eight. All of the students are low income, and the school has been designated a Title I School. The staff and faculty are African American and white, about 50 percent falling into each group. Both the principal and vice principal are African American men, and Tommy's teacher is an African American woman.

Although Tommy is in seventh grade, he has been assessed as reading at a third-grade level. This is particularly problematic because the content of most third-grade level passages are of little interest to Tommy. He gets frustrated with the third-grade reading passages and demonstrates his frustration in a number of ways, for example, misspelling words such as "day,"

---

[1]The author thanks Wanda Brooks who provided the case study of Tommy. Both case studies have been referred to in previous commentaries by the author.

"his," and "its," which he knows well, and forgetting to use basic rules of writing, such as capitalizing first words in sentences and ending them with punctuation. His seventh-grade reading and social studies books are too difficult for him to decode and to comprehend. As a result, Tommy completes almost none of his assigned classwork if it involves much reading and writing. Reading, language arts, social studies, and science are all subjects that "frighten him."

No one is quite sure how Tommy has managed grades one through six. Perhaps because he is extremely quiet and not a behavior problem, he has been passed on from grade to grade, despite his inability to read and write well. When he is sitting in class, the look on his face indicates his discomfort with what is occurring. Several teachers have commented about his "black-outs" or "aimless staring into space." Unlike many students, he does not act out his academic frustration aggressively by becoming disruptive in class. Instead, when he should be completing a writing assignment or reading pages from his assigned novel, he is writing rows of numbers over and over again on his paper. Tommy says this repetitive activity keeps him calm and helps him concentrate.

Tommy's teachers are unsure about how to help him. They indicate that he is very far behind and that the school, mired in inner-city academic failure and inadequate financial and personnel resources, is home to many children such as Tommy. Like Tommy, these children are years behind in their literacy development. Teachers comment that "many children need so much more than is humanly possible to give in one school year, even for the best of teachers." Tommy is offered, however, what his teachers are able to provide. For example, last year he attended tutoring one day a week after school, and this year he is assigned to the schoolwide reading specialist for remedial help in reading for one period a day.

In one class, Tommy works with two students identified as "special education" and other nonclassified students needing additional help with reading and writing. There are seven children in all who receive additional assistance. Tommy is performing at a level lower than the identified "special education" students. In his other seven classes, however, he is just one among thirty-three students hoping for a little individualized attention from his teachers. He is failing miserably in every subject except math. However, his school achievement records do not reveal the reasons for this performance. There is no evidence that Tommy has ever been the subject of an instructional support team's review.

Tommy's teacher provided a summary of whether the school and Tommy's teachers could promote positive outcomes for him. She indicated that with the help at home and some increased attention to his literacy problems at school, Tommy will most likely make some progress. This progress may not be enough, however, at this late stage. The chances of his catching up before entering eighth grade are slim. In fact, the chances of his being passed on to eighth grade are even slimmer. Yet, simply retaining him for one year may not eliminate but further perpetuate a cycle of failure that began when he first entered school seven years ago.

Since Tommy is approximately five grades behind in his literacy development, he would need an extensive amount of classroom support, in-school support, and home support to further develop his lagging literacy skills. For instance, all of his teachers, not only his reading and language arts teachers, would need to become involved in this effort. Classes such as science and social studies both require extensive amounts of reading and writing in the middle-school grades.

Once these teachers became aware of his problems, accommodations could be made in the classroom to have Tommy engage in partnered reading or offering him time before or after school to read the class material with the help of a teacher or tutor. Other accommodations in his reading and language arts classes can be made for Tommy as well, such as providing him with specialized spelling or vocabulary lists that match his learning needs. Additionally, individualized reading and writing activities would be beneficial to enhancing his literacy skills. Outside of the classroom, Tommy should receive tutoring and continue to see the reading specialist. However, the time spent in tutoring and with the reading specialists must be substantial and consistent, neither of which may be guaranteed. Lastly, the continued support of his mother is going to be crucial. She can monitor his homework and offer him literacy opportunities, like going with him to the library to select books he is interested in, checking his homework, reading to and with him, helping him study, and being in close contact with all of his teachers.

When asked what she might imagine for Tommy, his teacher responded:

> Considering how academically behind Tommy is, I hope he is able to complete high school successfully, without failing a grade or dropping out. He is completely disinterested in and overwhelmed by a school system that has essentially neglected many of his learning needs and devalued his potential as a human being. Tommy comes from a family where dropping out of school is not unusual and to end this cycle he will need to overcome a great deal of academic failure. At a minimum, I hope this is possible, and I hope that Tommy becomes a high school graduate rather than a statistic.
>
> My hopes for Tommy are not unlike the hopes and dreams his Mother holds for him. She dreams for him, however, through the eyes of a parent and not a teacher. As his mother, she sees in Tommy much of herself. She knows how uninspired he is because she too felt the same way in school. On the other hand, she also knows how difficult her life has been because she did not graduate from high school and, subsequently, she desires so much more for her youngest son. Tommy's mother blames herself for his academic failure and is attempting to improve her life by going back to school while at the same time changing the downward academic spiral her son is on by giving him additional support at home. Indeed our dreams for Tommy are similar, despite the fact that our understanding of who and/or what is to blame for his academic failure is, in some regards, quite different.

Ian

Ian is a second grader in a public elementary school, located in an affluent suburb outside of Philadelphia. He is one of approximately twenty children in his class, the only child of African descent in his class and grade, and one of a handful of children of African descent in his school. His parents are both African émigrés. Both are employed, and the family enjoys a modest middle-class lifestyle. His father works two jobs; his mother works and is completing studies toward a nursing degree. Both parents have verbal fluency in English. Ian has a younger brother.

Ian's parents decided to move to their current neighborhood because they wanted to ensure the safety of their children and expose them to "good" schools. The parents are consumed by the desire for Ian and his younger brother to be good readers and good students. They spend a considerable amount of time reading to them, buying books (particularly folktales about Africa) for them, taking them to museums, and engaging them in educational activities. They participate fully in all of the parent–child interactions that have been associated with successful readers and school achievement.

Ian is highly verbal in English and well read. He is a sensitive boy who is as comfortable talking about the history of his parents' homeland and the African continent as about the events of his day at school. However, although Ian appears to have "bought into" the belief that literacy is important and performs well on literacy measures, it is not clear that his facility with literacy will result in positive outcomes. He was recently the focus of an instructional study team review in response to his teacher's request. He tested average or above average on every measure. Yet, throughout the review, every school person other than the psychologist reminded the group, the parents, and me of his problematic behavior, which includes responding with a blank stare rather than verbally, not following the rules, and not always following directions (rather, remaking the assignment into something interesting for him). The teacher has interpreted Ian's not following the directions as his not understanding the task but has little information about what the dialogue is between Ian and him when these moments of misunderstanding occur.

Despite his love of reading and other literacy activities, Ian's literacy future and continued school achievement are, at best, tenuous. Ian reports that he feels isolated and alone in his school. He does not appear to fit in; he is not like the other children, and the teachers are intolerant of his "defiant" behavior. Ian has reported that he is treated differently by his teachers. By first grade had assigned a range of negative characteristics to black boys, indicating his displeasure at being a black boy: "No one likes black boys." He is developing literate abilities and likes to read, write, solve puzzles, and learn about African culture. Yet his literacy may not be enough, and his parents fear that his literate abilities will decline because of his overwhelmingly negative attributions to black maleness in his school. If Ian is to achieve positive outcomes, he will need a range of other social supports, particularly if he continues in his current school. His literacy well may not be enough.

What would it take to ensure positive outcomes for Ian? I recently began working with Ian, at the request of his parents, although I have been conversing with his parents about him for more than a year. They asked me to attend his instructional support team review; they were unsure of what to expect. In fact, they were so unsure that they did not seem to understand fully until the day of the review that there were strong inclinations to place Ian in a learning-disabled setting. His scores on the tests extricated him from this future, and possibly the hard questions that the parents asked advantaged him and eliminated the possibility of his being labeled.

My interests are not simply around Ian's literacy but also are connected to the reality that Ian, neatly located in a system with ostensible resources, may fail or feel so marginalized that he does not achieve the positive outcomes that are possible for him. His status as the son of émigrés, as a boy of African descent, as a nonconformist in some ways, as a "strong personality," and as a child from a lower middle-income, black immigrant family living in an upper middle-income community do not suggest a bright future. Ian's problems currently do not revolve around literacy alone; however, his literacy seems to be among the first abilities to suffer in his current state of discomfort and unhappiness. Neither the range of needs nor the range of resources is yet clear to those of us who are working with and who care about Ian.

The problems experienced by Tommy and Ian are similar: They are both experiencing learning problems in school, and both have the support of their parents. What distinguishes the two are the differences in their social class and their access to human resources who can interrupt or intervene professionally on their behalf. How different are Tommy and Ian's experiences from those of African American girls—in origin, course, and consequence? Reports such as the American Association of University Women (1995) find that African American girls' experience in school is as difficult if not more difficult than that of African American boys, particularly for girls in desegregated schools.

In Fordham's analysis, the experiences of the protagonists in her account, Katrina and Norris, reflect greater disparity in the ways in which society, schools, and African American families themselves understand, mediate, and explain difficult school and life experiences for boys versus girls. The question that Fordham poses is one of differentiated quality of motivational and cultural experience, cultural valuing, and cultural expectation and treatment. Such differentiated quality affects how African American girls such as Katrina fare in school and in society and how they ultimately come to feel about themselves. What Fordham suggests is that we begin to deconstruct the gendered experiences of African American girls, as similar to and different from those of African American boys, making more problematic than we have in past analyses the ways in which race defines and assigns options and life-course trajectories to African American girls within and outside of school.

Gender, Culture, and the School Lives of African American Male and Female Learners

Fordham's analysis of cultural discontinuities calls attention to the ways in which critical discourses around cultural studies, education, race, and the social sciences both use and preempt simplistic explanations for public understanding of issues affecting African American boys such as Tommy and Ian, and for invisible cadres of African American girls. It denotes the imaging of African American children as low achievers. By focusing on these issues, Fordham aims to elucidate several compelling ideas that, at the very least, can be considered provocative—both in the way she isolates the ideas (e.g., by examining the separate and gendered lives of the African American boys and girls she studies) and in the way she reconnects these ideas and images (e.g., by highlighting the shared experiences, perceptions, and treatment of boys and girls within schools, families, and communities).

Fordham artfully presents her argument through several lenses. The first is established at the outset of her chapter. She begins by presenting two sides of an apparently single coin: the consequences of high academic performance on the one hand and the centrality of being given the opportunity to fail on the other. In early statements, Fordham constructs a continuum along which achievement and failure may be defined and placed at a variety of points. For example, by asking that she be allowed to fail, Sonya's father used the dominant cultural perspective held of African American children's cognitive ability in order to recapture the opportunity for his daughter to succeed. By not acquiescing to the school's assessment, Sonya's father created the possibility of breaking the continuity (and traps) that often reduce the options for children like Sonya to achieve long-held aspirations for success in school and life.

I would suggest, however, that Sonya's father did not simply "challenge school experts" and enable his daughter to "realize her dream"; he seamlessly reinforced in his daughter a sense of her own identity as a capable learner and a persister with the personal agency to eliminate barriers. At the same time that he reinforced this message, he interrupted, perhaps only temporarily, the continuity of a school culture in which the possibilities for African American students are constrained by assumptions about their inadequacy as learners and for families, who often are perceived as limited in their ability to contribute to the cognitive development and intellectual life of the children in them.

The second lens focuses on resistance. In most of the remainder of her chapter, Fordham examines resistance and discontinuities as interchangeable concepts. Here, I differ with Fordham and suggest that cultural discontinuities and resistance not be represented as comparable or interchangeable concepts. Rather, resistance might be identified as a subset of cultural discontinuities.

It may be defined as emotional withdrawal and in specific and discernible ways by time, i.e., when resistance occurs, and by race, i.e., who is resisting versus who assigns the label, resister.

Fordham reminds us that "embedded in an oppositional identity, resistance was a primary finding of (her) study." She refers to "resistance and other discontinuities" and asks why they have:

> Become so central to the children of post-integration African-descended Americans? Why, despite improved social and economic conditions, are so few contemporary African American students succeeding in school? Why are the sons and daughters of upper- and middle-income African Americans performing in school in ways that closely parallel their more economically disadvantaged peers? Why is class distinction not a distinction in the performance of contemporary African-descended adolescents?

These are important questions that may be explained in part by examining cultural discontinuities but demand a more expansive analysis than Fordham provides.

The third lens is situated within a larger discussion, which Fordham examines within and outside of the fictive kin framework. This includes the differentiated experiences of, treatment of, and responses to black boys versus girls as valued within school and family contexts. Fordham distinguishes between the experiences of black boys and girls, both in the perceptions of girls as more academically responsible and less nurtured and in the perceptions that black girls hold of themselves as sufficiently obfuscated, ignored, minimized, and reduced in relationship to black boys—within schools and families. These girls, as in the case Katrina, may not simply be accused of "acting white" but seem to find a place of comfort, solace, and acceptance in an identity that is oppositional to their peer group and perhaps family expectations. This search by black girls for a place to be accepted and to be themselves results not simply in others referring to their performance and actions as "acting white" but also in their wanting to escape the cultural discontinuities that they feel they represent.

The issue of "acting white" has become a topic of scholarly and public interest, particularly since Fordham's interview in the "New York Times" in the early 1990s. At Capital High, a setting in which there is a predominance of African American students, the problem takes on a form that is unsettling to many of us. The problems look a little different for middle and upper middle-income students who attend predominantly white schools as well as for black children from low-income homes. The images of achievement as oppositional to the cultural lives of African American children are so effectively positioned that white teachers, and many from other ethnic groups (frequently including African American teachers), and white children assign any academic achievement of black children as "acting white." Such interchanges may offer at least partial sources of thought in responding to Fordham's question: Why are the sons and daughters of upper- and middle-income African Americans performing in school in ways that closely parallel their less economically advantaged peers?

In the fourth lens, Fordham focuses on "possible secondary discontinuities," which Ogbu describes as those that explain the experiences of minority groups such as African Americans: "These are the shared experiences of a particular social group and a dominating population, e.g., the oppositional identity of African Americans." Throughout the remainder of her chapter, Fordham engages us in examples from her work at Capital High, focusing on the gendered experiences of a boy and a girl, Norris and Katrina, and the tension that typified their school lives as they attempted to achieve academically. She appropriately, I think, aims to examine the larger issues of family as a context and as a source of the discontinuity. Using "fictive kin" as her conceptual framework, Fordham draws a parallel between historical fictive kin and present-day interactions within and among African-descended people. She distinguishes between the anthropological description in which people in a society who are not related by blood or marriage have some social or economic relationship and the common meanings of kin among many African Americans, including a sense of "brotherhood," "sisterhood," and so on, "a cultural symbol of collective identity of black Americans."

This framework allows Fordham to locate a range of behaviors, practices, and beliefs often said to typify black culture. She denotes an intergenerational connection by indicating that these ways of thinking, behaving, and believing are transmitted from one generation to another. She then argues that the notions of group identity clash with the individual fear of challenging black group identity. This confrontation between the group identity and the individual identity of the black student creates a need for academically talented young black males to distinguish themselves from their peers, to move back and forth between different and black codes of language and conduct, black codes of language and thought, to demonstrate ingenuity and to gain and sustain acceptance from students who have had less academic success. At the same time, the students become almost fraudulent in the multiple images and personalities that they are forced to present in order to survive.

What Fordham's argument presents is the way in which cultures construct meanings within a specified time. We have a sense of how the children in Capital High form meanings to which they ascribe a group identity. However, these meanings are not necessarily located within the historical meanings of group identity among African Americans. What Fordham does not address are the changes in these meanings and attributions to race and racelessness over time. Definitions of group identity have changed to represent clear polarizations among those who negotiate the world of whites to ensure their personal success and those who are less successful. The group identity that is formed seeks cultural continuity along lines that are as likely not to be linked with a shared African ancestry as are likely to be linked. Rather, many group identities are a mixture of other formulations of culture that can be linked to experiences in society which involve race and negative racialized portraits and representations. They are derived from exposure to television and misperceptions of others' lives; responses to negative popular images; poor treatment in school, and limited vision by those responsible for children's well-being.

In other words, these students are drawing on constructions of group identity that are both a historical and grounded in contemporary problems. Cultural continuities within African American families, as historians from Blassingame to Guttman to Anderson to Holt imply, are rarely formed around negativisms but around a common expectation of strength and possibility. In this way, the children in Capital High have created cultural meanings that are discontinuous from earlier, historical meanings of group, kin, and education as the means to success.

Closing Considerations

There are four areas of consideration that I would like to propose: (1) that notions of cultural discontinuities be replaced with greater investments and analyses of historical continuities within groups on which we can build (what historical strengths and communities existed that "inspired" and motivated children); (2) to explore more deeply what black culture includes and how we will interrogate issues of intra- and interculturality; (3) that issues of gender, of masculinity and of womanhood, be examined more critically and explicitly within school and family context; and (4) that issues of race be explicitly examined within a cultural discontinuity framework.

REFERENCES

American Association of University Women. (1995). *How schools shortchange girls.* New York: Marlow and Company.

Anderson, J. D. (1988). *The education of Blacks in the South, 1860–1935.* Chapel Hill: University of North Carolina Press.

Blassingame, J. W. (1972). *The slave community: Plantation life in the antebellum South.* New York: Oxford University Press.

Bowman, P. (1995). Education, schooling, and fatherhood. In V. L. Gadsden and W. Trent (Eds.), *Transitions in the life-course of African American males.* Philadelphia: National Center on Fathers and Families, University of Pennsylvania.

Cole, M. (1997). Gender and power: Sex segregation in American and Polish higher education as a case study. *Sociological Forum, 12,* 205–232.

Eisenberg, N., Fabes, R. A., Karbon, M., Murphy, B. C., Wosinski, M., Polazzi, L., Carlo, G., & Juhnke, C. (1996). The relations of children's dispositional prosocial behavior to emotionality, regulation, and social functioning. *Child Development, 67,* 974–992.

Gadsden, V., & Bowman, P. (1999). African American males and the struggle toward responsible fatherhood. In V. C. Polite & J. E. Davis (Eds.), *African American males in school and society: Practices and policies for effective education.* New York: Teachers College Press.

Gadsden, V. L., & Smith, R. (1994). African-American males and fatherhood: Issues in research and practice. In V. L. Gadsden & W. Trent (Eds.), *Transitions in the life course of African-American males: Issues in schooling, adulthood, fatherhood, and families* (pp. 23–38). Philadelphia: University of Pennsylvania, National Center on Fathers and Families.

Gadsden, V. L., Smith, R., & Jordan, W. J. (1997). The promise of desegregation: Tendering expectation and reality in achieving quality schooling. *Urban Education, 31,* 381–402.

Hill-Collins, P. (2000, August). Plenary at the annual meeting of the American Sociological Association meeting, Washington, DC.

Gutman, H. G. (1976). *The Black family in slavery and freedom, 1750–1925.* New York: Pantheon Books.

Hancock, T. E., Stock, W., Kulhavy, R., & Swindell, L. (1996). Gender and developmental differences in the academic study behaviors of elementary school children. *Journal of Experimental Education, 65*(1), 18–39.

Hawkins, K. W. (1995). Effects of gender and communication content on leadership emergence in small task-oriented groups. *Small Group Research, 26,* 234–249.

Meece, J. L., & Jones, M. G. (1996). Gender differences in motivation and strategy use in science: Are girls rote learners? *Journal of Research in Science Teaching, 33,* 393–406.

Myers, D. J., & Dugan, K. B. (1996). Sexism in graduate school classroom—Consequences for students and faculty. *Gender and Society, 10,* 330–350.

Sadker, M., & Sadker, D. (1994). *Failing at fairness: How America's schools cheat girls.* New York: Maxwell Macmillan.

Smedley, A. (1993). *Race in North America: Origin and evolution of a worldview.* Boulder, CO: Westview.

Updegraff, K. A., Eccles, J. S., Barber, B. L., & O'Brien, K. M. (1996). Course enrollment as self-regulatory behavior: Who takes optional high school math courses? *Learning and Individual Differences, 8,* 239–259.

11 Culturally Appropriate Pedagogy

Janice E. Hale

Closing the Achievement Gap

There has been growing alarm about the multitude of problems in the African American community that have circumscribed the life chances of African American children: crime, violence, teen pregnancy, poor school perform-ance, and early termination of education, to name a few. It is the perspective of this model that these maladies are symptoms of a complex web of social and historical problems that have festered for centuries. There are, of course, many underlying causes that are very difficult and expensive to fix.

This model offers a solution that places the school at the center of the effort to achieve upward mobility for inner-city African American children. The school is the appropriate focal point, because *everyone is required* to attend school. Everyone does not have a functional family, everyone does not attend church, but everyone is required to attend school.

The model is divided into three components, pictured in Figure 11.1. The foundational component is the *instructional model,* which will be described below. The other two components, *instructional accountability infrastructure* and *cultural uplift,* support the instructional model.

The guiding principles of the model are:

- Connecting children to academic achievement
- It takes a whole village to raise a child.
- Children learn what they are taught.
- School is interesting.
- Learning is fun.

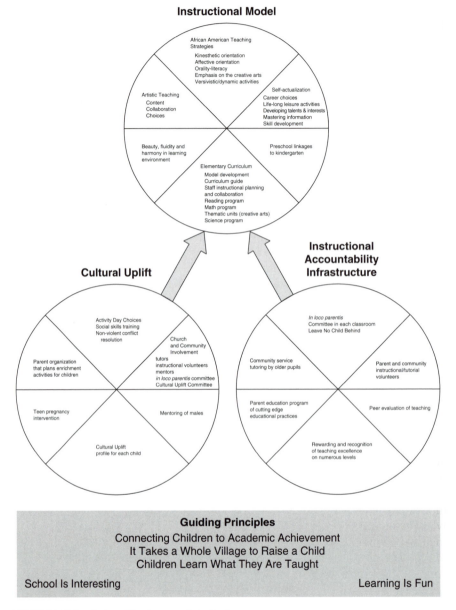

FIGURE 11.1 Culturally Appropriate Pedagogy

Conceptual Framework and Description of the Model

1. Instructional Component

This model makes the assertion that a key to improving the quality of the future for African American children is *connecting them to academic achievement*. Most African American children, particularly African American males, *do not like school.* Many drop out intellectually by the time they are in the fifth grade and make it legal at sixteen years of age. People who do not finish high school or those who finish with poor records are not able to obtain a job that is stable enough to support themselves or a family. Children who cannot conceptualize a future for themselves do not have the motivation to defer the gratification found in premature sexual activity or substance abuse.

The perspective of this project is that there are three purposes for educating children:

- Imparting skills such as the ability to read, write, spell, and calculate
- Creating information growth—there are things educated people know about the world
- Providing children with the opportunity to develop talents and interests that can lead to fulfilling leisure-time pursuits, the identification of careers, and an opportunity to make a creative contribution to the world

It is the perspective of this model that the way in which these purposes are achieved is just as important as what is taught. A process of education must be crafted that motivates African American children to regard academic activities to be interesting and fun. They must be guided on a journey to a lifelong love of learning.

Described herein are seminal ideas that lay the foundation for a new model that can create an educational process for African American children, which can build the bridges they need to enter the twenty-first century as independent, contributing members of our society. Ralph Ellison, author of *The Invisible Man*, has captured this craving that has come from African Americans throughout their sojourn in American for a culturally appropriate pedagogy:

> If you can show me how I can cling to that which is real to me, while teaching me a way into the larger society, then I will not only drop my defenses and my hostility, but I will sing your praises and I will help to make the desert bear fruit.

Theoretical Background of the Instructional Component

African American Teaching Strategies.   For the past thirty years, *remediation* programs have been the focal point for educational reform designed to benefit African American children. The critical issue now being raised is how we can create schools that educate African American children effectively wherever they are found. One theory is that there is a kind of "soulfulness" that characterizes African American life.

African American children are exposed to a high degree of stimulation from the creative arts. African American children learn from an early age the significance of perfecting performer roles. There are at least nine interrelated dimensions of African American culture outlined by Boykin (1983).

- Spirtuality, an approach to life as being essentially vitalistic rather than mechanistic, with the conviction that nonmaterial forces influence people's everyday lives
- Harmony, the notion that one's fate is interrelated with other elements in the scheme of things, so that humankind and nature are harmoniously conjoined
- Movement, an emphasis on the interweaving of movement, rhythm, percussiveness, music, and dance, which are taken as central to psychological health
- Verve, a propensity for relatively high levels of stimulation to action that is energetic and lively
- Affect, an emphasis on emotions and feelings, together with a special sensitivity to emotional cues and a tendency to be emotionally expressive
- Communalism, a commitment to social connectedness, which includes an awareness that social bonds and responsibilities transcend individual privileges
- Expressive individualism, the cultivation of a distinctive personality and a proclivity for spontaneous genuine personal expression
- Oral tradition, a preference for oral/aural modes of communication in which both speaking and listening are treated as performances and in which oral virtuosity—the ability to use alliterative, metaphorically colorful, graphic forms of spoken language—is emphasized and cultivated
- Social time perspective, an orientation in which time is treated as passing through a social space rather than a material one, in which time can be recurring, personal, and phenomenological

A. Wade Boykin (1979) suggests that the African American home environment provides an abundance of stimulation, intensity, and variation.

Therefore, African American children have an increased behavioral vibrancy and an increased psychological affinity for stimulus change and intensity. Boykin concludes that affective stimulation and vervistic stimulation are necessary for the African American child to be motivated to achieve in an academic setting. Boykin's research builds the case that in integrated settings the classroom organization that contains more stimulation would satisfy more students of both ethnic groups than the more monotonous settings in which most students are found today.

Specific Teaching Strategies Drawn from African American Culture

African American children are more kinesthetic than are white children and have a higher level of motor activity. Also, African American male children have a higher testosterone level than do white male children. Fewer demands should be placed on African American children in general and on African American male children in particular to sit still and engage in paper-and-pencil tasks for extended periods of time. Quiet activities should be alternated with active learning. Teachers should be trained to be patient with the rambunctious and outgoing nature of African American males. Conceptualizing these behavioral styles as normal will correct present tendencies to define African American males as needing medication and special education placement for emotional and psychological disorders.

There is strong affective orientation in child rearing in African American families. African American children learn best when their learning is "people oriented" as opposed to "object oriented." They will respond best when they are taught in small groups with a great deal of nurturing interaction between the teacher and the child and the child and his peers. In this model, a key activity will be to utilize parents and community volunteers to work with children with special needs, reducing whole class teaching and increasing the ability of the teachers to work with children in small groups. The "relief" time for teachers and instructional aids can be restructured so that they spend more time in direct instruction of children instead of in the activities that presently engage their time such as cutting out pumpkins, grading worksheets, and assisting the office clerical staff.

African American culture has a strong orientation toward oral communication, whereas the dominant culture has an orientation toward literacy. This difference needs to be bridged so that African American children are provided with the literacy experiences that the schools define as intelligence.

African American children are immersed in the creative arts. Infusion of the creative arts into instruction would increase the children's interest in activities and stimulate motivation to achieve.

Philosophical Background of the Instructional Component

Educators commonly affirm that learning environments for young children should be child centered and as homelike as possible. However, because there has been so much scholarship that has given pathological overtones to the African American home, this principle is often not applied to programs designed for African American children.

For example, it has been pointed out by A. Wade Boykin (1978) that African American culture is highly dynamic. A large amount of the stimuli African American children receive is variable, colorful, and rich. This makes it more difficult for them to tolerate instruction in a school that is monotonous, repetitious, and mundane.

An instructional model for African American children should diminish the use of dittoed sheets, workbooks, textbooks, and a skill-and-drill orientation. Emphasis should be placed on hands-on activities, projects, interrelated learning experiences, field trips, speakers, and classroom visitors. The intent is to create a learning environment that has elements of the culture of the African American community and stimulates higher-order thinking and creativity among African American children.

When children are engaged in skill-and-drill activities throughout their educational career, they become skill-and-drill *people*. The model of education that guides traditional urban schools where most African American children are found originated in early twentieth-century America. At the height of the industrial revolution, there was a need for a large population of unskilled workers to occupy blue-collar positions in factories.

Poorly educated people cannot obtain employment in the future as they once did in the past. It is possible now to identify the characteristics that will be required for people who will be economically viable in the twenty-first century. People will be needed who can think and who have imagination and can solve problems; people who are creative and innovative and have vision; and people who are self-starters, who can work independently and cooperatively.

For many African American children being educated in urban and rural schools, there is a disconnection between the abilities they will need to be economically viable in the future; to be able to function independently as adults; to be able to make a creative contribution to the society; and to have the abilities that are being developed as a part of the learning process on a daily basis in school.

There have been some well-intentioned efforts to improve educational outcomes for African American children by church organizations and groups such as the Nation of Islam. Some of these have been successful because the teachers sincerely cared for the children and taught them conscienciously. Often, however, these models had a rigid militaristic orientation and were characterized by children dressed in uniform, sitting in assigned seats doing seatwork at young ages, with the instruction oriented to tests. The children in these schools eventually made gains when they were compared to their counterparts in traditional schools. Moreover, there were few competing models for organizing instruction for African American children so, over time, this highly structured and rigid form of education was considered "the way" to produce outcomes for African American children.

It is proposed in this model to develop learners with intrinsic motivation by giving attention to the notion of *artistic teaching,* which incorporates elements delineated by Alfie Kohn (1993) in which children are motivated by the interesting manner in which content is presented; children are given opportunities to explore ideas and content in meaningful *collaboration* with their teachers and peers; and the children are given choices.

This model is designed in such a way that the children will receive a multidisciplinary exposure to the curriculum so that they will be able to develop their interests and talents in the process of mastering information and skills. The identification of talents and interests is the first step toward building careers that lead to lifelong satisfaction and self-actualization.

The time has come for educators to think about the kinds of people we are trying to produce through the educational process. For example, many school districts use the slogan, "Every child can learn." That sounds like a beautiful, inspirational sentiment on first reading. However, consider the goals of the Roeper School for Children, as stated by Chuck Webster, the head:

> Our goals for the children are for them to:
>
> - Understand themselves;
> - Find meaning in their world;
> - Construct their futures;
> - Have an impact on their world.

When the slogan "Every child can learn" is considered next to those goals, it seems condescending and one-dimensional. It is suggested that schools substitute the motto: "Leave no child behind" (Children's Defense Fund) and "Children learn what they are taught." More attention needs to be given to the kinds of African American children we are trying to produce. The question must be raised of whether we are interested in creating an educational process for African American children where they can have a creative impact on *our* society or whether we intend for them to iron other people's clothes and serve as a buffer for the economy.

On an ABC news documentary entitled, "Common Miracles: The New American Revolution in Learning," Peter Jennings stated:

> Education is how a society hands out its life chances. How it gives people options. Philosophers sometimes say the best definition of freedom is a good range of

options. A new revolution in learning would give many more Americans real freedom.

The time has come to clarify the values that must permeate the educational process. Most Americans agree that the schools should produce citizens who are responsible and honorable. Roeper has a goal of empowering children and enabling them to take responsibility for decision making in their lives. W. E. B. DuBois (1968) set the standard with the following words that were written in 1906 and still ring true today:

> And when we call for education, we mean real education. We believe in work. We ourselves are workers, but work is not necessarily education. Education is the development of power and ideal. We want our children trained as intelligent human beings should be and we will fight for all time against any proposal to educate black boys and girls simply as servants and underlings, or simply for the use of other people. They have a right to know, to think, to aspire. (p. 251)

Development of the Instructional Component

Elementary Curriculum

1. A curriculum guide must be written for the school and must include a vision statement and program objectives, as well as the following information:

   - Philosophical and theoretical framework
   - Goals for children in the various curricular areas and different stages in their development
   - Knowledge and skills for each curricular area and at various grades
   - Evaluation

   A curriculum guide is an essential document that enables teachers to crystallize an approach to learning and that provides a statement of content of instruction. Such a document can also serve as a spiritual focal point that gives the school a focus, an identity, and a vision.

2. Opening exercises should be created for the children at each grade level that include poems, songs, and physical activities that enhance concentration and focus their minds and bodies spiritually, ideologically, and physically for the work of the day.

3. Preschool linkages should be created to grade school. Teachers of preschool children should be involved in curriculum planning along with grade school teachers. A component of successful change for children is to create continuity between the preschool and grade school curricula and instruction. A curriculum guide should be written for the preschool

program in the elementary school that clearly states the philosophy, goals, objectives, and evaluation strategies.

4. Elementary curriculum. A companion piece to the creation of the culturally appropriate pedagogy is the identification of elementary reading, science, and mathematics programs that will achieve the optimal outcomes for African American children.

Reading program. Whole language is a program of instruction in which the teacher stimulates literacy through stories and literature that are read aloud to the children instead of using basal readers with controlled vocabulary. Whole language instruction also offers the attraction of providing involvement with rich, colorful literature, which is intrinsically motivating and interesting to children. On the other hand, there is strong evidence that children benefit from the solid structure of linguistic knowledge that stems from a good background in phonics. Therefore, this project will involve teachers in considering the merits of both approaches and in creating a fine-tuned instructional balance that meets the individual needs of the children in this school. Cultural salience is particularly important for African American male children. It is critical to expose them to written material that is stimulating and interesting. This can be a bridge that leads them to reading literature that is more Anglo-centric and the absorption of which is rewarded on standardized tests.

Mathematics program. The mathematics program must involve the children in hands-on active involvement with materials in contrast to heavy reliance on textbooks and paper-and-pencil activities. Also, there should be an integration of mathematics activities in all possible aspects of the children's day—record keeping, measuring, estimating, weighing, and so forth.

Science program. The science program should emphasize hands-on instruction and minimize the use of textbooks. Science process skills should be emphasized, such as observation, measurement (including estimation), inferring, and designing experiments. An important focus should be on creativity and inventiveness.

5. Thematic units should be created by elementary school teachers in the areas of social studies and science that will incorporate the arts and multicultural modalities for instruction. Units developed in social studies will include, but not be limited to, subject matter related to African American culture. The units will serve as a vehicle for increasing the vocabulary and level of information and knowledge of the learner about the world; broadening the drill and practice of reading and mathematics skills into a truly well-rounded educational experience; and providing students with an opportunity to identify talents and interests they can develop and extend into meaningful work.

6. Evaluation will be enhanced by utilizing *portfolio* assessment in which a child's actual work is collected and progress and growth are measured over time. The bell curve grading system in elementary school should be eliminated and emphasis should be placed on mastery of criterion-referenced material and growth.

7. Beauty and harmony must characterize the learning environment. An important activity of the study group will be to arrange the classrooms so that the environment is aesthetically pleasing to the children.

Instructional Accountability Infrastructure: Theoretical Underpinnings

Educators constantly decry the fact that parents of lower-income children often are not involved in the schools and do not attend parent conferences or even review children's progress reports. This situation is often described by exasperated teachers who feel that too much is expected of them when they do not have the support from parents that is customary in school districts that serve white-middle class children.

There have been major upheavals over the past thirty years in child rearing and parental education among white middle-class families that need to be understood in order for those who are involved in educating lower-income and African American children to understand what they are up against.

The creation of the Head Start Program in the 1960s brought to public attention an awareness of how much young children desire stimulation and want to learn. This interest in how to get lower-income African American children on the right track early grew out of the rebellions (also called riots) in urban areas in the 1960s. White middle-class families began to realize that the preschool experience was important for advantaged children as well, and early childhood education as we know it was born.

However, this interest in early childhood education went a step further, and the Super Baby movement was born. Affluent families began to play music to babies *in utero*; they began teaching babies to read with flash cards; baby gymnasiums were created; and elite preschools were opened that required letters of reference for 2-year-olds and intelligence test scores for admission.

There began to be a shift in the amount of time and energy affluent parents spent providing enrichment activities for their children. These parents left nothing to chance. They did not depend on the schools to teach their children to read and calculate. The children came to school reading, having been taught by their mothers. This commitment to education was expressed in the affluent public suburban school systems by parents who formed parent councils and volunteered to provide the programs they desired, such as science fairs, publishing centers, field trips, and so forth. Those who could afford private education created schools for gifted children to provide the enrichment they desired. Currently, however, an increasing number of families are turning to home schooling because they can thus control their children's education, which they primarily consider their own responsibility.

The point here is that parents have upped the ante in the past thirty years. Suburban public school systems and private schools cannot take the total credit for soaring standardized test scores based on the activity of the professionals in the classrooms alone. These jobs are plum teaching positions because the teachers do not have to focus on teaching the basic skills as much as on enhancing the learning of children who come to school already motivated and involved in the process of learning.

When parents desire more than the professionals offer, there is a cadre of white, nonworking mothers who can enter the schools as volunteers and complement the offerings of the schools. Further, there is a pressure on the schools to be conversant with movements such as home schooling and the exodus to private schools because many of the families in affluent school districts have such options. A major exodus from the public schools would be a threat to public financial support of the schools and to the value of property in those communities.

In inner-city communities, the families that are served by the public schools cannot as readily withdraw their children and enroll them in private schools. The working poor do not have the time and often the skills for home schooling to be an option. Therefore, the schools that serve inner-city children do not have to maintain the standards of the best schools in the community for fear that there would be a mass exodus to those schools by their constituents.

It cannot be emphasized too strongly here the advantage *white* middle-class children enjoy when the family can be *supported* by the earnings of fathers alone. This means that mothers, who are usually well educated, are free from having to earn salaries and can devote their talents and energy to child rearing and educating their children. Even though mothers in middle-class African American families are often as well educated or better educated than white middle-class women, they usually must contribute as much as half or more of the income necessary to sustain their families. The economic disparity between the incomes of African American males and white males places more pressure on African American mothers to direct their energy toward producing income.

When you consider the fact that approximately 17 percent of white families are headed by females and 63 percent of African American families are headed by females (and 85 percent of African American children in school are coming from female-headed households), the picture begins to emerge that whether African American mothers are married or not, they are not in a position to provide home schooling, extraordinary enrichment, and educating that are becoming routine for their white counterparts.

Therefore, it is the position of this model that an instructional accountability infrastructure is needed for school systems that serve African American and lower-income children (see Figure 11.1). Instead of educators constantly bemoaning the disparity in parent involvement in African American and lower-income school districts, they should accept the reality that middle-class African American mothers have greatly divided energies and are under a great deal of pressure to sustain their families and their communities; that working-poor mothers are under a great deal of pressure because they must use time-consuming modes of transportation and work hard, restrictive jobs, often with no benefits, vacations, or provisions for respite; and that mothers who are on public assistance often were or are teen mothers with a low level of education, sometimes abuse substances, often are abused by men, and have a compendium of pressures and problems that interfere with providing optimal parenting. This component would create an apparatus to ensure excellence within the school that emerges from an understanding of the existential situation of the parents.

2. Instructional Accountability Infrastructure Component: Strategies

A supervisory, evaluation, training, and reward system needs to be instituted at the building level so that excellent instruction is delivered to children, whatever the professionals deem to provide for them.

This component is designed to incorporate practices into the school that provide teachers with instructional support persons who can assist them in working with children in small groups and individually; institute peer evaluation of teaching so that good teaching practices become a part of the culture of the school that is peer reinforced rather than instituted from above; reward teachers for excellent outcomes for children on numerous levels; involve parents in inservice training and observation of schools where cutting-edge practices are employed; involve older children in the school in donating time for community service so that they can work with younger children; and identify a church that will adopt the school and provide community volunteers for tutoring, male mentoring, and enrichment activities.

The feature of this component, the *in loco parentis* committee, would take responsibility for the monitoring of child progress and for providing the support each child needs to perform on grade level. A committee would be created for each classroom and would include a teacher who teaches the same grade, a volunteer from the community, and a parent representative with a child in the classroom.

This committee would meet with the teacher at regular intervals and evaluate each child who is not performing on grade level in reading or mathematics to determine whether the child needs private tutoring, counseling, or alternative instructional strategies in the same way middle-class families intervene when their children are not progressing as they should be in school.

Older children in the school (or at a higher grade level outside the school but within the school district) could be involved in a program of community service wherein they allocate a percentage of their time to enrich the school. Older children could be involved in tutoring younger children in basic skills.

Parents in the school could be involved in volunteerism by tutoring children who need one-to-one support. Their own children would benefit when more of the teacher's time could be directed toward enrichment rather than remedial activities in the classroom.

Volunteers in the community could be organized from sororities, fraternities, or church and civic groups who are receptive toward adopting schools and providing support.

3. Cultural Uplift Component

It is important to provide children with enrichment activities at school and to orient parents to opportunities that are available and to the importance of getting their children involved.

The participants in the project will identify the resources in the community, such as African American churches, the YMCA, recreational programs, and so forth. This will be an effort to harness the community resources that already exist.

Male Mentoring. The names of the churches and community organizations able to assign mentors to the African American boys could be on record at a school. Then, when particular boys need support in the case of disciplinary referrals or poor academic performance, the mentors and pastors could be included in conferences and in designing solutions.

Teen Pregnancy Intervention. This project proposes devising intervention strategies that are compatible with the values of the community regarding teaching abstinence, family planning, and/or pregnancy termination.

Cultural Uplift Profile

A very important activity will be the creation of a cultural uplift profile for each child in the school. This will be an evaluation of the extent to which each child is involved in some co-curricular, extracurricular, church, or civic activity that will provide the intellectual enrichment and social and political skills that enable that child to achieve upward mobility.

It is also important to determine the categories of participation. Are the children involved in athletic activities exclusively? Is there a balance between sports and participation in debate, literary societies, art classes, science enrichment, drama guilds, music, dance, and civic organizations?

Teachers will also utilize this profile in conferencing with parents. Parents will be apprised of activities that are available in the school and community and they will be encouraged to involve their children in participating.

Parent Organization That Plans Enrichment Activities. Linkages will be created among parents so that they can trade services with each other to provide affordable cultural activities for their children. An organization modeled after Jack & Jill (an African American social club that provides enrichment experiences for middle-class children) can be created within the school wherein the parents plan cultural excursions within the metropolitan area that will broaden the exposures of their children.

A cultural uplift committee in each classroom will be composed of community volunteers (from the church and business community), teachers, and parents.

Activity Day (Choices). Providing children with choices strengthens their interest in creative and academic activities. Giving them choices of which topics they will study in greater depth or choices in the manner in which subjects will be explored strengthens intrinsic motivation and connects them to academic achievement.

Social Skills Instruction and Nonviolent Conflict Resolution. One of the results of the changing configuration of the family at the end of twentieth-century America is that many are not fulfilling the functions of families of years gone by. This is particularly evident in the area of the social skills children bring to school.

Consequently, an important feature of the cultural uplift component is identifying and developing a social skills curriculum for imparting those abilities.

A companion effort will be identifying and developing a curriculum for nonviolent conflict resolution. The perspective of this component is that when children are educated in an environment that respects them as being capable of making choices, respects their developmental characteristics, and treats them in a humanistic manner, they will eventually respond by respecting other people and things in the environment.

Children fall behind for a number of reasons. Upward mobility for African American families has had to be achieved within a very short time frame. Economic slavery (sharecropping) ended as late as 1948, rather than in 1865 as we have been taught. African American families have not had the gradual three-generational climb toward upward mobility that European immigrants have enjoyed. We have had to achieve upward mobility in one generation. Thus, we have had a very short time frame to connect with the "culture of power" and learn the fine points and nuances of mainstream America.

The economic castration of African American men has placed a heavy burden on African American women to generate income, do child rearing, and hold our families and community together. African American women do not have as much time for home schooling as white women do. And schools as they presently operate expect children to arrive at school at a high level of development, both intellectually and socially.

White Americans have become extremely aggressive in the past thirty years in providing educational advantages for their children *in utero* and certainly before they arrive at school. White Americans created the concept of "giftedness" when school desegregation began. (The simultaneous timing of these two events was pointed out to me by my brother, Phale D. Hale, Jr.) So, they created an academic discipline (gifted and talented) that produced a pedagogy for educating their children on the top floor of an integrated school while African American children were trained on the bottom floor.

White Americans have watched with delight as our focus for the past twenty years has been on finding our African roots while their focus has been on taking our places in college, professional schools, and the workplace.

White Americans have brought a high level of sophistication to bear on creating educational inequality that benefits their children to the detriment of ours. The African American community has not generated strategies to counteract the *de facto* segregation crafted in the 1950s. After *Brown v. the Board of Education,* we were stumped. Middle-class African Americans moved their children to the schools connected to the "culture of power," and inner-city African Americans were left to fend for themselves.

Public schools that service inner-city children have not produced outcomes because there is not an instructional accountability infrastructure that operates for parents who have not had the benefits of advanced education themselves. The African American middle class who have the information about cutting-edge educational practices have moved to suburban and private schools and taken their advocacy with them.

It is my considered opinion that we know how to train good teachers. We also know how to identify good teachers at work. What we have not addressed is how to erect support systems and supervisory strategies so that the teachers deliver to the children what they have been trained to do. Particularly, how do we get teachers to teach children effectively when the teachers have little interest in the achievement of the children they are teaching? How do we get teachers to teach children effectively when there are no external sanctions that prevent those children from falling through the cracks?

Instead of making teacher training the focus of school reform, the issue is really teacher supervision. Is the principal providing instructional leadership for the teachers in her building? This, in my opinion, is the cutting edge of school reform. The most important unit in education is the activity between the teacher and the child. If the parent does not have the skills to supervise the services rendered to the child, it becomes the responsibility of the highest ranking professional in the building to ensure that every child is taught effectively.

Recommendations for Civil Rights Groups, African American–Controlled Public School Boards, and Advocacy Organizations

1. There is a need for civil rights groups to marshal the political forces of the African American community and their allies in state legislatures to equalize school financing.

2. There is a need for these leadership groups to bring in African American intellectuals to contribute to the discussion around strategies to achieve quality education for African American children. Many of our leaders are politicians, not scholars. There should be seats at the table both for dialogue and to formulate solutions. When a scholar creates an organization to establish an agenda for the implementation of her ideas, the generation of ideas ends. There is a need for a partnership between those who build organizations and those who generate ideas.

3. Think tanks should be held at conferences. Instead of conferences consisting only of presentations being given separately, think tanks should also be organized so that scholars can talk to each other and to civil rights leaders, advocates, and politicians.

4. There is a need for these leadership groups to clarify that achieving equal educational outcomes is key to solving the most fundamental problems facing African Americans in this country. This should be given priority attention. Recently, it seems that our civil rights activity has focused on commemorating past marches and milestones rather than on conducting think tanks on carving out a path for our future.

5. There is a need for these leadership groups to incorporate into their agenda strategies to assist African American families who are having difficulty negotiating the schools. I submit that these difficulties cut

across socioeconomic levels and inner-city, suburban, and private school boundaries.

6. There is a desperate need for the creation of an educational aid society in African American communities throughout the country. Such an organization could be sponsored by the Urban League or by advocacy organizations. Just as Legal Aid provides legal services to lower-income families, the Educational Aide Society could provide subsidized or sliding-fee-scale services for families who are having difficulty negotiating the schools. It could be a referral service where African American families are provided with the names of psychologists, psychiatrists, counselors, educators, or social workers who can go to conferences with them and observe and evaluate their children from a culturally sensitive frame of reference.

REFERENCES

Boykin, A. W. (1978). Psychological behavioral verve in academic/task performance. Pretheoretical considerations. *Journal of Negro Education, 47,* 343–354.

Boykin, A. W. (1979). Black psychology and the research process: Keeping the baby and throwing out the bathwater. In A. W. Boykin, A. J. Franklin, & J. F. Yates (Eds.), *Research directions of Black psychologists.* New York: Russell Sage Press.

Boykin, A. W. (1983). The academic performance of AfroAmerican children. In J. Spence (Ed.), *Achievement and achievement motives.* San Francisco: W. Freeman.

Comer, J. P. (1988). *Maggie's American dream: The life and times of a black family.* New York: New American Library.

DuBois, W. E. B. (1968). *The autobiography of W. E. B. DuBois: A soliloquy on viewing my life from the last decade of its first century.* New York: International Publishers.

Hale, J. E. (1994). *Unbank the fire: Visions for the education of African American children.* Baltimore: Johns Hopkins University Press.

Kohn, A. (1993). *Punished by rewards.* Boston: Houghton Mifflin Co.

Kozol, J. (1991). *Savage inequalities.* New York: Crown.

Lewis, D. L. (1993). *W. E. B. DuBois: Biography of a race 1868–1919.* New York: Henry Holt & Company.

12 Comment

The Challenges of Cultural Socialization in the Schooling of African American Elementary School Children: Exposing the Hidden Curriculum

A. Wade Boykin

The academic plight of African American school children is well documented, especially for those from low-income backgrounds. Efforts to enhance the academic performance of such students has been a long-standing concern of educational practitioners and researchers, and for good reason. For surely African American communities and the larger society will benefit greatly if there are significantly greater numbers of academically skilled African American students. In spite of the persistent concern and obvious benefits that can accrue, all too many African American children continue to fare poorly in our nation's schools.

Over the years, Janice Hale has been a tireless warrior in the pursuit of better academic outcomes for African American children. She has written extensively on the subject. She has been a classroom practitioner as well as an educational researcher. She has lectured far and wide. She has offered conceptual vistas for understanding the problems and opportunities at hand. She has even established her own schools to serve young children of African descent. She is to be acknowledged, indeed commended, for her efforts.

In Chapter 11, "Culturally Appropriate Pedagogy," Hale provides one of her most comprehensive treatments to date on how to effectively address improving achievement outcomes for black children. Here, she persuades us that *achievement* cannot be narrowly construed to encompass only test scores and classroom grades, but must include career planning, cultural uplift, a commitment to lifelong learning, social and emotional development, and opportunities to impact positively on the wider society. In a phrase, as Hale states, we must pay attention as well to the ". . . kinds of people we are trying to produce through the educational process."

Other points of emphasis in Hale's chapter are worthy of note. She argues effectively that schools are the most appropriate institutions in which to intervene for systemically bettering the lives of children. She advocates approaches to classroom learning that link disparate subject matter through common themes, that place a premium on interest and engagement value, and that converge with assessment and evaluation procedures that encourage academic progress and mastery of content. She insists that families and community-based organizations must play a vital role in supporting the schooling process while schools become more involved in supporting their students' families and the surrounding community. She urges that the focus on children cannot be done to the neglect of the interests of teachers. She argues that the quality of the professional environment for teachers must be genuinely addressed. This should include the encouragement of proactive peer collaborations among teachers, as well as ample opportunities (coupled to incentives) for teachers to increase their capacity to deliver high-quality instruction. These are all very reasonable, progressive, and potentially fruitful directions for schools to take if they are serious about more effectively educating African American children.

This chapter continues in the line of Dr. Hale's scholarship, where she does not hesitate to take strong stands and make provocative claims as to what ails the educational process for African American children. This is done seemingly to shake the reader from complacency or the security of one's existing understandings, even at the risk of the occasional sweeping gener-alization.

Yet I would like to issue two cautionary notes. For one, while I resonate with the call to expand the range of in-school and outreach programs that are to serve the educational benefit of children, I believe it will require additional thinking and analysis on how to successfully pull this off. The administration and oversight that will be needed for effectively implementing and coordi-nating various student support and enrichment programs, not to mention parent and community participation components, may tax already overly burdened school personnel and spread too thinly a school's existing (likely meager) material resources. Also, I concur with the stress this paper places on building on the cultural assets and resources that African American children bring with them to school. Yet in citing my work, it is concluded that certain cultural factors are *necessary* for black children to be motivated to achieve in school. This inference from my work needs to be toned down. While I would assert that building on cultural assets can facilitate enhanced academic outcomes, the absence of such strategies does not doom a black child to failure. There are many other grounds for enhancing achievement for African American children. Many children will respond favorably to a caring, encouraging, demanding teacher. Evidence suggests that many black children respond favorably in school in order to please teachers (Ferguson, 1998). Many others will respond to high expectations held for them by their families. Others may respond to supportive peers as well. That many African American children respond favorably to certain culturally prescribed conditions does not mean that they cannot learn well otherwise.

This issue of culture deserves further exploration. We must all appreciate that what Dr. Hale proposes requires some profound changes in the ways extant schools currently operate. Indeed, any school reform effort that is to be authentic, systemic, and sustained implicates a fundamental change in the process of schooling. The school change process is daunting and complex and fraught with pitfalls and challenges. In raising the issue of culturally appropriate pedagogy, it must not be ignored that traditional schooling in America has always been and continues to be conducted in profoundly cultural ways. The vision and model of schooling that Hale offers must be factored against the existing cultural realities that are manifested in all too many schools that primarily enroll African American children.

In the American public education system, schooling is more than the confluence of reading, writing, and arithmetic, so to speak. Indeed while these activities are going on, the schooling process also conveys certain ways of viewing the world, ways of codifying reality. It conveys codes for prioritizing observations and experiences. Schooling makes certain themes salient. It offers blueprints for living and for acceptable ways of functioning. It works toward the attachment of meaning to events that transpire. It determines what is to be valued and esteemed and what are the proper forms of deportment and conduct. In short, there is a profound socialization agenda in schools, a cultural socialization agenda (Boykin, 1994; Hilliard, 1995; Banks & Banks, 1995). Thus, schools are not about reading, writing, and arithmetic *per se*. They are about the business of conveying such activities as they relate to certain cultural vantage points and as they are embedded in particular cultural substrates. Public schools never were conceived to be culturally neutral sites, and schooling was never conceived to be a culturally neutral exercise.

Indeed, the cultural socialization agenda for American public schools was once quite overt and blatant. One major purpose for the widespread implementation of mass education in the early twentieth century was to bring the values and behaviors of immigrant children from southern and eastern European nations into conformity with Anglo cultural ideals (Tyack, 1974; Kaestle, 1983). Thus, it was clearly evident that public schools were needed to get these children to appropriate such cultural themes as materialism, self-contained individualism, emotional containment, competition, and the like. In this regard, schools were conceived to serve a homogenization function that was fundamentally at odds with principles of pluralism and multiculturalism. This cultural socialization function, this mainstream acculturation function is no longer so overt, or at least not ordinarily. Now it is manifested in more subtle yet still pervasive ways. It is an integral part of what has been called the hidden curriculum of schooling, and it greatly informs the terrain on which education gets done (Vallance, 1974; Cornbleth, 1984). Although not ordinarily overt, this function will emerge whenever it is challenged by efforts to honor, or legitimate, other cultural forms or themes in our nation's schools.

This cultural socialization function works in concert with another function schools have served, that is, a talent-sorting function (Boykin, 2000; Oakes, Wells, Jones, & Datnow, 1997). Schools have come to serve the purpose of classifying and weeding out students, where discrimination in terms of putative intellectual abilities is a paramount concern. Schools all too often serve a sorting and classifying function, and all too often this sorting and classifying function is done ostensibly in terms of levels of reading, writing, and arithmetic ability. Yet it can be persuasively argued that students who are not easily socialized into mainstream cultural mores are denied ready access to literacy and numeracy attainment (Gilmore, 1985). The cultural socialization agenda in this regard serves as a mechanism for the sorting agenda. Children who ostensibly are failing with respect to the reading, writing, and arithmetic curriculum may actually have failed with respect to the hidden curriculum. Yet the denial of access to literacy and numeracy skills is construed as the children's own fault because they lack the ability to acquire these skills. In a similar vein, Lisa Delpit (1988, 1995) and others have argued that a "culture of power" prevails in schools. It represents the interests and rules of those who have power. The values, behavioral expressions, and interactional routines apropos for this culture of power are often only tacitly announced, thereby penalizing those children who do not have ready access to them or implicit awareness of their presence.

While we may be somewhat justified in referring to this curriculum as "hidden," in some respects children may in fact be aware of its presence. At some level of awareness children may be plugged into the cultural socialization agenda. Moreover, children do not come to school as cultural *tabula rasas,* waiting to be formed like cultural lumps of clay into the cultural images that schools attempt to impose. Instead, children, regardless of their background, bring preferences, experiences, lenses, themes and meanings, assumptions concerning proper conduct, and observation priorities that emerge in their everyday negotiations within the proximal environments of their homes, neighborhoods, and the corresponding social institutions of their communities. At some level, they also are aware of this social capital that they bring to school, and to some level they can articulate its manifestations; and their behaviors and perceptions in school often are reflective of this social capital (Stanton-Salazar, 1997). It is possible to understand and access this subjective understanding around matters of culture even in grade-school children. My colleagues and I have launched a line of research that speaks to this cultural phenomenology with respect to the schooling of African American children from low-income backgrounds. In turn, this work raises issues about the problematics and possibilities for the schooling of African American children who have been greatly underserved in our nation's public schools.

The conceptual framework that guides this work is predicated on the notion of *psychosocial integrity*. It is argued that there is *complexity, coherence,* and *meaning* contained in the proximal experiences of a preponderance of African American children from low-income backgrounds (Boykin, Allen, & Jagers, in press). As I have argued elsewhere (Boykin, 1986; Boykin & Ellison, 1995), part of this integrity is captured in terms of efforts to participate adequately, if not gainfully, within the mainstream of American life and within its corresponding institutions. Part of this integrity for African Americans is understood in terms of the participation demands of the minority experience. This is bound up in efforts to combat, buffer or cope with oppression, low status, marginalization, denial of opportunities, and lack of power. The integrity is also captured in terms of participation in the Afro-cultural experience. In this latter sense, this entails experiences that are substantially (but not entirely) captured in terms of prevailing fundamental cultural themes that characterize many of the interpersonal transactions, activities, and values of participants in the homes, neighborhoods, and community institutions that many African American children must negotiate. These themes represent aspects of Afro-cultural ethos rooted in traditional African cultural legacy. Themes deemed consistent with Afro-cultural ethos include a sense of communalism, a premium placed on movement expressiveness, spirituality, and verve—or receptiveness to relatively high levels of sensate (i.e., variability and intensity) stimulation. Themes like these are appropriated by many young black children by virtue of participation in their primary developmental experiences in their proximal environments outside of school. These themes consequently can occupy central places in these children's meaning systems when they come for formal schooling and help to frame their perspectives. They inform their sensibilities and priorities, and they give focus to the lenses through which they code their schooling experiences, and they give substance and structure to their cultural phenomenologies.

Important work on classroom cultural phenomenology vis-à-vis African American children has already been done. The work of John Ogbu (1994) and his colleagues is particularly noteworthy. Ogbu and others have argued that subjective perceptions of many African American school children lie at the heart of their schooling difficulties. He has argued that many black children participate in a culture that operates in opposition to mainstream cultural dictates. This is done to serve as a protective buffer against the caste status that is imposed through the exigencies of racism in America. Since the mainstream puts great value on the attainment of high scholastic achievement, African Americans are said to reject this objective, because individual striving for academic success would have no utility value for black people in the American social order. To this analysis, Fordham and Ogbu (1986) have added that many African American students reject high achievement for fear of being accused of "acting white." They ostracize their high-achieving peers for "acting white." High-achieving peers, as a protective mechanism, develop identities that take on a "raceless" persona.

To many, this argument has merit, and evidence has been garnered in its support. But the full picture of the schooling experiences of many African American children is not fully told through this depiction. We would argue that it speaks more so to negotiation through the minority experience. There is also the Afro-cultural experience. Consequently, we advance the argument that there are certain fundamental cultural themes that have been appropriated by many African American children from low-income backgrounds that contribute to their phenomenological understanding of their classroom experiences and consequently affect the nature of their participation in the formal schooling process. Since they may not be coming into schools as cultural *tabula rasas* and since the cultural lenses through which they approach their schooling experiences may not extrapolate well to the mainstream acculturation agenda of schools, a likely consequence is that this aspect of their cultural meaning system will be dishonored by the schooling experience. To the extent that this happens, it may lead to resistance in these children to the cultural socialization agenda of schools and in turn may create problematic transactions between students and teachers and problematic attitudes that many children may hold toward the schooling experiences. Of course, all this makes the sorting-out function of schools that much easier to enact for all too many of these children.

If this argument has merit, then many African American students may not be rejecting high achievement or high-achieving peers *per se* but the cultural context in which high achievement is typically embedded and the cultural modalities through which high achievement is typically displayed. This in turn contributes to the schooling difficulties faced by many of these children, and without recognition of this challenge, schooling difficulties for many of these children will remain impervious to change.

In the line of research that we have conducted, we have sought to test out aspects of these claims. The basic paradigm is relatively straightforward. We have constructed differing written scenarios that depict classroom activities or the achievement of children in classrooms. The scenarios differ in terms of the salient cultural theme depicted for classroom activities or the achievement modalities of the student. We then ask targeted samples to answer questions pertaining to the child in the scenario or the classroom depicted, to determine if the depicted child or classroom is being accepted or rejected.

In one study (Boykin, Bailey, Miller, & Albury, 1999), we gave fourth-grade African American children from low-income backgrounds a set of four scenarios, each depicting a different high-achieving child. They were to assume that the child depicted in the scenario was a student in their class.

They were told to answer a set of four questions about the child depicted in each scenario. The questions tapped into the subjects' willingness to have positive social contact with the depicted high-achieving child. Examples were "Would you like x to be your good friend?" or "Would you like to play with x at recess or after school?" In one scenario, the child achieved highly through individualistic means; in a second, the child achieved highly through competition; in a third, the high-achieving child did so via a verve orientation; and in the fourth, the high-achieving child did so through communal means. Each question was responded to in a yes/no format. One point was given for each yes answer, and zero points for a no answer. Thus, scores could range from zero to four. An average score over two indicated that the sample was more socially accepting of the depicted child. A score less than two would be in the rejection range. The results were that the two achievers who achieved highly via Afro-cultural themes were overwhelmingly endorsed, and the two who achieved highly via Euro-cultural themes were resoundingly rejected. Thus, high achievers were not rejected out of hand, but only those who did so in conformity with mainstream cultural dictates. Similar results were obtained with low-income African American students in middle and high school as well (Marryshow, 1995).

In another study (Walton, 1993), these same four scenarios were given to classroom teachers in two grade schools in a medium-sized northeastern city. Both schools had over 90 percent enrollment of African American children from low-income backgrounds. This time the scenarios were stripped of any reference to high achievement. Teachers were asked to assume that the child depicted in each scenario was a student in their class. They were to judge what that child's achievement status would likely be and what would be that child's level of classroom motivation. The results revealed that these teachers on average felt that in their classrooms the academic standing and motivation levels would be substantially higher for the children who functioned more consistently with individualism and competition. This, of course, is the opposite of what was found in terms of the student perceptions in the previous study. The possibility of clashing cultural agendas seems high given the comparison of the results from these two studies. Moreover, in more recent studies, it has been shown that it is more the rule than the exception that in schools serving African American students from low-income backgrounds classroom instructional activities are conducted within individualistic and competitive theme contexts (Boykin & Miller, 1997; Watkins-Lewis, 1998). Moreover it has been shown that elementary-level African American children are quite cognizant of the potential for cultural clash (Miller, 1997).

In another project (Martin, 1997), we questioned a group of students about their preferences for four different classrooms that differed in terms of learning and instructional activities. The classroom activities in each scenario corresponded to a different one of the four cultural themes described in the previous studies. Children were also shown illustrations of classrooms that were physically laid out to be consistent with a given one of the four cultural themes. Tested children were African American fourth and sixth graders from low-income backgrounds. It was found that students more greatly prefer classroom activities as well as classroom physical arrangements consistent with the Afro-cultural themes.

Taken together, the results seem to indicate that there is systematic character to the cultural phenomenologies of many African Americans from low-income backgrounds. These children have uncovered the hidden curriculum and they have definite opinions about it. Schooling for many African American children can thus be conceived as conducted in a culturally contested realm. This work does not imply that mainstream acculturation should be abandoned, but it does suggest that problems may accrue when teachers disproportionately privilege mainstream cultural themes and frames of reference at the expense of other legitimate cultural forms. As Hale and others (Delpit, 1995; Dyson, 1999) have argued, schools must involve all children in the learning process and, once involved, strive to extend their capabilities across multiple contexts. Culturally appropriate pedagogy helps to accomplish this end, when coupled to the extended goal of getting children to become proficient at the multicontextualization of their intellectual skills. In doing this, it is my hope that we may one day realize the ambitions of a talent-development approach to schooling (Boykin, 2000), such that all children truly can succeed in a demanding curriculum and to high standards, while they become proactive contributors to their communities and to society at large. But, of course, more research, development, and transformations need to be done.

REFERENCES

Banks, J., & Banks, C. (1995). *Handbook of research on multicultural education.* New York: Macmillan.

Boykin, A. W. (1986). The triple quandary and the schooling of Afro-American children. In U. Neisser (Ed.), *The school achievement of minority children* (pp. 55–72). Hillsdale, NJ: Lawrence Erlbaum.

Boykin, A. W. (1994). Harvesting culture and talent: African American children and school reform. In R. Rossi (Ed.), *Schools and students at risk: Context and framework for positive change* (pp. 116–138). New York: Teachers College Press.

Boykin, A. W. (2000). The Talent Development model of schooling: Placing students at promise for academic success. *Journal of Education for Students Placed at Risk, 5,* 3–25.

Boykin, A. W., Allen, B., & Jagers, R. (in press). *The psychology of African American experiences: An integrity-based perspective.* Needham Heights, MA: Allyn & Bacon.

Boykin, A. W., Bailey, C., Miller, O. A., & Albury, A. (submitted). The influence of culturally distinct learning orientations on the achievement perception of African American and European American grade school children. Manuscript submitted for publication.

Boykin, A. W., & Ellison, C. (1995). The multiple ecologies of Black youth socialization: An Afrographic analysis. In R. Taylor (Ed.), *African American youth: Their social and economic status in the United States* (pp. 83–128). Westport, CT: Praeger.

Boykin, A. W., & Miller, O. A. (1997). In search of cultural themes and their expressions in the dynamics of classroom life. Paper presented at the Annual Meeting of the American Educational Research Association, Chicago, IL.

Cornbleth, C. (1984). Beyond the hidden curriculum. *Journal of Curriculum Studies, 16,* 29–36.

Delpit, L. (1988). The silenced dialogue: Power and pedagogy in educating other people's children. *Harvard Educational Review, 58,* 280–298.

Delpit, L. (1995). *Other people's children.* New York: Norton.

Dyson, A. (1999). Transforming transfer: Unruly children, contrary texts, and the persistence of the pedagogical order. In A. Iran-Nejad & P. Pearson (Eds.), *Review of research in education,* Vol. 24 (pp. 141–171). Washington, DC: AERA.

Ferguson, R. (1998). Teachers' perceptions and expectations and the Black-White test score gap. In C. Jencks & M. Phillips (Eds.), *The Black-White test score gap* (pp. 273–317). Washington, DC: Brookings Institution Press.

Fordham, S., & Ogbu, J. (1986). Black students' school success: Coping with the burden of "acting white." *Urban Review, 18,* 176–206.

Gilmore, P. (1985). "Gimme room": School resistance attitude and access to literacy. *Journal of Education, 167,* 111–128.

Hilliard, A. (1995). *The maroon within us.* Baltimore: Black Classic Press.

Kaestle, P. (1983). *Pillars of the republic: Common schools and American society.* New York: Hill & Wang.

Marryshow, D. J. (1995). Perception of future economic success and the impact of learning orientation on African American students' attitudes toward high achievers. Doctoral dissertation, Howard University, Washington, DC.

Martin, S. (1997). Students' attitudes toward four distinct learning orientations and classroom environments. Doctoral dissertation, Howard University, Washington, DC.

Miller, O. A. (1997). Cultural influences on the classroom perceptions of African-American grade-school children. Master's thesis, Howard University, Washington, DC.

Oakes, J., Wells, A., Jones, M., & Datnow, A. (1997). Detracking: The social construction of ability, cultural politics and resistance to reform. *Teachers College Record, 98,* 482–510.

Ogbu, J. (1994). From cultural frames to differences in cultural frames of reference. In P. Greenfield & R. Cocking (Eds.), *Cross-cultural roots of minority child development* (pp. 365–392). Hillsdale, NJ: Lawrence Erlbaum Associates.

Stanton-Salazar, R. (1997). A social capital framework for understanding the socialization of racial minority children and youths. *Harvard Educational Review, 67,* 1–40.

Tyack, D. (1974). *The one best system.* Cambridge, MA: Harvard University Press.

Vallance, E. (1974). Hiding the hidden curriculum. *Curriculum Theory Network, 4,* 5–21.

Walton, T. (1993). Teachers' attitudes toward Black students who display differing cultural orientations. Master's thesis, Howard University, Washington, DC.

Watkins-Lewis, K. (1998). The cultural bases for teachers' perceptions of their classroom practices: Implications for Black students who display differing cultural orientations. Master's thesis, Howard University, Washington, DC.

13 Education and Socialization

A Review of the Literature

Michele Foster

Introduction

This chapter addresses questions concerning the effect of children's educational experiences on their adult decisions, specifically, in their choice of residence, employment, voting, civic participation, attribution of social problems, and views of social justice. Additionally, I discuss whether education inevitably involves transmitting the dominant society's social outlook; analyze the extent to which teachers consider diversity an asset in the classroom; analyze how the racial composition of the school affects student socialization; and finally suggest what major research questions remain to be answered about the role of education in the socialization of students. I include data from large-scale quantitative, longitudinal, and cross-sectional data bases, as well as from smaller studies that utilize either quantitative, qualitative, or ethnographic methods or that employ mixed methods. Because the focus of this chapter is educational experiences, it considers the effects of nonschool settings as well as school contexts. Much of the evidence that bears on this topic does so only indirectly. As a result, I have often drawn on several sources to elucidate a point.

What effect does a child's educational experience have on adult decisions such as choice of residence, employment, voting, civic participation, attribution of social problems, or views of justice? This section considers each of these topics in turn.

Some researchers suggest that desegregation has a positive effect with respect to several adult outcomes, including choice of residence. According to these researchers, young people who experience desegregated schooling versus segregated schooling are more likely to live pluralistic adult lives in several arenas: in their choice of post secondary institutions, housing and neighborhoods, workplace environments, and friendship patterns. Where data have been available, these findings hold for African Americans, Latinos, and whites. Second, for African American students as well as for Latinos, where data are available, school desegregation seems to facilitate access to better and higher-paying jobs (Braddock, Dawkins, & Trent, 1994).

Residential Choices

Data from national surveys collected since 1958 indicate that whites' attitudes toward integration, specifically their responses to two questions, "if black people came to live next door" and "if black people came to live in great numbers" in their neighborhood, have become more positive. When asked in 1997 if they would move if blacks moved next door, only 1 percent of whites said they would, compared to 44 percent in 1958. The percentage of whites saying they would move if blacks moved into their neighborhoods in large numbers also declined from 80 percent in 1958 to 18 percent in 1997 (Council of Economic Advisors, 1998). The results of these surveys suggest that white attitudes toward living in integrated neighborhoods are more positive. When polled, 85 percent of African Americans also indicate that they prefer living in racially mixed neighborhoods (*New York Times*, April 1, 1987).

Despite the changing attitudes of whites and a decline in the residential segregation of African Americans from other groups between 1970 and 1990, except for whites who in 1990 lived in neighborhoods whose composition was approximately 84 percent white, African Americans are still more likely than any other ethnic minority group to live in neighborhoods with members of their own group. Among ethnic groups for whom 1990 national data are available, Latinos resided in neighborhoods whose composition was approximately 32 percent Latino, Asians in neighborhoods that were approximately 21 percent Asian, and African Americans in neighborhoods that were approximately 65 percent African American (Council of Economic Advisors, 1998). In the Washington metropolitan area, for instance, white and Latino poor are widely scattered throughout the region's suburban neighborhoods, whereas poor African Americans live in highly concentrated pockets of poverty in the central city. An analysis of census data reveals the severity of the District region's residential segregation. Poor non-black families are significantly more likely to have access to housing opportunities in low-poverty communities than are their African American counterparts, who are far more often confined to the poorest and most distressed neighborhoods. Blacks are four times more likely than the non-black poor to live in the District and fourteen times more likely to live in a neighborhood with a high concentration of poverty. Moreover, as an increasing share of jobs migrate to the suburbs, poor African American communities in the central city are being cut off from access to economic opportunities (Turner, 1997).[1]

We cannot predict how the educational experiences of today's youth will affect their future choice of residence. Despite a growing number of affluent neighborhoods that are predominantly African American, as well as other neighborhoods that are ethnically mixed, the evidence currently available on the topic of residential integration is unambiguous and inconsistent with the changing attitudes reported in surveys. With few exceptions, the research on residential choices demonstrates that whites will not move from a neighborhood as long as the percentage of African American families does not exceed 8 percent, but whites will not tolerate an African American population that approximates the percentage of the national population of 12 to 13 percent. Once the percentage of African American residents in a neighborhood approaches between 10 and 12 percent, whites will begin to move even when socioeconomic class is held constant (Jaynes & Williams, 1989).

Employment

Poor high school preparation and limited access to a college education are directly related to employment opportunities. As job growth in the industrial sector declines, there is a growing demand for highly skilled and highly educated workers, while those workers with fewer skills and less education are consigned to a declining standard of living (Reich, 1991). Ethnic minority groups, particularly African Americans, continue to suffer the damaging effects of past and present racial discrimination in education (see Miller, 1995, for a discussion). The National Research Council found that students in racially segregated public schools with high concentrations of poor minority students typically have low achievement test scores, high dropout rates, and limited opportunities for jobs and college admission after graduation (Jaynes & Williams, 1989, p. 378; Orfield, 1993). In its survey of the status of black Americans, the Council concluded that despite school desegregation and increased federal financial assistance, "there remain persistent and large gaps in the schooling quality and achievement outcomes of education for blacks and whites" (Jaynes & Williams, 1989, pp. 377–378; see also, Darling-Hammond, 1997, 1998). The Council determined that "separation and differ-

---

[1]Data from other cities, southern and northern, reveal that African Americans live in racially secluded neighborhoods. See, for example Douglass S. Massey and Nancy A. Denton, *American apartheid: Segregation and the making of the underclass* (Cambridge: Harvard, 1993), and Reynolds Farley and William H. Frey, "Changes in the segregation of whites from blacks during the 1980s: Small steps toward a more integrated society," *American Sociological Review,* 1994 (vol. 59: pp. 23–45).

ential treatment of blacks continue to be widespread in elementary and secondary schools and in different forms in institutions of higher learning" (Jaynes & Williams, 1989).

Although the college-going rates of African Americans have increased since the early 1980s, they are still lower than for whites. In 1994, 13 percent of African American adults (25 years of age and older) had a bachelor's degree compared with 8 percent in 1980. Corresponding percentages for whites were 23 percent in 1994 and 18 percent in 1980. One third of African American 18- to 24-year-old high school graduates and 42 percent of comparable whites were enrolled in college in 1993. Only 40 percent of African Americans in a 1980 cohort of sophomores enrolled in college immediately after graduating from high school compared with 51.1 percent of whites (Nettles, 1997). Moreover, since "the 1970s, the college-going chances of black high school graduates have declined, and the proportion of advanced degrees awarded to blacks has decreased" (Jaynes & Williams, 1989). Although college education has become increasingly important for success in the job market, college enrollment among black high school graduates has declined since the mid-1970s, when college enrollment rates for whites and blacks were approximately equal. The Southern Education Foundation recently reported that while blacks account for 25 percent of the college-age population in twelve southern and border states (states bordering on the old Confederate states) that formerly maintained *de jure* racially segregated colleges and universities, blacks make up only 16 percent of full-time university freshmen and 10 percent of bachelor of arts or bachelor of science recipients. In addition, the formerly all-white colleges and universities in these states remain largely segregated; in eight of the twelve states, fewer than 10 percent of all black first-year students are enrolled in the most prestigious, predominantly white universities (Southern Education Foundation, 1995).

The transition to post secondary education is more difficult for African American students who not only attain lower levels of education but are less likely to attain the level of education they once desired than their white counterparts.[2] Of two cohorts of students who were sophomores in 1980 and 1990, a much smaller percentage of African Americans than of whites enrolled in higher education in the fall following their graduation. Since educational attainment is higher for individuals who enter post secondary school immediately after high school, it should come as no surprise that even a decade later, African Americans have attained lower levels of education than their white counterparts; only 43.5 percent of African Americans have some credential beyond high school, compared to 52.7 percent of whites. There are several causes for the decline in college attendance by black students, some located in the system of post secondary education, but others originating in the K–12 system of education. One reason for the decline is the

---

[2]This entire section is drawn from Nettles (1997a, 1997b).

steep increase in the cost of a college education (college costs have increased by 138 percent since 1980) coupled with the decline in the availability of financial aid, the result of challenges to merit-based scholarships for black students.[3]

Another reason that the transition to post secondary education is lower can be found in test-taking patterns. According to recent data, African Americans are less likely to take undergraduate admissions tests (African Americans represent 9.1 percent of PSAT/NMSQT examinees, 11 percent of SAT examinees, 11 percent of ACT examinees, and 4.4 percent of advanced placement examinees) relative to their proportion in the college-age population (14.3 percent); and even after controlling for family income and parental education, those that do take admissions tests score far below their white and Asian counterparts and somewhat lower than Latino students.[4] African American students who take the SAT have taken fewer honors courses and less academically rigorous course work than white students. Female students represented the majority of African American undergraduate test takers, a fact that shows up in high school completion patterns and post secondary enrollment.

The percentage of African Americans aged 25 years old who have attained a high school diploma has increased between 1994 (73 percent) and 1980 (51 percent), but compared to whites, a higher percentage of African American high school graduates were unemployed during the year following their high school graduation for individuals in both the 1980 and 1990 sophomore cohorts. Among both cohorts, a higher share of African Americans than of whites were unemployed or out of the work force in the year following their scheduled high school graduation. The reasons for this higher rate of unemployment are not clearly understood. But since this disparity exists regardless of socioeconomic status, father's educational attainment, high school diploma status, high school program, high school type, urbanicity, or

---

[3]The Banneker Scholarship Program at the University of Maryland, challenged in Podberesky, provided merit-based scholarships for qualified black students. The Banneker Program was adopted as part of a desegregation plan mandated by the U.S. Department of Health, Education, and Welfare to increase the number of black students at the University of Maryland. It accounted for only about 1 percent of the university's total financial aid budget. The Fourth Circuit's decision, and the Supreme Court's refusal to review and reverse it, established an adverse precedent that may jeopardize targeted minority student aid that is critical to increasing minority university enrollment. Neither color-blind merit-based scholarships nor color-blind need-based scholarships are adequate substitutes for race-based student aid. In Podberesky, the University of Maryland had extensive experience with both forms of color-blind scholarship assistance, and neither one had worked to significantly increase black student enrollment. As a result of this case, other states have moved to dismantle their race-based student aid programs.

[4]The average 1996 verbal and mathematics scores for the following groups were: whites, 526/523; Asian Americans, 496/558; Mexican Americans, 455/449; Puerto Ricans, 452/445; other Latinos, 465/466; African Americans, 434/422.

poverty level of the high school student body, it is easy to conclude that this disparity is related to racism.[5]

African American men were overrepresented in the armed services among both 1980 and 1990 sophomore cohorts. African Americans represented only 5.9 percent of the cohort but 15 percent of those in the military, 13.8 percent in 1986 and 16.9 percent in 1992. African American men composed only 6.7 percent of the 1990 cohort, but represented 11.3 percent of those engaged in the military service in 1992, 14.5 percent in 1993, and 15.8 percent in 1994.

On almost all indicators—percentages of students taking college entrance tests, scores on college entrance tests, high school curricular choices, on-time high school completion, unemployment, successful transition to post secondary education, levels of post secondary education, overrepresentation and overconcentration in lower ranks in the military, lower earnings of high school graduates, congruity between educational aspiration and educational attainment—African Americans fare poorly.

Voting

Studies of voting behavior have found that in general voters have more schooling than nonvoters; wealthier people tend to vote more than the poor; younger people do not vote in high numbers; older groups have higher voter turnout; and whites have a higher turnout than blacks. Yet, according to a recent report by Democracy South, large voter turnout is critical to creating more equitable economic and social conditions.[6] This report found that economic and social equity improves when a larger share of adults vote. The states with the best twenty-year record of voter turnout generally have fuller employment, a less regressive tax system, and a smaller income gap between their richest and poorest families. These states also have less crime, a lower high-school dropout rate, and a higher potential for residents to reach old age. These high-turnout states are not richer than those with the lowest voting rates, but they enjoy the smallest gaps in the nation between "haves" and "have nots." Ten of the top twelve states for turnout also rank among the top twelve states on a set of equity indicators compiled for the Democracy Index; eleven of the worst fourteen for turnout are at the bottom on the equity scale. The fourteen worst turnout states include eight southern states and five others with large ethnic minority populations, all states with histories of disenfran-

---

[5]More African American students than white students who were eighth graders in 1988 were likely to be unemployed and not students in 1993, a year after their scheduled high school graduation.

[6]Democracy South is an arm of the Institute for Southern Studies.

chising people of color and frequently low-income whites. Coincidentally, only one of these states allows voter registration within twenty-nine days of election day. States with high voter turnouts, by contrast, have long traditions of making voting easy. An important conclusion to be drawn for this study is that when more people feel included and are motivated to shape their government, the benefits of jobs and public policy get spread around more evenly.

Although this is not directly addressed in the research on education, to the extent that African American students are not successful in school and end up being incarcerated, many will be politically disenfranchised. According to a report by Human Rights Watch and the Sentencing Project of the American Civil Liberties Union, 13 percent, one of seven, or some 1,460,000 African American males out of a population of 10.4 million eligible to vote were legally barred from voting due to a prior felony conviction, many for relatively minor drug offenses. Over half a million black men are permanently ineligible to vote, while another 950,000 are unable to vote due to laws barring voting by prisoners, probationers, or parolees (American Civil Liberties Union, 1997). Nationwide, according to this report, 3.9 million people— or one in fifty adults—are temporarily or permanently disenfranchised because of a felony conviction.

The state-by-state analysis indicates that laws on voting rights for criminals differ among the states. All except four states—Maine, Vermont, Massachusetts, and Utah—bar prisoners from voting. Other states suspend voting rights until a felon has completed probation or parole. Fourteen states—Alabama, Arizona, Delaware, Florida, Iowa, Kentucky, Maryland, Mississippi, Nevada, New Mexico, Tennessee, Virginia, Washington, and Wyoming—take away some or all felons' voting rights permanently. In Texas, voting rights are suspended for two years after a sentence is completed. The greatest percentages of disenfranchised black men are in Alabama and Florida, where one in three cannot vote. Although many of these individuals will regain their voting rights after completion of their sentence, the cumulative impact of large numbers of persons being disenfranchised from the electoral process clearly dilutes the political power of the African American community.

Civic Development and Participation

The findings from a recent government study of the civic development of high school students are relevant to this paper (Niemi & Chapman, 1999). In this study, civic development consisted of five elements: political knowledge, attention to politics, political participatory skills, political efficacy, and tolerance of diversity. The study found definite relationships between students' characteristics and their civic development. Approximately 19.5 percent of students surveyed were able to correctly answer at least four of five questions assessing their political knowledge. The percentage of high school students who reported reading the national news weekly equaled the percentage of those who reported watching or listening to the national news. Fifty-five percent of students say that they understand politics, and 64 percent feel as though their families has a say in government, both measures of participation skills. A majority of students express confidence in their political participation skills.[7] With respect to tolerance of diversity, 85 percent of students are tolerant of speech against religion and 57 percent of students uphold the idea of permitting controversial books in a public library.

There were, however, important differences in the civic development of students that were related to grade, gender, social class, type of school attended, participation in school and out-of-school activities, and racial-ethnic background. For instance, eleventh- and twelfth-grade students were better able than those in ninth and tenth grades to answer four or five political knowledge questions, were more likely to read the news at least once a week than were students in lower grades, and had more confidence in their ability to speak at a public meeting than students in lower grades. Eleventh- and twelfth-grade students were also more confident in their understanding of politics and more tolerant of speech against religion and the presence of controversial books in public libraries. With respect to gender, greater percentages of male students reported reading the news weekly and watching the news daily than female students, and the former knew more political facts than females and reported having a greater understanding of politics than females. Female students, however, expressed more confidence in their ability to write to government officials than did male students. With respect to ethnicity, white students were much more likely than students from other racial-ethnic groups to answer four or five political items correctly. White students expressed more confidence in their ability to understand politics than students from other racial-ethnic groups, and while white students were more accepting of allowing controversial books in public libraries than other groups, they were more likely than Latinos but as likely as blacks to be tolerant of speech against religion. Students from all racial-ethnic groups were alike in their beliefs in their participatory skills and just as likely to believe that their families have a say in what the government does.

Student civic development was highest among students with the most educated parents and lowest among students with the least educated parents. With only two exceptions, the relationship between having highly educated parents and high levels of civic development holds. These two exceptions concern the area of attentiveness to politics. While there is a positive relation-

[7]In this study, political participation skills were defined as the ability to write a letter to a government office and the ability to make a statement at a public meeting. Ninety-three percent of students felt they could do the former, whereas 82 percent believed they could do the latter.

ship between reading the national news and education, this difference does not obtain for watching national news. Finally, students who attended private schools scored higher on measures of civic development than their counterparts in public schools.

It is possible to argue that students who are more engaged in extracurricular activities both in and of out of school and students who as high school students are engaged in some form of community service are more likely to be engaged in civic participation when they become adults. The research on community service activities is far from conclusive, but a synthesis of the findings of the research on community service activities reveals that high-quality programs not only have a positive effect on academic achievement and personal development, but also on political efficacy and future civic participation, two areas of interest. Although studies that examine the effect of community service activities on academic achievement are limited, several studies have found improvements in grades under two conditions: when students considered "at risk" for educational failure or students with initial low levels of academic achievement are engaged in experiential learning such as internships or community-based education or when they participate in service-learning programs centered on tutoring (Wade, 1998).

Although the findings are uneven and vary with respect to gender, grade level, instrumentation, and scales, several studies have also noted modest gains on measures of social and personal development. Although previous literature reviews analyzing the effects of service on political efficacy have been mixed, in part because many of the community service projects are not linked directly to political issues, among those studies that found positive effects, some had noted that these changes were more likely to occur when programs are squarely focused on political issues, local government, or social actions (Wade & Saxe, 1996). However, in the government study reported above, with the exception of tolerance, participation in community service was positively related to civic development. Given previous work that suggested no relationship between community service and political knowledge, it is noteworthy that this new study found definite relationships between political knowledge and political efficacy (Niemi & Chapman, 1999). It should be noted, however, that community service projects that were integrated into classroom experiences did not show improvements in civic development.

The results are also inconsistent regarding the effect of community service on increasing the involvement of students as adults in the civic life of their communities. A number of studies have shown no improvement. However, two national studies by the independent sector suggest that early participation in community service activities is a strong predictor of volunteering for both teens and adults (Hodgkinson & Weitzman, 1997). This same study also found that schools were an important factor in promoting community service activities as those students whose schools sought student participation in community service activities were three times more likely to participate than were students who were not asked. Other studies that have polled adults have found that those who were involved in community service activities in high school were more likely to be politically and socially active in their communities than those who did not participate in community service activities in high school (Wade & Saxe, 1996). Supporting this research is the finding from a major study of intergroup understanding in two diverse communities of youth aged 12 to 18 that engaging in community service was positively related to young people's designed to promote intergroup understanding as well as with their commitments to public interest goals (Flanagan, 1998).

According to Nettles (1997a), about 44 percent of 1992 seniors participated in community service during their last two years of high school. Girls participated at higher rates than boys. African Americans generally participate at lower rates than their white counterparts (34.3 percent versus 45.9 percent). Although most community service was voluntary for most of the seniors surveyed, this was the case for a smaller share of African Americans than of whites (77.3 percent versus 87.1 percent).

Test scores appear to be related to the likelihood of community service, with those having lower scores participating at less than half the rate of higher-scoring seniors (24.1 percent versus 57.5 percent overall). Among students in the three lowest test quartiles, participation rates were comparable for African Americans and whites, but among those with the highest test scores, a smaller share of African Americans than of whites participated (42.7 percent versus 59.3 percent).

Overall more than one half of high school seniors in the highest socioeconomic group participated in community service, compared with only one third of those in the lower socioeconomic group (58.8 percent versus 31.3 percent). Participation rates were comparable for African Americans and whites with the lowest socioeconomic status (29.5 percent versus 30.5 percent). But at higher levels of socioeconomic status, African American high school seniors appear to participate at lower rates than their white counterparts (49.4 percent versus 58.9 percent).

A greater share of girls than boys engaged in community service among both whites and African Americans in urban, suburban, and rural high schools. Regardless of school location, a smaller share of African American than of white students took part in community service activities. Among African Americans, 39.4 percent of those in urban schools, 29.5 percent of those in suburban schools, and 31.9 percent of those in rural schools participated in the community, whereas 54.0 percent of whites in urban schools, 45.4 percent of whites in suburban schools, and 42.1 percent of whites in rural schools participated. Overall, one half—50.4 percent—of students attending schools at the lowest levels of poverty (as measured by the share of students who received free or reduced-cost lunch) participated in community service, compared with about 37.7 percent of students attending schools with the greatest poverty levels. Rates of participation were comparable for African Americans and whites attending schools with the least poverty (50.5 percent versus 49.9 percent). But at schools in which at least 6 percent of the students received free or reduced-cost lunch, a smaller share of African Americans than of whites participated. About two thirds, 65.2 percent, of high schools seniors attending Catholic high schools participated in community service, compared with less than one half (42.4 percent) of seniors at public high schools. In public schools, African American participation in community service lagged behind that of whites (33.1 percent compared with 44.2 percent). But participation rates of African Americans and whites were comparable at Catholic (60.6 percent compared with 65.3 percent) and other private schools (47.1 percent compared with 59.7 percent).

While the research literature does not demonstrate an explicit link between extracurricular or nonschool activities and civic participation, there is some evidence that participation in extracurricular and/or nonschool activities is related to growth in student self-esteem, competence, and personal and social responsibility factors that are linked to some of the outcomes of interest. Consequently, the significant decline in the African American students' participation in such activities should concern us. Data indicate a sharp decline between eighth and twelfth grades in the proportion of African American students who participate in academic subject clubs, the school newspaper and yearbook, and academic honor societies. In 1988, a greater percentage of African American than of white eighth graders participated in academic subject clubs (e.g., foreign language, math, science) (28.4 percent compared with 18 percent), but by the time these students had reached high school, their participation in these clubs had dropped to 20.3 percent compared with 25.4 percent. From 1988 to 1992, similar declines were apparent in participation in academic honor societies and involvement in the school newspaper and yearbook. In 1988, a higher percentage of African Americans than of whites were members of academic honors societies (16.8 percent compared with 12.1 percent). But by the time most 1988 eighth graders were high school seniors, only 13.6 percent of African Americans were members of academic honor societies, compared with 19.2 percent of whites. In 1988, involvement with the school newspaper or yearbook was greater for African Americans than for whites (23.1 percent compared with 19.5 percent). But by 1992, the involvement with the school newspaper or yearbook was lower for African Americans than for whites (14.0 percent compared with 19.3 percent).

African American students are less involved in nonschool activities than are white students. Overall, nearly two thirds—63.5 percent—of 1988 eighth graders participated in nonschool activities, such as scouting, religious organizations, 4-H clubs, or other youth groups. A smaller percentage of African American eighth graders than of whites participated in nonschool activities in 1988—57.9 percent compared with 67.2 percent (Nettles, 1997a).

When the government study mentioned earlier examined the relationship between student activities, both in and out of school, and civic development, it found that on all measures, students' civic development is higher in schools that have an active student government than in schools that have none. This same study also found that participation in other kinds of school activities and nonschool activities is associated with greater political knowledge, political attentiveness, participatory skills, and political efficacy (Niemi & Chapman, 1999).

On average, African American students watched more television than did white students. In 1988, 13.2 percent of overall eighth graders watched more than five hours of television each weekday and 26.1 percent watched more than five hours per day on weekends. In 1988, 80 percent of African American eighth graders, compared with 63 percent of whites watched more than two hours of television each weekday. Nearly one third—30.1 percent—of African American students watched more than five hours of television each weekday, compared with only 10.5 percent of whites.

The proportion of African American students who watched more than five hours of television each weekend day was more than twice as large as that of whites (49.9 percent versus 22.4 percent). Regardless of race, the average number of hours of television watched by 1988 eighth graders declined between 1988 and 1992. In 1992, however, when most 1988 eighth graders were high school seniors, African Americans continued to watch more television than their white counterparts. In 1992, 69.7 percent of African Americans watched at least 2 hours of television each weekday, compared with 49 percent of whites. More than one fifth—22.3 percent—of African American students but only 6.4 percent of white students watched more than five hours of television each weekday. The proportion of African Americans who watched at least five hours of television each weekday was nearly three times as large as the proportion of whites, 41.4 percent compared with 14.7 percent (Nettles, 1997a, pp. 97–105). This finding is consistent with other research that has found that youth from ethnic minority backgrounds rely more heavily on television media for both entertainment and education (Romer & Kim, 1995). Indeed, some researchers have argued that television serves as an important agent of socialization for African American youth, who rely on television as a source of guidance for defining appropriate behaviors in a variety of different social settings such as during dates, in classrooms, and in peer groups (Poindexter & Stroman, 1981; Stroman, 1986).

Attribution of Social Problems and Views of Justice

In 1996, The Carnegie Corporation awarded sixteen grants for research on improving relations among African American, European, Latino, and Asian American elementary, middle, and high school students. These grants to university researchers and independent organizations in nine states were for two types of studies: intergroup perception and behavior and the effectiveness of intervention strategies. The research reported here includes both quantitative, qualitative, and ethnographic studies, many emphasizing the social processes that occurred inside schools and classrooms and to a lesser extent the social forces of the surrounding community. Several of these studies are discussed in the following section because they have a direct bearing on the topic of civic participation, attribution of social problems, views of justice, and other related issues.

One of the relevant Carnegie studies examined intergroup relations among youth in the context of Facing History and Ourselves (FHAO), a program that uses the Holocaust as a starting point for discussing violence, anti-Semitism, and racism, as well as courage, compassion, caring, and justice. The evaluation/outcome study employed a quasi-experimental design and combined quantitative and qualitative methods and examined a number of psychosocial competencies assessed by a series of questionnaires and scales.[8] Nine teachers and 409 eighth-grade students took part in fourteen FHAO sections, each consisting of ten-week units and eight comparison sections. A number of the findings from this study are relevant to the attribution of social problems and views of justice. Compared with those in the comparison group, students who participated in FHAO showed increases on measures of relationship maturity and decreases in racist attitudes and self-reported fighting behavior. In contrast, FHAO participants did not show greater gains on measures of moral reasoning, civic awareness, or participation than control group students.

A few findings, complicated by interactions, are worthy of a brief explanation. One concerns measures of racist attitudes; while participation in FHAO was related with a decrease in racist attitudes among girls, it was not in boys. A second concerns differences between measures of ethnic identity and ethnic minority group membership. Compared with white students, students of ethnic minority backgrounds showed greater increases in measures of ethnic identity, a measure related to self-esteem among the latter, but not among the former. On the other hand, students of ethnic minority backgrounds showed greater increases in other group orientation, which the researchers conclude is evidence of ethnic minority group students' openness to others. A final finding was that teachers rated FHAO students higher on

[8]The following measures were employed: The GSID Relationship Questionnaire, a 24-item questionnaire designed to assess children's and adolescents' social competence, defined as relationship maturity; a Multigroup Ethnic Identity Measure, a 14-item instrument designed to assess aspects of ethnic identity; scales adapted from the National Learning Through Service Survey designed to assess aspects of civic attitudes and participation; The Modern Racism Scale designed to measure racial attitudes; Defining Issues Test designed to assess moral reasoning; and a FHAO teacher rating scale, a 15-item inventory designed to tap teachers' assessments of student attitudes and behavior.

particular elements of interpersonal and civic character and significantly lower on teasing and discrimination than comparison group students (Schultz, Barr, & Selman, 1998).

Another Carnegie-funded study systematically set out to examine adolescents' perceptions of intergroup relations and how this interacts with their views of citizenship, their ideas of what constitutes a "just world," their beliefs about justice and opportunity in America, and the factors associated with these views (Flanagan, 1998). A total of 1,119 students—115 African Americans, 115 Arab Americans, 140 Puerto Ricans and Dominicans, and 749 European Americans—aged 11 to 19 from four communities (three urban and one rural) participated. The socioeconomic status in the four communities of different ethnic composition was low middle and middle income.

Family, community and school influenced students' views concerning justice in America. Older students as well and those from educated families were less likely to view America as a just society. African American and European American students were slightly less likely to believe America was a just society than other groups, although this difference was not statistically significant. Personal experiences of prejudice toward oneself or toward family members were strongly related to adolescents' views that America was an unjust society. Community factors, including youths' reports that the police were fair to everyone, were positively related to assessments that America was a just society. Students' perceptions of a democratic school climate—fair treatment of all students by teachers, equal expectations for all students' achievement, and teacher intervention in incidents of peer intolerance—were related to students' perceptions that America was a just society.

Fifty-four percent of the students believed that all groups faced prejudice equally in comparison with 46 percent who believed that some groups faced more prejudice than others. Among the students who believed some groups experience more prejudice than others, the categories they gave were (in order of importance) discrimination based on race, language, religion, gender stereotypes about different groups, and power. Regarding their own or their family members' encounters with prejudice, 66 percent of African Americans, 66 percent of Arab Americans, 50 percent of Latinos, and 47 percent of European Americans answered affirmatively. Experiences of prejudice were higher for ethnic minority students, but among European American students a proximal awareness of prejudice was associated with a stronger desire to promote intergroup relations. Among African American students, those who had experienced prejudice were more likely to want to advocate for their groups, and among Latino Americans and Arab Americans, experiences with prejudice were related to lower levels of patriotism.

As briefly mentioned in an earlier section, this study found consistent relationships between adolescents' engagement in voluntary work and their commitments to promoting intergroup understanding as a life's goal. This relationship was found for African American, Latino, and European Americans, but not Arab Americans. Volunteering was associated with higher patriotic goals among European and Latino students. Among the former, volunteering was related to lower self-interest, and among the latter, it is was related to a desire to advocate for their group.

While the findings from these studies are encouraging, they must be interpreted cautiously. One reason is that both of these studies tap changing attitudes, which do not always correspond to changed behavior, a pattern that is seen from the evidence presented on "residential apartheid," to borrow a phrase from Hacker (1992, p. 35). Another reason for exercising caution when interpreting these findings is that in some schools the rhetoric surrounding these issues may not correspond to the day-to-day reality within schools. At least one other Carnegie-funded study found that although some schools are actively engaged in "doing diversity," that is, they regularly sponsored various activities designed to promote an appreciation of cultural diversity, issues of equity, fairness, and inclusion did not pervade the daily life of the schools (Foster, 1998).

Rather than endorsing a particular approach or program such as FHAO, the findings reported above suggest that schools and other socializing institutions must take affirmative steps to promote an understanding of democracy, racism, civic awareness, participation, opportunity, justice, and injustice, not only in discussions of these topics, but in the way that administrators and teachers model these values in their schools.

Student Diversity and Student Socialization

Despite trends toward resegregation in many urban school districts that have resulted from white flight and judicial reversals of desegregation orders, large numbers of students are currently enrolled in racially and ethnically mixed schools (Orfield, 1983; Orfield, Montfort, & Aaron, 1989). In fact, because of segregated residential patterns, it is in school that many students have their initial, most frequent, most enduring, and most extended contact with peers from different racial and ethnic backgrounds. A great deal of research on intergroup relations in schools has been undertaken over the years; however, because the context of these studies was school desegregation with its narrow focus on the relationships between black and white students, much of it is not germane to today's schools. Today schools have much larger numbers of Latino and Asian students. Although this increase is most evident in states like Texas, Florida, and California, since 1970 sharp increases in the ethnic minority populations have occurred in all regions of the United States (Council of Economic Advisors, 1998).

Complicating the situation are the high poverty rates of many of the nation's school children. African American, Native American, and Latino children have higher poverty rates than do white and Asian families, in some cases reaching as high as 40 percent in school districts (Council of Economic Advisors, 1998). As American schools enter the twenty-first century, understanding the relationships between ethnic minority and white students, but also the relationships between students who increasingly come from diverse ethnic, cultural, and linguistic backgrounds, will be critical. Understanding what contributes to productive relationships among students of color is critical because there are now many cities where the only intergroup contact that occurs takes place between different groups of ethnic minority students, between and among new immigrant groups, or between established residents and new immigrants. Whether the development of friendships among individuals of different racial ethnic groups ought to be a priority for schools is contested, yet almost everyone agrees that stereotyping and hostility between groups not only can result in tremendous costs to the society, but can limit that the ability to work productively with individuals from different backgrounds, which is a necessary skill in a highly pluralistic society.

Intergroup relations in schools are influenced by many factors that are both internal and external to the schools themselves. Common institutional practices such as tracking, homogeneous grouping, cooperative work groups, use of multiethnic curricula, and racially ethnically mixed faculty are examples of the social processes within schools that can affect intergroup relations. Students' preferred seating patterns in the cafeteria, choices of extracurricular activities, and playground playmates also influence the amount of contact between different groups of students, but it is unclear to what extent student choices are influenced by the institutional practices of schools. Particular aspects of language, cultural values, ideologies, and behavior may also have consequences for how children interact and perceive each other. The larger political, social, and cultural community forces also shape what goes on in schools and classrooms. In some communities, for example, the privileged status of a white majority group encroaches on the institutional practices in schools and classrooms.

Interventions can reduce this bias, but even after interventions designed to reduce bias toward students of color, some studies have found that white children still may hold higher levels of bias toward their group (Katz, 1998). As children get older and enter middle childhood, they begin to express more negative attitudes toward other groups, report having fewer cross-race friendships, and gravitate toward peers of their own racial and ethnic background even if they previously had friends from other groups. In part this is a function of the developing adolescent identity (Carlson, 1998; Foster, 1998; Hughes, 1998). But it is also a function of the organization of middle schools, which begin to track students at this level. Pervasive in middle and high schools, tracking often stratifies students by race even when they come from similar socioeconomic backgrounds (Carlson, 1998; Hughes, 1998).

By the time students enter high school, patterns of relations and affiliation take on a different character. The peer group becomes increasingly important and students begin to identify more with their respective social or reputational groups than with particular racial and ethnic groups. In high schools that have two extremes of poor and wealthy students and where these extremes map onto students' racial and ethnic categories, class divisions are more likely to be an obstacle to intergroup relations. Moreover, insofar as tracking corresponds to socioeconomic and associated racial and ethnic categories, it tends to inhibit cross race and ethnic relationships. Although groups of students may congregate with students from similar racial and ethnic background, and different groups may hold stereotypes about each other, in communities with high immigration levels, most often new immigrants, the newcomers who because of their unfamiliarity with American popular culture, language, and styles of dress, are singled out for the harshest criticism (Schultz, Barr, & Selman 1998; Stepick, 1998; Yu, 1998). Also from early ages, students are exposed to media images that depict various groups negatively, and these depictions have an effect on adolescents' developing attitudes toward others (Flanagan, 1998).

Interventions such as films to reduce prejudice, programs such as Facing History and Ourselves, and media campaigns can produce changes in attitudes, measures of maturity, and knowledge, but these changes are not necessarily carried over into everyday student behaviors (Graves, 1998; Schultz, Barr, & Selman, 1998; Katz, 1998). More than programs, intergroup contact holds the possibility of reducing prejudice; however, according to Alport's contact hypothesis, this is likely only when groups of equal status sanctioned by authority figures are engaged in activities in which they are working toward a common goal. Sports teams and other activities that bring students together on an equal basis are more likely to promote positive group relations (Greenfield, 1998; Stepick, 1998). Under the wrong circumstances, however, these activities can just as easily exacerbate tensions and lead to conflict among groups. Positive intergroup relations are most likely to be engendered—negative comments suppressed, groups work well together, and group unity conspicuous—when the adults treat members without favoritism, respond to conflict as a group rather than an individual problem, handle interpersonal and intergroup problems in a direct and public manner, and identify as part of a community that prides itself on tolerance and diversity. If, on the other hand, adults behave in a contrary manner, the groups will be marked by ethnic conflict, hierarchical groups will be erected creating ethnic conflict, and the effectiveness of the group will be compromised (Greenfield, 1998).

Contrary to assertions of conservative critics who claim that multicultural events are divisive, multicultural events—particularly those that positively highlight the role of subjugated groups—give students from these groups the opportunity to evaluate themselves positively. But while such activities are necessary, they must be complemented by activities that bring students together to work cooperatively in order to build solidarity among groups (Stepick, 1998). The lesson here is that unmediated intergroup contact can also intensify tensions, heighten conflict, and reinforce stereotypes. However, given the stratification within society and particular communities that is often mirrored in schools, the conditions for equal contact between groups rarely obtain. Tracking or streaming exacerbates existing tensions (Stepick, 1998; Yu, 1998; Hughes, 1998).

Intergroup contact among children and youth is insufficient. By their actions, teachers play important roles in promoting positive intergroup relations by intervening in bullying incidents or other acts of student intolerance and by not favoring or mistreating some groups over others (Flanagan, 1998; Pinderhughes, 1998). While there is a range of things schools can do to improve intergroup relations, programs and events alone will not change things if other things do not change. And since as children get older the peer group takes on increasing importance, in order to have a lasting effect changes must be targeted to the peer group (Pinderhughes, 1998).

Teachers and Diversity

Despite the opportunities that are presented by having a culturally diverse student body, and although when questioned most teachers agree that student diversity is desirable, the majority of teachers, most of whom are Anglo females in their early twenties from lower middle-income to middle-income families (Cazden & Mehan, 1989), are not adequately prepared to deal with a diverse student body. Both current and prospective teachers' responses to diversity indicate their lack of knowledge about students different from themselves. Teachers tend to rely on racial and cultural stereotypes and explanations of dysfunction, deficiency, and deprivation and/or insist on adopting a color-blind approach to dealing with students (King, 1991; Ladson-Billings, 1995; Delpit, 1994; Paine, 1989; Sleeter & Grant, 1988; Burstein & Cabello, 1989; Schofield, 1982; Sleeter, 1992; Tatum, 1997). A recent study that examined prospective teachers' perceptions of the teachability of students of different ethnic groups found that white teachers' assessments of students varied according to students' ethnic backgrounds. Teachers in this study consistently rated white and Asian American students higher than Latino and African American students on cognitive and motivational measures (Tettegah, 1996). Thus, despite teachers' declarations about equity and fairness, most of them simply do not have the dispositions, knowledge, and skill necessary to teach in today's culturally diverse classrooms.

Changing teacher attitudes toward student diversity is a difficult and gradual process (Sleeter, 1992; Schofield, 1982), prompting some to argue that rather than trying to change teachers' attitudes about diversity, schools of education should select individuals who are less racist in their outlook and possess the dispositions to teach students of diverse backgrounds (Haberman, 1991, 1992).

Two points remain to be discussed. The first I have interpreted as a rhetorical question, in part because the answer seems self-evident. Does education necessarily involve transmitting the dominant culture's outlook? To answer this question, I quote Mwalimu Shujaa (1994), who in a book entitled *Too Much Schooling, Too Little Education*, defines the terms schooling and education. He writes:

> Schooling is the process intended to perpetuate and maintain society's existing power relations and the institutional structures that support those arrangements. Education, on the other hand, is a process that prepares the young to understand themselves in relation to others and to provide the emotional, social and intellectual tools to act meaningfully and ethically in the world. (p. 14)

Adopting the views of the dominant culture is not preordained. In fact, a study that compared white and African American female adolescents' view about body image and weight concerns found that despite their awareness of the prevailing idealized white conceptions of beauty, African American female adolescents rejected these in favor of conceptions of beauty rooted in the African American community (Parker, Nichter, Nichter, Vuckovic, Sims, & Ritengaugh, 1995). Another study (Duncan, 1996) found that male adolescents also held views that contravened those of the dominant society.

Unanswered Questions

There are many unanswered questions regarding the role of the school in the socialization of students. In fact, there are more unanswered than answered questions. While many of the studies reviewed in this paper tap changes in attitudes, few of them are able to chart changes in behavior. Part of this is methodological. Because it is easier and most cost effective to administer questionnaires and surveys to large groups of students than it is to observe their day-to-day behavior, as well as the preference in the field of educational and social science research for studies that can achieve statistical significance, most of the extant studies are quantitative ones that tend to focus on attitudes rather than on behavior.

That being said, there are a number of areas where additional research would be helpful. Because of space limitations, I mention them only briefly. One area is related to how children's educational experiences influence voting behavior. Political scientists argue that when African Americans experience high empowerment and are faced with critical issues, their voting behavior is relatively equal to or greater than those of nonblacks (Gilliam & Kaufman, 1999). We need a better understanding of the educational forces and factors that encourage black students to see the value in sociopolitical involvement.

Is voting behavior influenced by the presence of critical issues? What are the correlates and factors that sustain voting in the absence of critical incidents?

We need insight into what young people know, how they feel, and what they think can be done about the manifestations of racism in the larger society. For example, are they aware of the class action lawsuit that the black farmers filed in 1997 against the United States Department of Agriculture, charging racist treatment? Are they aware of the settlement? Or the fact that it is the first time that the government has agreed to compensate the farmers as a group for racial bias? That this racial bias has been documented and cited by civil rights advocates and organizations such as the NAACP and the Congressional Black Caucus as one of the major reasons for the diminishing ranks of black farmers? (Fletcher, 1999). Are they aware of the recent airings of Denny's Racial Tolerance Ads and the reason underlying their airing? To what forces do students ascribe the higher incarceration rates of African Americans? Do they understand the implications of the 1994 Crime Bill? Do students have a grasp of the problems of poor people? Do schools deepen or constrain students' understanding of the cutting-edge issues facing their communities? Have students fallen victim to the same views about social justice as members of the dominant group? Do middle-class and working-class students hold similar attitudes toward social issues? Are schools social-izing middle-class and successful students to dissociate themselves from their poorer, less-educated brothers and sisters in order to move into the middle class? As they move into the middle class, which aspects and mores of the majority culture are students being urged to adopt? Or are they learning that getting involved will conflict with their long-term self-interests? We know from surveys, for example, as well as from popular treatises of the subject that middle-class African Americans are more cynical and less optimistic and perceive more hostility than their lower-status counterparts (Cose, 1993; Hochschild, 1998).

We need to understand how today's parents, particularly black middle-class parents, themselves both the beneficiaries and sometimes victims of desegregation, teach their children about racism. We know that teaching children about racism has been a central feature of life for blacks in America. Given the changes in the manifestations of racism, especially important in the post-desegregation era when racism has become less overt, less predictable, and less blatant, we need to know whether and how these lessons have changed. We have a few books (see, for example Beal, Villarosa, & Abner, *The Black Parenting Book*; Wright, *I'm Chocolate, You're Vanilla*; Comer & Poussaint, *Raising Black Children*) that deal with this issue, several anecdotal accounts, and a small number of research accounts (see, for example, O'Connor, 1997), but as far as I could ascertain this topic is not supported by a large research base. More systematic analysis is needed of the various strategies that parents of all social classes use to deal with this complex issue, as well as of the effect that these various approaches have on the views that children develop about social justice and the attribution of social problems.

These are but a few of the questions that need to be investigated in order to give us a fuller picture of how children's educational experiences affect their socialization.

REFERENCES

American Civil Liberties Union (January 30, 1997). Intended and Unintended Consequences: State Racial Disparity in Imprisonment. www.aclu.org.

Beal, A. C., Villarosa, L., & Abner, A. (1998). *The black parenting book: Caring for our children in the first five years.* New York: Broadway Books.

Braddock, J., Dawkins, M. P., & Trent, W. (1994). Why desegregate? The effect of school desegregation on adult occupational desegregation of African Americans, Whites, and Hispanics. *International Journal of Contemporary Sociology, 31*(2), 273–283.

Brown, D. L. (January 13, 1999). No easy lessons on race: Black parents find new ways to prepare children. *The Washington Post,* pp. A–1.

Burstein, N. D., & Cabello, B. (1989). Preparing teachers to work with culturally diverse students: A teacher education model. *Journal of Teacher Education, 40*(5), 9–16.

Carlson, C. (1998). Intergroup relations among middle school youth. Paper presented at the Workshop on Research to Improve Intergroup Relations Among Youth. Washington, DC: Institute of Medicine, National Research Council, Commission on Behavioral and Social Sciences and Education, Board on Children, Youth and Families, 9–10 November.

Cazden, C. B., & Mehan, H. (1989). Principles from sociology and anthropology: Context, code, classroom, and culture. In M. C. Reynolds (Ed.), *Knowledge base for the beginning teacher* (pp. 45–75). Elmsford, NY: Pergamon Press.

Comer, J. P., & Poussaint, A. F. (1992). *Raising black children: Two leading psychiatrists confront the educational, social, and emotional problems facing black children.* New York: Plume.

Cose, E. (1993). *The rage of a privileged class: Why are middle class blacks angry and why should America care?* New York: Harper Collins.

Council of Economic Advisors (September, 1998). Changing America: Indicators of social and economic well-being by race and Hispanic origin. Washington, DC: United States Government Printing Office.

Darling-Hammond, L. (1997). *The right to learn.* San Francisco: Jossey-Bass.

Darling-Hammond, L. (September, 1998). Unequal opportunity: Race and education. *Brookings Review,* pp. 28–32.

Dawkins, M. P., & Braddock, J. H. (1994). The continuing significance of desegregation: School racial composition and African American inclusion in American society. *The Journal of Negro Education, 63*(3), 394–405.

Delpit, L. (1995). *Other people's children. Cultural conflict in the classroom.* New York: The New Press.

Duncan, G. A. (1996). Space, place and the problematic of race: Black adolescent discourse as mediated action. *Journal of Negro Education, 65*(2), 133–150.

Flanagan, C. (1998). Intergroup understanding, social justice, and the "social contract" in diverse communities of youth. Paper presented at the Workshop on Research to Improve Intergroup Relations Among Youth. Washington, DC: Institute of Medicine, National Research Council, Commission on Behavioral and Social Sciences and Education, Board on Children, Youth and Families, 9–10 November.

Fletcher, M. A. (January 6, 1999). USDA, black farmers settle bias lawsuit. *The Washington Post,* pp. A–1.

Foster, M. (1998). A tale of two towns: Intergroup relations in communities and classrooms. Paper presented at the Workshop on Research to Improve Intergroup Relations Among Youth. Washington, DC: Institute of Medicine, National Research Council, Commission on Behavioral and Social Sciences and Education, Board on Children, Youth and Families, 9–10 November.

Gilliam, F. D., & Kaufman, K. M. (1999). Is there an empowerment life-cycle? Long-term black empowerment and its impact on voter participation. Los Angeles: Department of Political Science, University of California.

Graves, S. B. (1998). Different and the same: A study of the impact of a prejudice-reduction video series on children. Paper presented at the Workshop on Research to Improve Intergroup Relations Among Youth. Washington, DC: Institute of Medicine, National Research Council, Commission on Behavioral and Social Sciences and Education, Board on Children, Youth and Families, 9–10 November.

Greenfield, P. (1998). How can sports teams promote racial tolerance and positive intergroup relations? Key lessons from recent research. Paper presented at the Workshop on Research to Improve Intergroup Relations Among Youth. Washington, DC: Institute of Medicine, National Research Council, Commission on Behavioral and Social Sciences and Education, Board on Children, Youth and Families, 9–10 November.

Haberman, M. (1991). Can cultural awareness be taught in teacher education programs? *Teacher Education, 4*(1), 25–31.

Haberman, M. (1992). Does direct experience change education students' perception of low-income minority children? *Midwestern Educational Researcher, 5,* 28–31.

Hacker, A. (1992). *Two nations: Black and white, separate, hostile, unequal.* New York: Scribners.

Hodgkinson, V., & Weitzman, M. (1997). *Volunteering and giving among teenagers 12 to 17 years of age.* Washington, DC: Independent Sector.

Hochschild, J. (Spring, 1998). American racial and ethnic politics in the 21st century: A cautious look ahead. *Brookings Review,* pp. 43–46.

Hughes, D. (1998). The Early Adolescent Development Study. Paper presented at the Workshop on Research to Improve Intergroup Relations Among Youth. Washington, DC: Institute of Medicine, National Research Council, Commission on Behavioral and Social Sciences and Education, Board on Children, Youth and Families, 9–10 November.

Jaynes, G. D., & Williams, R. M., Jr. (Eds.), (1989). *A common destiny: Blacks and American society.* Washington, DC: National Academy Press, 1989.

Katz, P. (1998). Fostering positive intergroup attitudes in young children. Paper presented at the Workshop on Research to Improve Intergroup Relations Among Youth. Washington, DC: Institute of Medicine, National Research Council, Commission on Behavioral and Social Sciences and Education, Board on Children, Youth and Families, 9–10 November.

King, J. E. (1991). Dysconscious racism: Ideology, identity, and the miseducation of teachers. *Journal of Negro Education, 60*(2), 129–169.

Ladson-Billings, G. (1995). Multicultural teacher education: Research, practice, and policy. In J. A. Banks & C. A. McGee Banks (Eds.), *Handbook of research on multicultural education.* (pp. 747–759). New York: Macmillan Press.

Miller, L. S. (1995). *An American imperative: Accelerating minority educational achievement.* New Haven: Yale University Press.

Nettles, M. (1997a). *The African American education data book. Volume II: Preschool through high school education.* Fairfax, VA: Frederick D. Patterson Research Institute.

Nettles, M. (1997b). *The African American education data book. Volume III: The transition from school to college and school to work.* Fairfax, VA: Frederick D. Patterson Research Institute.

Niemi, R. G., & Chapman, C. (1999). The civic development of 9th through 12th-grade students in the United States: 1996. Washington, DC: National Center for Education Statistics, US Department of Education Office of Educational Research and Improvement.

O'Connor, C. (1997). Dispositions toward (collective) struggle and educational resilience in the inner city: A case analysis of six African-American high school students. *American Educational Research Journal, 34*(4), 593–630.

Orfield, G. (1983). *Public school desegregation in the United States, 1968–1980.* Washington, DC: Joint Center for Political Studies.

Orfield, G. (1993). School desegregation after two generations: Race, schools, and opportunity in urban society. In H. Hill & J. E. Jones, Jr. (Eds.), *Race in America: The struggle for equality* (pp. 253–260). Madison: University of Wisconsin Press.

Orfield, G., Montfort, F., & Aaron, M. (1989). *Status of school desegregation 1968–1986*. Alexandria, VA: National School Boards Association.

Paine, L. (1989). *Orientations toward diversity: What do prospective teachers bring?* East Lansing, MI: National Center for Research on Teacher Education.

Parker, S., Nichter, M., Vucokovic, N., Sims, C., & Ritengaugh, C. (1995). Body image and weight concerns among African American and white adolescent females: Differences that make a difference. *Human Organization, 54*(2), 103–114.

Pinderhughes, H. (1998). Forging a multicultural school environment: An examination of intergroup relations at an inner city high school—The P.R.O.P.S. Program. Paper presented at the Workshop on Research to Improve Intergroup Relations Among Youth. Washington, DC: Institute of Medicine, National Research Council, Commission on Behavioral and Social Sciences and Education, Board on Children, Youth and Families, 9–10 November.

Poindexter, P. M., & Stroman, C. A. (1981). *Blacks and television: A review of the literature*. Washington, DC: Job.

Reich, R. B. (1991). *The work of nations: Preparing ourselves for 21st-century capitalism*. New York: A. A. Knopf.

Romer, D., & Kim, S. (1995). Health interventions for African Americans and Latino youth: The potential role of mass media. *Health Education Quarterly, 22*(2), 72–189.

Schofield, J. W. (1982). *Black and white in school: Trust, tension, or tolerance?* New York: Praeger.

Schultz, L. H., Barr, D., & Selman, R. (1998). An outcome study of facing history and ourselves: The value of a developmental approach to evaluating innovative educational programs. Paper presented at the Workshop on Research to Improve Intergroup Relations Among Youth. Washington, DC: Institute of Medicine, National Research Council, Commission on Behavioral and Social Sciences and Education, Board on Children, Youth and Families, 9–10 November.

Shujaa, M. (1994). *Too much schooling, too little education: A paradox of black life in white societies*. Trenton, NJ: Africa World Press.

Sleeter, C. E. (1992). *Keepers of the American dream: A study of staff development and multicultural education*. Washington, DC: Falmer Press.

Sleeter, C. E., & Grant, C. A. (1988). *Making choices for multicultural education: Five approaches to race, class, and gender*. Columbus, OH: Merrill.

The Southern Education Foundation. (1995). *Redeeming the American promise: A report on the panel on educational opportunity and postsecondary desegregation*. Atlanta: The Southern Education Foundation.

Stepick, A. (1998). Immigrant and native minority adolescent interaction: Miami. Paper presented at the Workshop on Research to Improve

Intergroup Relations Among Youth. Washington, DC: Institute of Medicine, National Research Council, Commission on Behavioral and Social Sciences and Education, Board on Children, Youth and Families, 9–10 November.

Stroman, C. A. (1986). *Black families and the mass media.* Washington, DC: Institute for Urban Affairs and Research, Howard University.

Tatum, B. (1997). *Why are all the Black kids sitting together in the cafeteria? and other conversations about race.* New York: Basic Books.

Tatum, B. D., & Brown, P. C. (1998). Improving interethnic relations among youth: A school-based project involving teachers, parents, and children. Paper presented at the Workshop on Research to Improve Intergroup Relations Among Youth. Washington, DC: Institute of Medicine, National Research Council, Commission on Behavioral and Social Sciences and Education, Board on Children, Youth and Families, 9–10 November.

Tettegah, S. (1996). The racial consciousness attitudes of white prospective teachers and their perceptions of the teachability of students from different racial/ethnic backgrounds: Findings from a California study. *Journal of Negro Education, 65*(2), 151–163.

Turner, M. A. (May 18, 1997). Segregation and poverty: Segregation by the numbers. *The Washington Post,* pp. C–3.

Wade, R. C. (1998). Community service-learning: Collaborating with the community as a context for authentic learning. Paper presented at The Ohio State University.

Wade, R. C., & Saxe, D. W. (1996). Community service-learning in the social studies: Historical roots, empirical evidence, critical issues. *Theory and Research in Social Education, 24,* 331–359.

Wright, M. (1998). *I'm chocolate, you're vanilla: Raising healthy black and biracial children in a race-conscious world.* San Francisco: Jossey Bass.

Yu, H. C. (1998). From intolerance to understanding: A study of intergroup relations among youth. Paper presented at the Workshop on Research to Improve Intergroup Relations Among Youth. Washington, DC: Institute of Medicine, National Research Council, Commission on Behavioral and Social Sciences and Education, Board on Children, Youth and Families, 9–10 November.

14 Comment

Schools as Contexts for Socialization

Cynthia Hudley

The effort to examine the role of the school as a socializing agent is as important as it is difficult. Researchers in fields as diverse as education, psychology, economics, and urban geography have generated substantial bodies of literature on the topic of schools as contexts for socialization, yet we still have so little conclusive knowledge. Michele Foster's review of the literature on education and socialization eloquently sets out both the strengths and limitations of the diverse literature base. Although she has been tireless in her search for work that has bearing on the connection between the quality of the school experience and children's later life outcomes, that connection remains mostly obscured. I would like to consider some of the possible reasons why this is so.

Studying Schools as Socializing Contexts

One thing is quite clear; the school is a critical context for children's socialization. The work of Alexander and Entwistle (1988, 1996) in Baltimore, and that of the Cairns (Cairns & Cairns, 1994) in the southeastern United States has amply demonstrated that the early years of formal schooling establish a stable developmental history. A child's early years affect later schooling and eventual adult outcomes; history guides and constrains future social behavior in important ways that we should consider here. However, we must hold on to an appreciation of the multiple pathways, both positive and negative, that are available to individual members of groups; stability in group level outcomes says nothing about individual outcomes. Think of Waddington's (Jantsch & Waddington, 1976) model of a tree lying on its side to visualize how, from the same starting point, relatively small differences at early choice points can branch out to quite different developmental outcomes. Early circumstances can seriously constrain the future pathways that will be available. School plays a role in creating and defining both the kinds of pathways and the access to pathways along which children's development proceeds.

Unfortunately, as clearly as we know that school is a critical context for children's development, developmental research has too often misrepresented certain segments of our society, including our poorest children, our ethnic minority children, and children growing up in "nontraditional families." These overlapping populations of children have been typically studied from the perspective of pathology; only recently has a burgeoning literature begun to document the unique strengths of the urban poor, African American families, and female-headed households (e.g., Swadener & Lubeck, 1994). We know much more about the construct of risk than we do about the fundamental strengths in African American children, families, and schools. Therefore, our understanding of the mechanisms by which schools might create multiple paths to positive outcomes as well as enhance access to these positive pathways also remains inadequate. Much research has exhaustively catalogued the multiple stressors and defects of African American children and families as well as the schools that educate them. We must turn an equally searching lens on their assets and successes.

Understanding Multiple Causality

I would assert that our lack of clarity in understanding the role of the school as a context for socialization has much to do with how we frame the questions. In a pluralistic environment like the United States, the framework for discussion, that is, the discourse, will be largely structured by the culture and influence of the dominant group. Thus, questions about schooling in inner-city America have been framed in the dominant discourse, and that discourse may have little or nothing to do with the contemporary reality of the lives of many families, children, and schools.

Our dominant educational discourse has focused on a succession of single-factor theories to explain child outcomes. We have moved from locating causes of educational outcomes within the child (the psychometric model) (Gould, 1981) to locating causality for outcomes within the family (the deficit hypothesis) (Zigler & Muenchow, 1992), to locating causes within the schools (cultural difference model) (Au & Kawakami, 1991). However, one cannot and should not look to schools or to children or to any single factor to understand complex developmental phenomena.

Single-factor models ignore the dynamic nature of the relationships between children and families, schools, and societies and cultures (Dornbusch & Glasgow, 1996). To complicate matters further, this nexus of relationships is constantly changing across time. These relationships exist, whether they are positive or negative, engaged or neglectful, and in their totality they afford an explanation of child outcomes. By viewing child outcomes as nested in relationships, we see them more clearly as system outcomes, or societal outcomes, that must be located at the nexus of child, family, school, community, culture, and historical time.

School Contexts and Life Outcomes: Some Examples and Questions

Consider employment status as a single example of the socializing role of school contexts. Research conducted in the 1980s suggested that African American graduates of desegregated schools were more likely to work in desegregated environments (Braddock, Crain, & McPartland, 1984), and this effect was probably due to these students' developing more racially diverse social networks than African American students attending segregated schools. Unfortunately, there was much less attention paid to the type, status, and compensation of the employment available to these African American children (Fine, 1991). Access to employment and advanced preparation for highly skilled careers was and continues to be restricted for African Americans in our society due to constraints of culture (institutional racism), community (lack of training opportunities or transportation to get to training), or family (limited financial resources). Further, our current national debate on affirmative-action programs suggests that simple access to the opportunity structure will continue to be a struggle for African Americans. Thus, employment outcomes (opportunities, status, history) in adulthood are not simply a function of how effectively schools might shape children's decisions about which careers to pursue.

Neighborhood of residence is another obvious example of social and cultural influences on individual decisions. The quality and type of the neighborhood in which one lives are less a personal choice and more a negotiation between the individual seeking housing and the community in which the housing is sought. Foster's literature review does an excellent job of illuminating this tension between individual decision and social outcomes. African Americans may decide to live in racially mixed neighborhoods; however, the ultimate racial composition of any neighborhood will be determined by the decisions of members of various ethnic groups to remain or to move over time. Although reported attitudes may have changed, behavior has not.

We will become much more effective in our efforts to understand schooling contexts as socialization contexts when we begin to frame our questions in a discourse that appreciates multiple causality. Another question posed for this symposium topic, on civic participation, may be a useful example. Whether a resident participates in the civic life of the community is not always a matter of a volitional decision. Participation can be constrained by a variety of factors, be they social (e.g., refusal to allow "those people" into the local league or committee), institutional (inconvenient working hours, inadequate public transportation), or cultural (language barriers). Therefore, to examine civic participation we might better ask, "What outlets available in the community for civic participation (if any) are valued consistently by home and school and made available to which children? And how do these early experiences affect children's efforts to participate in their communities as adults through outlets that are available at the time (if any)?"

The literature reviewed by Foster on this specific topic of civic participation is illustrative of this point. The clearest findings of a relationship between early school experience and later life civic participation seem to link adult behavior to children's early opportunities to volunteer in their own communities with school support of projects that both child and family deem important (Wade & Saxe, 1996). To look only at whether the child participates, in the absence of assessing opportunities the school provides, political issues that are active in the community, or family responsibilities that are entrusted to the child or other similar contextual mediators, almost ensures that findings from study to study will be inconsistent.

Another example of multiple pathways embedded in a nexus of relationships is drawn from the longitudinal work on effects of early intervention. The High Scope/Perry preschool project (Lazar, Darlington, Murray, Royce, & Snipper, 1982; Schweihart, Barnes, & Weikart, 1993) has data that suggest that children in resource-poor communities who received high-quality preschool enrichment programs in the early 1970s were much less likely in the late 1980s to be on welfare or to have been arrested than their peers who did not receive such intervention. The mechanisms that seem to buffer the preschool project participants from later negative life outcomes had to do with social competence—the ability to engage in positive social interactions with both adults and peers, rather than significant gains in IQ or standardized achievement scores. Similarly, work on teacher–student relationships emphasizes the beneficial influences of social and affective support (Werner & Smith, 1982; Pederson, Faucher, & Eaton, 1978). In this instance, although the dominant educational discourse seems to be fixated on test scores, national assessment programs, and competency testing, the social dimension of schooling may have created important mechanisms that support children along pathways toward successful developmental outcomes.

These brief examples have attempted to demonstrate that a direct relationship among early school experiences, individual decisions, and later life outcomes is not a reasonable expectation. Particularly for African Americans, a host of cultural, social, and individual factors mediate both decisions and outcomes. We remain severely limited in our understanding of how schools might facilitate access to certain pathways in life, including a specification of those pathways that are not within the ability of the school to impact.

Lee Cronbach, a highly esteemed former president of the American Psychological Association, once said that the special task of each generation of social scientists is to pin down and realign culture's view of people with the people's contemporary reality (Cronbach, 1975). Thus, the goal now for social sciences is understanding the diversity of the lived experiences of families and children, schools, and communities that will allow us to more accurately frame inquiry into the role of schools as a socializing agent. As I said earlier, multiple pathways are present that lead individuals to similar outcomes; it is equally true that similar early pathways may lead to remarkably divergent outcomes.

Teachers, Schools, and Society

Once we agree that social relationships in schools are resources for sustaining children's healthy development, then understanding how teachers interact with students from ethnic backgrounds different from their own becomes of paramount importance. The research base again is well represented by Foster's review. However, we should also remember that teachers are embedded in educational systems that many would agree have not changed much in almost a century (Goodlad, 1984). Teaching is a highly isolated activity that most often goes on behind closed doors, and this is especially true in schools that serve African American children in inner cities. Technological innovation (the Internet as a teaching tool), reforms that bring changes to the governance structure (school site councils), and redesigns of teacher-preparation programs (to name but a few changes that have occurred) have hardly transformed the actual work of teachers in classrooms or the relationships between teachers and administrative personnel.

If anything has changed, it is the increased rigidity in recent years of the sorting function that schools have historically fulfilled (Shepard & Smith, 1989). Assessments carry more high-stakes consequences at increasingly early levels of schooling, retention is on the rise, and mandated curricula increasingly constrain teachers' instructional decision-making opportunities. All of these indicators reflect a Zeitgeist that endorses a "get tough" stance toward students, teachers, and schools who cannot measure up to assessments imposed from above. In this context, the nature of teacher attitudes toward students from diverse ethnic and cultural backgrounds is yet another manifestation of our society's inability to successfully enact social justice. Schools do not operate in a vacuum; they reflect the stress and strain of the society in which they operate (Bracey, 1992).

Developing schools that value diversity requires changes in families, communities, schools, and larger social systems. Certainly, diversifying the teacher pool and recruiting teacher candidates who are committed to justice and equity, as Foster has described, are important goals. Curriculum materials that prepare teachers to value and interact appropriately with students from backgrounds other than their own are increasingly available and of increasing quality for both preservice and inservice teacher education. However, we must also hold teacher educators, school boards, and citizens in communities across America accountable for finding ways to celebrate diversity and to disavow racism. Valuing diversity is not a goal specific to schools. It must be simultaneously the most systemic and the most deeply personal commitment that our pluralistic society and each of its individual members is prepared to undertake.

Students Together

How a school's racial composition affects the development of its students is perhaps the most compelling question we might address in this forum. Recall from my earlier comments that the literature on desegregation has suggested that there are some differences in the content of social networks for students in desegregated schools. However, the nature of racial composition in schools has changed dramatically over the past decade. Foster has again cogently targeted the limitations of the intergroup relations literature in its focus solely on black/white relations. In increasing numbers of schools, the ethnic composition is entirely people of color; in California, the ethnic mix in public schools is often Latino, black, and Southeast Asian, with each group itself containing a rich mix of ethnicities.

Foster and I also agree that the question of student socialization cannot be addressed solely from the perspective of the school. As I said earlier, schools reflect the societies in which they are embedded. Two longitudinal studies on student life in multiethnic secondary schools may serve to illustrate the point. Peshkin (1991) described a small-town, multiethnic high school that achieved relatively positive interpersonal relations across ethnic lines, mostly out of necessity. This was the only high school in an old, established town that was actively working to improve its image and attract employers and retail customers from surrounding, more affluent, recently constructed housing developments. Schofield (1989) described an urban magnet middle school that began as a multiethnic school but became 75 percent African American within five years. African American students there reported feelings of alienation, and African American parents were engaged in protests over tracking policies. The larger community stigmatized the school as a "low-achieving, black school." These two brief examples demonstrate the power of the multiple relationships among schools, families, and communities. The social relationships that exist within communities, as well as the quality of the home-school relationships, will jointly determine the quality of interethnic relationships on school campuses. The socialization of students must be considered in the context of the community and the families as well as the school, all the while maintaining an understanding of how relationships between the three systems change across time.

Unanswered Questions

I am in complete agreement with Foster's statement that "there are more questions unanswered than answered" on this topic of schools as contexts for socialization, and she has posed an excellent range of questions to guide future research. I would add another possible research agenda that focuses on the training of education professionals, be they teachers, administrators, pupil services personnel, or support staff. We need to better understand ways of attracting more ethnic minority people to the profession. That is, what factors influence ethnic minority students' decisions to pursue a teaching career; what features of teaching are particularly attractive to what groups of people; and what are the barriers to entering the teaching profession and how can these be addressed? We also need to better understand how to attract and train prospective teachers who are committed to social justice, regardless of their ethnic background.

Overall, the role of school as a socializing agent is not well understood. The path to clearer insights will be one that travels through the families, communities, cultures, and time periods in which those schools are embedded.

REFERENCES

Alexander, K. L., & Entwisle, D. R. (1988). Achievement in the first two years of school: Patterns and processes. *Monographs of the Society for Research in Child Development, 53* (20, serial No. 218).

Au, K. H., & Kawakami, A. J. (1991). Cultural and ownership: Schooling of minority students. *Childhood Education, 67*(5), 280–284.

Bracey, G. W. (1992). The second Bracey report on the condition of public education. *Phi Delta Kappan, 74,* 104–117.

Braddock, J. H., Crain, R. L., & McPartland, J. M. (1984). A long-term view of school desegregation: Some recent studies of graduates as adults. *Phi Delta Kappan, 66,* 259–264.

Carins, R., & Cairns, B. (1994). *Lifelines and risks: Pathways of youth in our time.* New York: Cambridge University Press.

Cronbach, L. (1975). Beyond the two disciplines of scientific psychology. *American Psychologist, 30,* 116–127.

Dornbusch, S. M., & Glasgow, K. L. (1996). The structural context of family-school relations. In A. Booth & J. F. Dunn (Eds.), *Family-school links: How do they affect educational outcomes?* (pp. 35–44). Mahwah, NJ : Lawrence Erlbaum Associates, Inc.

Fine, M. (1991). *Framing dropouts: Notes on the politics of an urban public high school.* Albany: State University of New York Press.

Goodlad, J. I. (1984). *A place called school: Prospects for the future.* New York: McGraw-Hill.

Gould, S. J. (1981). *The mismeasure of man.* New York: W. W. Norton.

Jantsch, E., & Waddington, C. H. (1976). *Evolution and consciousness: Human systems in transition.* Reading, MA: Addison-Wesley.

Lazar, I., Darlington, R., Murray, H., Royce, J., & Snipper, A. (1982). Lasting effects of early education: A report for the Consortium for Longitudinal Studies. *Monographs of the Society for Research in Child Development, 47* (2–3, Serial No. 194).

Pederson, E., Faucher, T. A., & Eaton, W. W. (1978). A new perspective on the effects of first grade teachers on children's subsequent adult status. *Harvard Educational Review, 48,* 1–31.

Peshkin, A. (1991). *The color of strangers, the color of friends: The play of ethnicity in school and community.* Chicago: The University of Chicago Press.

Schofield, J. W. (1989). *Black and white in school.* New York: Teachers College Press.

Schweinhart, L. J., Barnes, H., & Weikart, D. P. (1993). *Significant benefits: The High/Scope Perry Preschool study through age 27.* Ypsilanti, MI: High/Scope Press.

Shepard, L. A., & Smith, M. L. (1989). *Flunking grades: Research and policies on retention* (pp. 214–236). New York: Falmer Press.

Swadener, B. B., & Lubeck, S. (1994). *Children and families "at promise."* Albany: State University of New York Press.

Wade, R. C., & Saxe, D. W. (1996). Community service-learning in the social studies: Historical roots, empirical evidence, critical issues. *Theory and Research in Social Education, 24,* 331–359.

Werner, E., & Smith, E. (1982). *Vulnerable but invincible.* New York: Wiley.

Zigler, E., & Muenchow, S. (1992). *Head Start: The inside story of America's most successful educational experiment.* New York: Basic Books.

INDEX

academic motivation, 192
achievement gap, 173
achievement orientation, 103, 132–133, 136, 147, 151–153
  academically, males, 153–155
  adolescent females, 141–143, 148–151
  parental involvement in, 168
achievement outcomes, definition of, 190–191
"acting white," 145–147, 169, 195
adolescence
  academic achievement, females, 141–143, 148–151
  African Americans, 100–101, 103, 117, 140
  body image, females' view of, 218
  danger, attitudes about, 122
  development, 102, 131–132
  developmental psychology, 104
  females, 140, 141–143, 148–151, 218
  gender-identity formation, 132, 160–162
  male African American, 100–101, 103, 117
  sex, attitudes about, 122
  sexual activity, premature, 175
  teen pregnancy intervention programs, 185
  violence, attitudes about, 121
affirmative-action programs, 227
Africa
  ancient cultures, 49–50
  colonization by Europeans, 15–16
African American
  academically successful males, 153–155
  child-rearing, 106
  cultural genocide of, 14–15
  cultural orientation, 57
  culture and history used in curriculum, 4, 177
  education, early history of, 40
  family make-up, statistics of, 117

  female adolescents, 140
  home environment, 176
  male adolescents, 100–101, 103, 117
  names used, 9–10
  protest by, 50
  students' instructional model, 178
  women, negative attitudes towards, 118
Afrocentric curriculum, 55–59
agricultural education, 46
Algebra Project, 91–92, 96
American Negro Academy, 51
American popular culture, 216
ancient cultures, Africa, 49–50
apartheid, American, xi, 25, 44
Armstrong, Samuel, 43–44
Ascher, Marcia, 92
Asian Americans, 89, 97
  neighborhoods, 201
  teachers, 91
Atlanta Compromise, 44

behavioral styles of children, 177
boys. *See* Male adolescents
Burroughs, Nannie Helen, xi

capitalism, 49, 52
Carnegie Corporation, 211–214
Catholic high schools, 210
Chicago Urban League, xii
child development, 5
child-rearing tasks, 106, 119
Citizenship Schools, 79
civic participation as a function of educational background, 206–211, 225, 227–228
Civil Rights Era, education in, xi
Civil Rights Groups, 188–189
Civil Rights Movement, xii, 50, 54
classroom experience, response to by culturally different children, 4
classroom organization, 177
cognitive maturation, 105
collective identity, 102

233

political power tool, 9–12, 17, 35–37
politics, global, 18–19
racial identifications, 35
racial identity, 114
racially discriminatory policies of
    schools, 34
racism, xii, 19, 162
    economics of, 14–15
    measures of racist attitudes, 212
    science used to legitimate, 17, 21
reactive coping response, 104, 108
reading curriculum, 181
Reconstruction Era, 41
recruitment of teachers, 217
referent identity group, 104
reflectivity, 73
research on curriculum, 69
residential choices, 201–202
resilience, 111, 114
risk contributors, 112
ritualized warfare of dominant American adolescent males, 156

satellizers, 73
SAT exams, 204
scholastic evaluation, 182
school boards, 188–189
school districts, unitary status, 3
schools
    as an agent of socialization, 225
    cultural discontinuities in, 169–170
    cultural socialization agendas, 192,
        195
    desegregation, 200
    enrollment, statistics of, 120
    gender research within, 160
    integration, progress of, 3
    parental involvement, 182
    policies, racially discriminatory, 34
    segregation, racial, 3
    selection of curriculum, 40
    viewed as culturally hostile, xi
science curriculum, 181
    ethnoscience, 92
segregation of neighborhoods, 201–202,
    214
self-actualization, 179
separatism, black, 51, 53

sex, attitudes about in adolescent
    males, 122
sexual activity
    premature, 175
    teen pregnancy intervention programs, 185
sharpeners, 73
signifying, 78, 94
skill-and-drill activities, 178
slavery, 48, 50
social connectedness (communalism),
    176
socialization
    between children, in schools, 5
    sex role, 104
    of students by schools, 214–217, 225
    of teachers and students, 83
social reward system, female-specific,
    148–151
social skills instruction, 186–187
social studies curriculum, 181
social systems
    organization of, 47
    subjugation of peoples, xii
social time perspective, 176
Spencer Foundation, xii
spirituality, used in teaching strategies,
    176
sports teams, 216
standardized achievement tests, 79
Steele, Claude, 2
stress engagement, 108, 112
student government, 211
students. *See also* names of different social groups
    attitudes of racism, 212
    democratic values of, 59
    experience linked with classroom
        content, 81
    Latinos, 80
    learning styles, 73–75
    portfolio assessments of achievement,
        182
    underachieving, 151–153
    views on justice, 212–213
substance abuse, 175

"talk-story," 76